Introduction to UNIX

George Meghabghab
Valdosta State University

Introduction to UNIX

Copyright © 1996 by Que ® Education & Training.

Library of Congress Catalog No.: 95-74881

ISBN: 1-57576-054-1

00 99 98   4 3 2

Interpretation of the printing code: the rightmost double-digit number is the year of the book's printing; the rightmost single-digit number, the number of the book's printing. For example, a printing code of 96-1 shows that the first printing of the book occurred in 1996.

Screens reproduced in this book were created using Collage Plus from Inner Media, Inc., Hollis, NH.

Publisher: Robert Linsky

Director of Product Marketing: Susan L. Kindel

Copy Editors

Susan Christophersen, Noelle Gasco, Patrick Kanouse

Book Designer

Gary Adair

Cover Designer

Jay Corpus

Acquisitions Coordinator

Elizabeth D. Brown

Production Team Supervisor

Brad Chinn

Production Team

Steve Adams, Carol Bowers, Mona Brown, Judy Everly, David Garrett,
Jason Hand, Sonja Hart, Michael Henry, Clint Lahnen, Louisa Klucznik,
Steph Mineart, Nancy Price, Bobbi Satterfield, Laura A. Smith,
Tina Trettin, Todd Wente, Colleen Williams

Composed in *Stone Serif* and *MCPdigital* by Que Corporation.

Acknowledgments

Que Education and Training is grateful for the assistance provided by Larry Schumer, Dr. Robert Siegfried, Scott Parker, and Brad Doty.

Trademark Acknowledgments

An *Instructor's Manual* (ISBN 1-57576-070-3) is available to the adopters of *Introduction to UNIX*, upon written request. Please submit your request on school letterhead to your local representative or to S. Dollman, Macmillan Computer Publishing, 201 W. 103rd Street, Indianapolis, IN 46290-1097.

Contents at a Glance

Table of Contents

7 Electronic Mail   143

Part III   Shells and C Programming   167

8 Shells and Shell Scripts   169

11 UNIX System Administration   251

12 Working with UNIX and the Internet   281

Preface

Que Education and Training is the educational publishing imprint of Macmillan Computer Publishing, the world's leading computer book publisher. Macmillan Computer Publishing books have taught more than 20 million people how to be productive with their computers.

This expertise in producing high-quality computer tutorial and reference books is evident in every Que Education and Training title we publish. The same tried-and-true authoring and product development process that makes Macmillan Computer Publishing books best-sellers is used to ensure that every Que Education and Training textbook has the most accurate and most up-to-date information. Experienced and respected college instructors write and review every manuscript to provide class-tested pedagogy. Quality-assurance editors check every line of programming code in Que Education and Training books to ensure that it is accurate and that instructions are clear and precise.

Above all, Macmillan Computer Publishing and, in turn, Que Education and Training have years of experience in meeting the learning demands of computer users in business and at home. This "real world" experience means that Que Education and Training textbooks help students understand how the skills they learn will be applied and why these skills are important.

Introduction

As a student, you need to adopt a more serious attitude toward computers, and that means understanding UNIX. UNIX is part of every college student's life, from courses given in business schools to classes on computer information systems and computer science. Why should you consider this particular book essential? After you have finished reading some of the chapters, you may be more convinced of this textbook's value as an in-depth coverage of the latest commands of UNIX System 5 Version 4 (SVR4).

This book is intended for students who know a little about UNIX but would like to learn more. Is it necessary for you to have a book on UNIX to understand how to use this operating system? Ask the programming wizards among your UNIX classmates, and they will tell you they have little need for a book. Ask more probing questions, and you will find that these students have already developed a strategy to learn about an operating system as elegant as UNIX. Developing such an approach to learning UNIX is the focus of this book: A strategy to discover the multifaceted rich environment that constitutes UNIX.

This book will also be beneficial to UNIX administrators and networking experts who installed UNIX; although they may know a few aspects of UNIX well, they may have little or no familiarity with other facets of this system. *Introduction to UNIX* covers topics that will help you understand UNIX in general and may provide essential information for specific uses of this system. (For example, UNIX is the basis for POSIX. POSIX is required for some government contracts.)

Ten years ago, UNIX was considered to be highly mysterious. Practically the only way to learn about UNIX was to be initiated as if it were a secret society. You learned the passwords and the secret handshakes, and you could say "grep" and argue whether "vi" was pronounced "vye" or "vee-eye" (or maybe "six"). Now UNIX seems to be everywhere. Even the little girl in the movie *Jurassic Park* knows about UNIX. What happened?

In short, UNIX became "respectable." The system that had been largely a creation of research laboratories and academia grew up, got dressed in a suit and tie, and moved into the business world. It's everywhere, from businesses to defense-related industries. UNIX is now the de facto standard for minicomputer operating systems, and very few minicomputer manufacturers today would think of marketing a new computer that cannot use UNIX. Most major computer manufacturers have embraced UNIX (some grudgingly) because the market demanded it. Products like Univel's UnixWare and Berkeley Software Design's forthcoming 4.4 BSD (Lite) put UNIX on a desktop PC. Even Microsoft's media juggernaut has to take UNIX into account when marketing its NT operating system. UNIX runs on PCs and mainframes, micros, and minis.

From its humble beginnings, the UNIX market has mushroomed. UNIX has become many things to many people. To some, it is simply a tool for getting work done; for others, it is an elegant expression of how a computer should be organized, or is the basis of a community. This popularity has brought UNIX out of its shell (so to speak) and caught the attention of many people who never have seen the system at work.

Why an Introductory Book about UNIX?

UNIX was once famous as the best-documented "undocumented" operating system. Although the source code was well-documented, the user guides and the tutorials were of erratic quality and presentation. Sometimes it seemed as if you had to completely understand the system before you could learn anything about it. Now, books about UNIX fill shelves in large bookstores. Articles about it appear in computer and business magazines. Why? UNIX hasn't changed (that much). Instead, the users have changed.

At one time, the typical UNIX user had some roots in academia or research, some experience with the theoretical underpinnings of an operating system, and substantial experience with computers. In recent years, however, UNIX has ballooned past its original users; like an expanding empire, it has set its boundaries far beyond them.

When UNIX entered the "real world," it met users who just want to get the job done and who don't want to delve into the details of the system. To help this set of users, introductory UNIX books were published.

Imagine a UNIX system as a tiny academic city within your own real city. It's a place to work, read, write, and even play games. It has its public services, administrative staff, a post office, and even a janitorial staff. To be truly comfortable—that is, to really enjoy your new tiny city within your real city—you must learn the rules. You must find the locations of objects, learn whether you can bump into your professor's directory without reading the exams, discover where the latest projects are hidden, and avoid

getting caught while attempting to visit the virtual exams/assignments/
projects that surround you in the real world.

Introduction to UNIX is your guided tour through UNIX. The novice student will find refuge in its pages, and everyone will leave the virtual city
with a better understanding of its narrow syntax yet wider impact on the
real city.

Although *Introduction to UNIX* strives to provide the latest information,
UNIX won't hold still. It keeps changing and growing under pressure from
the marketplace and the users. This past year, there has been a strong push
to put the UNIX platform on a desktop computer.

Who Should Use This Book?

If you are a new UNIX user who wants an overview of the capabilities and
features of UNIX, you should find this book quite helpful. It provides the
foundation for using UNIX painlessly, whether you are on a single-user
desktop machine or a character terminal with a hundred other users. Specifically, this book is geared toward anyone who is new to UNIX and running a UNIX machine:

- Students who are enrolled in an introduction to an operating system
  class on a UNIX machine, or an introduction to a C class on a UNIX
  machine

- System administrators who must coexist with Novell NetWare and
  UNIX

- Computer novices

If you have *limited* experience with UNIX, you will find this book especially useful because of its coverage of the following topics:

- Shells and shell scripts

- C programming in a UNIX environment

- System administration

- Networking

Regardless of the version of UNIX you are using, you can use *Introduction
to UNIX*. The depth of coverage in the discussions of the command lines
apply across all UNIX versions.

If you are already familiar with the common features of UNIX (such as vi and Bourne shell programming) and are looking for new tools (such as C shell scripts, C programming on a UNIX machine, and the emacs editor), you should consider using this book. The questions and exercises at the end of each chapter help you understand the material covered in the chapter. In addition, instructors will find it easy to grade those assignments with the help of the *Instructor's Manual*.

How Is This Book Organized?

Introduction to UNIX builds your knowledge of UNIX from the basic (What is the kernel of the UNIX operating system?) to the advanced (How do you use a C program to issue system calls and interact with the kernel of UNIX?). The order in which topics are covered can be easily altered to fit any course structure.

For this book, it is assumed that you have a UNIX system nearby already up and running. The book leads you from your first exploration of computers and UNIX through managing the details of your own system. You don't have to read the chapters in sequence. If you already know how to log in to a UNIX system, jump to Chapter 3 and begin with the in-depth use of files, directories, and permissions. Part III delves into shells and shell scripts, as well as C programming. If you have already covered the basics, but you have never administered a UNIX system before, begin with Part IV.

Part I: UNIX Basics

Part I provides the basic information you need to start using and understanding UNIX. What is an operating system and why is UNIX special? How do you get started and how do you quit? Part I also introduces the "meat" of UNIX—its file and directory system. What are files and how are they organized? How do you create, move, and delete them?

Chapter 1, "Introduction to the UNIX Operating System," discusses UNIX as an operating system, describes important UNIX features, and provides a brief informal history of the system. It points out the differences between some of the "flavors" of UNIX and provides some UNIX terminology. If you are a total novice to computers, you will want to read this chapter.

Chapter 2, "Getting Started with UNIX," assumes that you've just sat down at a configured and functioning UNIX terminal, and shows you how to begin working with the system. The chapter discusses how to start the system, log in and out, figure out what kind of system you're using, manipulate the user interface, and obtain help. When you have finished this chapter, you will be able to start and stop your system, as well as begin and end a user session on the system.

Chapter 3, "Understanding the UNIX File System," covers the basics of understanding how your system is organized. What is a file? Why are files in UNIX different from the ones in DOS? How do directories differ from files? What is the directory tree? Can you really name a UNIX file *?:!;? After reading this chapter, you will know the answers to these questions.

Chapter 4, "Working with Files and Directories," explains how to control your system's files and directories. How do you create directories and files? How do you copy them? How do you find a file you have misplaced? How do you get rid of a file with a funny name like *?:!;? After navigating Chapter 4, you will be confident of your abilities to make, destroy, find, and alter files and directories.

Chapter 5, "Understanding Permissions and Other System Information," explains how UNIX works for multiple users, how users own things, and how they can share programs and files. It ties together the information learned in the previous four chapters by showing you how to dig out system information, and analyzing what that information means.

Part II: Working with Applications

Part II describes the tools that form the background for much of the work performed in UNIX. How do you create or change the contents of a text file? How do you send a message to someone? How do you read your mail? Part II demonstrates ways to improve your productivity with UNIX by connecting you with the rest of the world. These chapters show you how to start your applications by using common system tools, such as the vi and emacs editors, as well as UNIX shell tools for electronic mailing.

Chapter 6, "Using the *vi* and *emacs* Editors," introduces the vi editor, which resembles a stripped-down word processing program used mostly by programmers. The vi editor works on text files instead of word processing files. Because so much of UNIX configuration involves text files, it's useful to know how to use a fast editor with many capabilities. This chapter walks through the basics (reading a file, writing a file, moving the cursor, and adding and deleting text) before touching on other capabilities such as searching, searching and replacing, copying blocks of text, and formatting text in the editor.

Chapter 6 also describes the basics of the emacs editor, including the same capabilities that were discussed for the vi editor. This discussion establishes a sound basis for comparing both text editors. The exercises make it clear that a strategy is needed to help you uncover new text editors and to analyze their impact on learning a new text editor.

Chapter 7, "Electronic Mail," introduces you to electronic mail, a productivity aid that is revolutionizing business. After discussing what electronic mail is and what it looks like, the chapter leads you through addressing, sending, and reading electronic mail, with the standard mailx Mail utility. By the time you have finished this chapter, you will understand how to recognize electronic mail addresses, what messages are, how to send and read mail, how to read mail before it hits your mailbox, how to prevent people from sending you mail, and how to organize your .mailrc file.

Part III: Shells and C Programming

Part III shows you how to look beyond files and directories on your UNIX machine. This part includes a chapter on shells, providing an introduction to the Bourne Shell and the Korn shell, as well as a detailed study of a C shell. Part III includes a discussion of how to write C shell scripts using all the features of the C shell.

Part III also keeps you excited about aspects of programming on a UNIX machine, other than using your shell scripts. C is a highly functional language that is transportable from one UNIX operating system to another. You can use C to create databases, perform intense math calculations, create reports, and so on. C is fun to learn and will give you more control over your programs than shell languages.

Chapter 8, "Shells and Shell Scripts," introduces shells, including the Bourne, Korn, and C shells. The chapter details all aspects of C shells, from aliases and process information to job control and C shell scripts. The exercise section provides a comparative assessment of all three shells and investigates how to benefit from all three.

Chapter 9, "C Programming in a UNIX Environment," is a brief introduction to writing programs under UNIX using the C programming language. In this chapter, you write your first C program and then examine its parts. You learn how to control the flow of your program, and you examine some of the basic elements of C, including types, variables, loops, and functions.

Part IV: Networking

Part IV describes customizing and maintaining your UNIX system. How do you connect your system to other computers? How do you configure a printer? When working with your UNIX system, you make decisions that can strongly affect how your system performs and how it behaves. The information in this part lets you customize your UNIX system until it better serves your goals. Part IV is about the "once in a while" tasks that are an important part of any system.

Chapter 10, "UNIX Networking," demystifies one of the great strengths of UNIX—its networking capabilities. This chapter describes the fundamentals of networking, including TCP/IP and NFS networks. After reading this chapter, you will understand the basics about networks and be able to configure both TCP/IP and NFS networks.

Chapter 11, "UNIX System Administration," describes the role of the system administrator. A system administrator is a combination of manager and janitor, both boss and employee, responsible for making sure that the system runs smoothly and that problems are prevented or cleaned up. As part of the administrator's job, new accounts are created, old accounts are removed, and files are backed up regularly. After reading this chapter, you will have a basic understanding of the important tasks of the system administrator.

Chapter 12, "Working with UNIX and the Internet," discusses the rapidly changing world of the Internet and explains how UNIX is used with this information superhighway. Included in this chapter are tips for interacting with e-mail, interest groups, and newsgroups, and for locating and retrieving information with Gopher and World Wide Web. After reading this chapter, you will be able to access the many services and resources available through the World Wide Web and create your own home page.

Conventions Used in This Book

Introduction to UNIX uses several conventions to help you understand its discussions. These conventions are listed here for your reference.

UNIX commands, files, and messages displayed by the computer are printed in monospace. Note an example:

All the information about your user account is kept in the file /etc/ passwd.

Special keys you must press are indicated by name and capitalized, such as Enter or Esc. Your keyboard may have different names for some keys—for instance, Enter is often called Return, PgUp may be spelled out (Page Up), and so on. Key combinations are joined by a hyphen (-). While holding down the first key, you press the second key. Ctrl-d, for example, indicates that you are to hold down the Ctrl key, press the d key, and then release both keys.

Information that you should type appears in **`boldface and monospace`**. Type this information exactly as it appears. Remember that UNIX is case-sensitive—you must type upper- and lowercase letters exactly as they appear in the text. If the text instructs you to enter a command, type the indicated command and press Enter.

Information that is a placeholder for other information appears in *`italic and monospace`*. As you type the command, you replace the italic monospace word or words with the appropriate word for your system or your task. For example, "At the login prompt, type *`yourlogname`*" indicates that you should type your login name at the prompt as a replacement for *`yourlogname`*.

UNIX Basics

1

Introduction to the UNIX Operating System

Topics Covered

- What Is an Operating System?
- UNIX Features
- Parts of a UNIX System
- Some UNIX Terminology
- A History of UNIX

This chapter helps you understand the tasks performed by an operating system that are vital to your computer. The chapter also discusses how UNIX performs these tasks. In addition, the chapter provides a brief history of UNIX, which helps you understand why UNIX has its present form, and provides a survey of the major "flavors" of UNIX available today. Finally, the chapter discusses the parts of the UNIX operating system and lists some of UNIX's terminology.

What Is an Operating System?

A computer without software—the machine as it rolls off the assembly line—is incapable of performing many common tasks without a great deal of assistance. "Simple" tasks, such as printing information to the screen or transferring data to disk, require complex sequences of instructions. In the old days (in computer terms, about 25 years ago), every program was responsible for controlling every task, and programs were much more complicated to write than they are now. For example, to save a piece of information in memory, some computers required you to know *where* in memory you were going to store the information. In the same way, communications between the user and the computer were much more tedious in the past; users often entered commands by flipping toggle switches and received responses in the form of rows of lights.

People expect more from computers now. Using computers today is relatively easy partly because of improvements in operating systems. An *operating system* is the software that supervises and assists you and the programs you run on your computer. The computer's operating system handles the details of common operations, allowing you and your programs to concentrate on less technical concerns—the reasons you bought your computer—such as balancing your books, finishing that letter to Aunt Peggy, or selling more cars.

Most people who use a computer don't think about the operating system, even when they're using it. They use a computer to accomplish some real-world task, usually by using an *application program*—software written to perform that task, such as word processing or accounting. The operating system is a necessary tool for the computer to run applications.

An operating system, like a waiter or a police officer, is something you notice when it is *not* doing its job. Different operating systems offer different features, but all systems share the following roles:

- *Traffic cop.* The operating system coordinates the sequence of events, especially on large computers where many users try to work simultaneously. The operating system ensures that each user gets a fair share of the computer's attention.

- *Servant.* The operating system controls the computer's resources. It's a servant to programs, carrying out tasks for them. On today's computers, application programs don't have to directly control such operations as printing data to disk and displaying characters on-screen. The operating system contains software to perform these tasks, and application programs ask the operating system to carry out these functions for them.

- *Accountant.* The operating system controls system resources. The term *resource* refers to any component or service provided by the computer that is in limited supply, including memory, disk space, and various pieces of hardware. The operating system handles the purse strings, ensuring that all users share resources, and that no two users use the same resource at the same time. (Actually, the operating system is more like a nursery school teacher, ensuring that everyone in the sandbox plays fair.)

- *Guardian.* The operating system protects files and data, enforcing the security of the system. It may set locks on certain files to prevent accidents; it may even control who can use the machine.

- *Toolkit.* An operating system includes a collection of programs that accomplishes common tasks such as copying files or printing reports. Among UNIX users, these programs are known as *tools* because they provide an important means of accomplishing work, just as a carpenter uses tools to perform a job.

- *User interface.* An operating system provides a standard mechanism for accomplishing tasks such as maintaining files and running programs. You can "fit" user interfaces into this mechanism.

UNIX Features

UNIX is an operating system rich with features for the programmer and the user, features unique among the available operating systems. With UNIX's multitasking and multiuser capabilities, device independence, and tools approach, experienced UNIX users can be more productive than users on other operating systems that lack these features. The error-handling capabilities of UNIX reduce data losses when a program fails to work. The portability of UNIX provides users, managers, customers, and business planners with a greater range of choices than is available with any other operating system. This section helps you understand these features and compares them with other operating systems such as MS-DOS, MVS, VMS, OS/2, and Windows NT.

Multitasking

UNIX can perform more than one task at a time for each user, a capability known as *multitasking*. Through a process known as time sharing, the computer seems to be devoting its full time to each task, although it actually spends only fractions of a second with any job before switching its attention from one job to another. As one of its many responsibilities, UNIX continuously decides which job to run next, and how long to spend on each job. This process occurs so quickly that it is usually invisible to the user. Several forms of multitasking are available:

- *Windowing capability*. Some sophisticated terminals, such as X-Terminals, enable you to divide the screen area (known as real estate) to display a different activity in each area. You can watch several tasks simultaneously produce results and can send keyboard input to any task desired.

- *Background processing*. You can run jobs that require no human interaction (such as formatting a disk or sorting a data file) in the background. Background tasks receive a share of the computer's attention, but don't use the keyboard, thus freeing the keyboard for use for another task.

- *Task switching*. Using a UNIX variant, such as Linux, on your PC, you can begin several tasks and then press a combination of keystrokes to switch between them. Other UNIX systems let you stop jobs, start them, and move them between the background and the foreground.

Multiuser Capability

Besides being able to run more than one *task* at a time, UNIX can serve more than one *user* at the same time. Unlike operating systems such as MS-DOS and OS/2—but like the PICK, VMS, and MVS systems—UNIX allows each user to be involved in completely unrelated tasks while seemingly holding the computer's undivided attention. UNIX handles multiple users through time sharing, although multiuser operation goes beyond parceling out processing time. Each user works at a terminal, which is merely a keyboard and screen connected to the computer by a cable. Terminals resemble PCs in appearance (and you can buy programs that enable your PC to act as a terminal), but in most cases the terminal doesn't contain its own processor. A terminal of this type is sometimes called a more descriptive but derisive name: dumb terminal. A terminal's only purpose is to send characters from the keyboard to the computer, and then to receive characters from the computer and display them on-screen.

Some terminals include processors to aid in transferring data between the user and the computer. For example, X-Terminals contain graphics processors to display windows and other graphics. Processors are typically hidden from the user.

On most machines, especially small systems, each terminal connects to the computer through a serial port, a connector that provides access to the computer's communication circuitry. PCs have only a few serial ports, although you can use the computer's built-in monitor and keyboard as a terminal. Minicomputers may contain dozens of serial ports. On large mainframes, *controllers*—small computers in their own right—coordinate the input from groups of terminals, taking some of the load off the main computer.

A multiuser operating system, such as UNIX, offers several advantages over single-user systems:

- *Low cost per user.* On a multiuser system, such as UNIX, each user needs only a dumb terminal (even an obsolete PC and an inexpensive terminal program work), which can cost only a few hundred dollars. These terminals are connected to a single computer. If single-user computers are used instead, each user has a "personal computer" costing thousands of dollars. Now that UNIX is available for PCs, a group of users, each using an older, inexpensive PC with a terminal program, can connect to a single UNIX box. UNIX provides an extremely cost-effective method for providing computer access for many people.

- *Central administration.* If each user doesn't have his or her own computer, or if the computers are linked in a network, the company can have a single person perform the routine computer chores such as backups and maintenance.

- *Shared resources.* Users on multiuser systems can share information and interact with each other in ways not possible on single-user systems. Users can exchange electronic mail messages, trade data, and share equipment such as modems, printers, disk drives, and faxes.

Single-PC UNIX systems, such as UnixWare, provide fewer advantages unless the PCs are connected as part of a network. By connecting several UNIX machines in a network, a single administrator can handle backups and jobs can be distributed among machines.

Multiprocessing Capability
UNIX systems scale well up to about 12 to 16 processors. Sun claims almost linear scalability of Sybase System 11 running on a 16-way SPARC center 2000. Some vendors have even introduced 32-way and 64-way UNIX SMP systems. Sequent has announced a UNIX system architecture that can be configured with up to 256 Pentium Pro processors.

Accessing scalability is tricky. Scalability depends on a number of factors, including the hardware architecture, application software, and the operating system itself.

Clustering offers another way to scale. Of course, users cluster systems primarily for increased availability rather than performance gains—approximately 80 percent of users who cluster UNIX systems do so for higher availability; only 20 percent cluster for performance gain.

Device Independence

Most computer operations involve moving data to and from files or devices. A *file* is a collection of related pieces of information, and can be compared with a file folder. For example, information that makes up the file-listing program in UNIX is stored in a file named ls. A *device* is any input, output, or storage mechanism attached to the computer, including terminals, hard drives, modems, printers, and CD-ROMs. UNIX attempts to handle these operations in a device-independent manner, letting you use files and devices interchangeably. If a file normally writes its output to the screen, you can send the results to the printer or a file instead; similarly, you can tell a program to read its input from a file instead of the keyboard.

In a sense, UNIX treats devices as special kinds of files and gives them names; thus, you can use a device name anywhere you can use a file name. This flexibility doesn't mean that you can perform any operation on any file or device; some operations don't make sense in some contexts. For example, you can use printers only for output, not input. An attempt to read data from a printer would fail.

DOS takes a similar approach to files and devices. The drive letters (A:, B:, C:) are the names of disk drives, just as LPT1 is the name of the printer. In DOS these names are predetermined. If your printer in UNIX was named /dev/laser, these two commands are equivalent for DOS and UNIX, respectively:

```
COPY DIARY.TXT LPT1
cp diary.txt /dev/laserCurrent C-head at bottom of page
```

Devices are usually given file names in the directory /dev.

Most devices also have unique capabilities. You can format disks, rewind tape drives, and adjust various terminal settings. UNIX provides special commands and programming functions for performing these operations.

Tools

From its earliest days, UNIX has relied on what is called "the tools approach" to solving problems. Rather than have every program try to perform every task,

UNIX provides the means to connect tools. By combining tools in various ways, you can accomplish complex tasks.

To connect tools, UNIX provides a feature called a pipe. A *pipe* lets data flow out of one program and into another. Each program can modify the data in some way. The pipe is represented on the UNIX command line by a vertical bar (¦), which looks like a pipe.

For example, suppose that you maintain a file called clients. Each line of the file contains information (name, company, and phone number) about a business associate. Using different combinations of tools, you can extract many types of information from this file. Perhaps you need to call those clients who work for Ace Trucking, so you want to display names and telephone numbers for clients working for Ace. You also want the list in alphabetical order by last name. After considering the tools available, you might use the grep command to find the lines in the file that contain the phrase Ace Trucking, the cut command to pick out only the names and telephone numbers, and the sort command to arrange the information in alphabetical order. Using pipes, you can type a single command that invokes all these tools in concert. The command might have the following format:

```
grep "Ace Trucking" clients ¦ cut -fl,3 ¦ sort +1
```

Each of these tools—grep, cut, and sort—accomplishes a single, simple task. By combining tools, you can perform larger, more complex tasks than you can with a single tool.

An apocryphal story from early UNIX days demonstrates the power of the tools approach. A certain company wanted a complex sorting job done, so it called its Information Services staff. After considering the task, the company's own programmers said, "That would cost hundreds of thousands of dollars to write because we don't have the expertise." The company then went to a consulting programmer, who said, "I can write that program in six months for several thousand dollars." An employee for the company mentioned the problem to her husband, who happened to be a UNIX programmer. In minutes, he had written a 10-line command that did the job using existing UNIX tools! (The story doesn't mention whether he was paid thousands of dollars, or whether the company switched to UNIX.)

The tools approach provides several advantages over collections of more complex programs:

- *Flexibility*. Because UNIX provides so many general-purpose tools, you can accomplish the most complex tasks by combining already available tools.

- *Speed*. You can accomplish tasks quickly because all the building blocks have already been created.

- *Structured approach*. Because all UNIX users start with the same building blocks, the tools approach encourages all users to solve problems in similar ways.

The tools approach also makes UNIX confusing to novices: Instead of having one way to carry out a process, UNIX can accommodate hundreds of approaches. Tools using graphical user interfaces go a long way to solve this problem, but they also insulate new users from the power of the tools approach.

Error-Handling

Because UNIX is a multiuser system, it must handle errors well. On a single-user system such as MS-DOS, it's only an inconvenience if you must turn off the computer and restart it; on a multiuser system, rebooting the system is an expensive inconvenience to several people and costs much more time and money. Not surprisingly, then, UNIX strives to prevent dangerous errors.

UNIX tries to keep ill-mannered application programs from writing in sections of reserved memory, attempts to prevent users from accidentally deleting files that don't belong to them, and provides strong interrupt-handling. The following list discusses these safeguards, starting with the least serious problem and moving to the most serious issues:

- UNIX makes it easy for you to keep other users from accidentally changing or deleting your files. The operating system has ways of assigning ownership and permissions to files that control who can read and write to those files. (Chapter 5, "Understanding Permissions and Other System Information," has more information on file permissions.)

- UNIX offers ways for most programs to handle interrupts. An interrupt is any signal that changes how the system runs. If you type a command and then decide you don't want to execute it, pressing Ctrl-c usually stops the job. (Some programs, such as the vi editor, will even send you mail, reminding you that you were editing a file when the job was interrupted and asking if you'd like to restore the file.)

- When an application program attempts to do something "bad" (in terms of internal data organization), the UNIX operating system catches it. The user gets the (admittedly cryptic) message Segmentation violation, and a file named core is created. The core file allows programmers to find out what went wrong; if you're not a programmer, you can safely remove the file.

- When things go very wrong, the UNIX system saves all the information it can about the current state of the operating system (a process called *panicking*) and quits. A skilled programmer can go through this information and find out what went wrong. It's very rare for a UNIX machine to panic.

Serious errors occasionally occur in UNIX: The operating system isn't perfect. Nonetheless, errors occur only rarely, making users less likely to lose important data.

UNIX versus DOS

How does UNIX compare with DOS, which is currently the most widely known operating system? More important, why would you want to use UNIX as the operating system for your PC rather than DOS (or OS/2 or Windows 95)? Table 1.1 compares the features of several operating systems.

Table 1.1	UNIX Compared with Other Operating Systems				
Operating System	Different Manufacturers?	Hardware Required	Primary Multiuser?	Multi-tasking?	Market
MS-DOS	Yes	IBM PC or compatible	No	No	PCs
OS/2	Yes	IBM or PC compatible	No	Yes	PCs
Windows NT	No	Various	Yes	Yes	PCs
PICK	Yes	Various systems	Yes	Yes	Small businesses
VMS	Only DEC	DEC VAX architecture	Yes	Yes	Minis and superminis
MVS	Yes, mostly	IBM mainframe	Yes	Yes	IBM
UNIX	Yes	Various	Yes	Yes	Workstations

Briefly, UNIX is the only operating system that offers multitasking, graphics, and cross-platform compatibility. UNIX users already enjoy file-sharing, network-printer services, remote-application execution, client/server program support, multiuser access, and a graphical user interface. If you need to work in a networked computer system, UNIX is currently the only operating system that combines all these elements.

Parts of a UNIX System

This section describes some of the parts of the UNIX system. This summary isn't meant to be exhaustive; it simply provides the background you need when working with computer systems. If you already have experience with computers, you may want to skip the hardware discussion and glance at the software descriptions.

Every computer system consists of hardware and software. The hardware is the physical portion of the system—the actual computer box, screens, printers, and so on. The software consists of the programs that make use of the hardware. The UNIX operating system itself consists of software that works very closely with the hardware.

Hardware varies from system to system and from manufacturer to manufacturer, but usually includes a processor, one or more terminals, and any number of peripherals.

The processor unit (or system unit) is the box that does the computing. This unit acts as the brain of the computer, storing and processing information. The processor may range in size from a few circuit boards to hundreds of square feet of cabinets. Included in the processor are the following items:

- The central processing unit (CPU), which processes data according to instructions provided by software. Some computers have more than one CPU.

- Random-access memory (RAM), which provides temporary data storage for running programs and their associated data.

Most processor units also include a disk drive or some other storage medium, but (strictly speaking) these items are peripherals.

Users communicate with the computer through a *terminal*, which is usually a unit consisting of a screen and keyboard. A single UNIX system may have only one terminal, or it may have thousands of terminals located around the world. Although terminals by themselves superficially resemble whole computers, most lack any kind of processor. Although most terminals merely serve as conduits for entering and displaying characters, some may carry out more complex functions.

X Window System terminals, for example, include processors that are more powerful than many older PCs.

A *console* is a terminal connected directly to a special connector (called a *port*) on the computer. The port—not the terminal—distinguishes the console: The console is the system administrator's control station. If a severe error occurs, UNIX displays the appropriate message on the console, and some activities, such as shutting down the system or performing maintenance, can be performed only on the console. Besides performing these special functions, the console can be used for the same tasks as any other terminal. Some UNIX machines, especially PCs, have no terminals other than the console.

Peripherals include other equipment you can hook up to the computer. The list of peripherals grows daily: disk drives, printers, floppy disk drives, CD-ROM drives, modems, voice synthesizers, fax boards, and dozens of other types of equipment.

By itself, hardware does nothing. To accomplish a task, the hardware must be given instructions—which is where software takes over. To visualize the software on a UNIX computer, imagine that it consists of several parts working together: the kernel, shell, tools, and applications. The relationship of these parts is shown in Figure 1.1.

The *kernel*, which is named for the inner seed of a nut, is the central core of UNIX. The kernel is where the computer's activities are coordinated and controlled. After you boot (start up) a UNIX computer, its first major job—after perhaps running some diagnostics on the machine—is to load the kernel. The kernel remains in the machine's memory until you shut down the computer. It controls every facet of the hardware's operation and acts as a protective layer surrounding the hardware. Programs can communicate with the hardware only by using the kernel as an intermediary.

The kernel is both servant and master for the programs running on the machine, which are called *processes*. The kernel supervises the processes, but it also performs tasks that the processes request.

Programs communicate with the kernel through system calls. When a program needs to create a file, write to a printer, communicate with another program, or perform any of dozens of other possible actions, the program uses a system call to ask the kernel to take the appropriate action. Because all UNIX systems use the same system calls, UNIX programs are very portable. (In this context, portability doesn't mean that the same program can be copied to another machine and run; it means that a programmer can make the program run on another machine with few or no changes.)

1

Figure 1.1

The parts of a UNIX system.

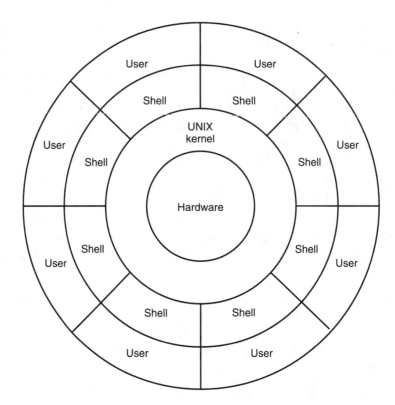

The *shell* is a program that acts as the user interface to the kernel—the shell is the part you actually see and use. Traditionally, shells have taken the form of command-line interfaces, but newer versions of UNIX also provide graphical user interface (GUI) shells. The UnixWare desktop is an example of a GUI shell.

UNIX systems also include a wide variety of utility programs called *tools* or commands. Most tools are small and relatively simple, and each accomplishes a single task or group of related tasks. These tasks, such as copying files or making backups, are usually secondary to the computer's main work. Although you didn't buy your computer to perform these tasks, they are necessary activities.

People buy computers to run applications, not to communicate with the operating system or to use UNIX tools. *Application programs* earn the computer's keep by balancing budgets, storing and retrieving customer lists, helping in the composition of documents, and performing many other useful functions.

Most UNIX systems don't come with application programs, although older versions of UNIX included text-processing software. Applications usually must be purchased, either from the computer manufacturer or from third-party vendors. Thousands of UNIX packages are available, including conversions of PC applications to UNIX.

Some UNIX Terminology

This section defines some important terms used in UNIX.

- *Advertise*. Another term for export.

- *Background execution*. Running a UNIX program that doesn't interact with the screen or keyboard. Background execution is used to perform tasks that require significant time but that don't require interaction with the user such as sorting a file or formatting a file for printing.

- *Console*. A terminal found on all UNIX systems, which is unique in that system error messages are displayed on it. A console isn't physically different from any other terminal; on traditional multiterminal systems, the console is simply the terminal plugged into a special port.

- *Current directory*. Also known as the current working directory. This directory is where your activities are located and is the directory from which all relative path names start. You run a cd command to make a directory the current directory.

- *Device driver*. A software module within the UNIX kernel that controls the operation of a specific type of device such as a disk drive, terminal, or tape drive. A device driver is included for each type of hardware on the system; it contains the instructions to perform operations such as reading and writing data.

- *Directory*. A file that contains a table of contents for other files. From your perspective, directories serve as a place on-disk where you can store files.

- *Export*. To make a resource (such as a directory) available to other systems on the network. Some networking systems use the word *advertise* instead, to indicate that, although the resource is available, it may not necessarily be used.

- *File*. A group of related data organized into a single unit and stored on the UNIX file system under a file name. UNIX has four types of files:

    Regular files (the type you most commonly see and use)

    FIFO files ("first-in, first-out" files or "pipes")

    Character device files (devices such as terminals)

    Block device files (devices such as disk drives)

- *Foreground execution.* The operation mode in which a program accepts input from the keyboard and displays data on-screen. By default UNIX programs run in the foreground. Programs that run in the foreground are also said to be interactive.

- *I-node.* Stands for information node. An area of a disk that contains important information about a file, including the file's mode, number of links, user identification information for the owner, size of the file, time and date stamps, and information telling where the data associated with the file or directory are located on disk.

- *Kernel.* The central core of UNIX in which the computer's activities are coordinated and controlled. The kernel remains in the machine's memory as long as the computer is running.

- *Multitasking.* The capability to perform more than one task at a time for each user.

- *Multiuser.* An operating system that enables more than one person to use the computer simultaneously.

- *Network.* A set of linked computers that can share data. The links between computers may be temporary and initiated on request (for example, a UUCP network), or they may be permanent (for example, an Ethernet network).

- *Parallel.* Operations running simultaneously. Computers with parallel programs run the programs at the same time; computers with parallel processors have two or more processors working concurrently. The parallel port on a computer sends more than one piece of information at a time, compared with a serial port, which must send one bit of information at a time.

- *Pipe.* A way to use the output of one command directly as input to another command. A pipe is symbolized on the command line by a vertical bar (¦), as in the command who ¦ sort.

- *Shell.* A program that links the internal portions of UNIX (the kernel) with the user, thereby providing the interface between the kernel and you. You issue commands, which the shell translates into system calls for the kernel, and information returned by the kernel is displayed on-screen by the shell in a form understandable to the user. The word *shell* is typically used to indicate a command-line interface, although technically the UnixWare desktop is a GUI shell.

- *Source code.* Instructions in a programming language that can be turned into a program.

- *Terminal.* A device with a screen and keyboard that enables you to communicate with the computer. Terminals superficially look like computers, but most of them lack a processor.

A History of UNIX

You don't have to know the history of the operating system to use UNIX. (If you're in a hurry, skip this section for now and come back to it later.) However, the history of UNIX is entertaining (as histories of operating systems go) and is helpful in understanding why various components work in certain ways within the UNIX environment. Although the histories of many operating systems begin with the words "Manufacturer X got together a large team of designers...," the opposite is true of UNIX.

The Game of Space Travel

In the 1960s, most operating systems were designed for batch processing—users provided programs and data to the computer, the computer processed the data, and results were printed. The user typically prepared a set of punch cards, sent them by interoffice mail to the computer operator, and got results back the next day. Very little human interaction with the computer was required or even possible.

By the late 1960s, however, AT&T Bell Labs in Murray Hill, New Jersey, was developing a new operating system called Multics. Multics was a joint effort with General Electric and Massachusetts Institute of Technology. In this interactive operating system, the computer and user essentially carried on a conversation with one another (the user typed at a keyboard, and the computer's responses were printed on a teletype machine). An interactive environment had much more potential than a batch system, and the developers at Bell Labs were becoming used to the capabilities Multics offered; Multics proved to be very expensive, however, and by 1969, Bell Labs decided to remove itself from the project. By March 1969, the computer used for Multics was gone.

The ill-fated Multics project had captured the attention of a handful of programmers who liked the interactive environment Multics offered. Two of these programmers—Ken Thompson and Dennis Ritchie—later became the primary players in developing UNIX. The group suddenly found itself without a computer, and attempts to requisition one were rejected as too expensive.

18

Ken Thompson had a powerful motive for finding a new computing environment: He was working on a game called "Space Travel," a simulation of the movements of the planets and major moons. In the game, the player guided a spacecraft around the objects of the solar system. Thompson found an abandoned DEC PDP-7 on which to continue development of "Space Travel," but the computer lacked an operating system. To make the computer usable, he turned his attention from the game to the development of a new operating system. Thompson and Ritchie sketched the beginnings of a new file system, a crucial component of what was to become UNIX. With input from Rudd Canaday, he implemented a very basic version of the new operating system on the PDP-7 as the 1960s came to a close.

This original operating system is barely recognizable when compared with today's UNIX. The file system was primitive and unwieldy by today's standards, and it was a single-user system with no time-sharing capabilities. Brian Kernighan, another Bell Labs researcher, suggested the name UNIX in 1970 in what Ritchie described as "a somewhat treacherous pun on Multics."

The environment in which the initial operating system was developed would shape UNIX forever. For instance, the early terminals transmitted information at 110 baud (9,600 baud and higher are common now); it took three seconds to print the message "Operation successfully completed." Wherever possible, Thompson and Ritchie (and other UNIX developers) used the shortest possible command names and the shortest possible messages. If a UNIX command succeeds, it usually gives no message at all!

In 1970, DEC introduced its new PDP-11 computer, and Thompson and his crew managed to obtain one. They moved UNIX to the PDP-11 and, the following year, applied the system for the first time in the Bell Labs Patent Department. Along with providing Thompson and Ritchie a computer on which to continue their work, the system provided text processing (known today as word processing) facilities for three typists who prepared patent applications. This first version of UNIX was known as UNIX First Edition.

At this point, UNIX was written in assembly language, as were all operating systems. Assembly language is the most efficient language in which any program can be written, and efficiency is particularly important for an operating system. However, each machine has its own assembly language, and converting assembly programs from one type of computer to another is difficult and expensive. As a result, UNIX written in assembly language for the PDP-11 computer was confined to that computer.

The next milestone in UNIX's development began independently of UNIX. In 1971, Dennis Ritchie began developing a new programming language called C, which is derived from an older language called B. (It seemed natural that the follow-up to B should be called C; this sort of word play is a hallmark of many UNIX tools.) C was notable for two reasons: It produced very efficient programs—sometimes 90 percent as efficient as assembly language—and C programs could be made to run on a wide range of computers with little or no modification. In 1973, Thompson, Ritchie, and others rewrote UNIX almost entirely in C.

The use of the C language transformed UNIX from an operating system that could run only on a PDP-11 into an operating system that could run on any machine for which C was available. Since 1973, UNIX has spread to many different makes and models of computers largely because so few changes are necessary to move it to a new computer. To this day, all versions of UNIX are written in C.

Two packages of programs released internally by Thompson's team are worth mentioning. The Programmer's Workbench included many of the programming tools that later earned UNIX a reputation as a powerful program-development environment. The Documenter's Workbench consists of a collection of text processing tools that made it possible to produce reasonably sophisticated documents on the computer.

Throughout much of the 1970s, UNIX was considered by AT&T as a tool for internal use. The Sixth Edition, released in May 1975, was the first version of UNIX widely available outside Bell Labs. AT&T licensed it to universities, an action that eventually changed the whole look of UNIX.

UNIX and Universities

A multiuser, multitasking system is ideal for a university. Students can be given accounts on one large computer rather than buying each student a separate computer. AT&T provided the source code for the entire UNIX operating system and charged academic programs only the cost of reproducing the source code and the manuals. (UNIX licenses for educational institutions are still comparatively inexpensive.) Students were attracted to UNIX because it had sophisticated document processing capabilities, including programs for typesetting mathematical equations and advanced tools for programming.

Students weren't just using UNIX—they were also writing programs for UNIX. Unlike programmers who work for corporations, students and professors have little reason to keep source code a proprietary secret. Following the example of the original Bell Labs developers, students and professors shared the programs they were writing for UNIX. Other users modified the source code itself. (In fact, the famous hacker ethic—information is free!—remains quite strong among old-time UNIX programmers and led to the development of the GNU project and the Free Software Foundation, which are discussed later in this chapter.) Unlike software for DOS, most UNIX programs are distributed as source code, and then turned into a program by someone at the buyer's end.

With most operating systems, only the manufacturer can fix problems, because only the manufacturer has access to the source code. With UNIX, anyone who finds a problem can look at the files, find the instructions that cause the problem, and fix it—creating a new and improved version of the UNIX operating system. Many of the fixes that were introduced in this informal manner have eventually found their way into the "official" AT&T UNIX. Programs were also added this way, including vi (which is described in Chapter 6, "Using the *vi* and *emacs* Editors").

Today, 80 percent of universities have UNIX systems. When students graduate and move into the workforce, they want to work on systems with which they are familiar. Although programmer preferences are not the only reason many small businesses have computerized with UNIX, they are a contributing factor in the movement of UNIX into many businesses not otherwise likely to consider the system.

The combined efforts of these programmers, students, and professors have provided UNIX with its current extensive tool set. As a side effect, however, UNIX commands are not completely consistent. For example, programmers at one university might be taught that all commands should include a help option (perhaps -?), whereas programmers at another university believe that a command should give a help message only when an unknown option appears.

Some universities went beyond producing programs—they modified the operating system itself. In fact, in 1976, the University of California at Berkeley released its first set of enhancements to UNIX; in 1981, the university released the 4.1 BSD (Berkeley Software Distribution) UNIX, an enhanced version of UNIX with added tools and capabilities. BSD, in conjunction with the U.S. Department of Defense, served as the force that linked UNIX machines into networks.

Networks and Workstations

As computers became smaller and less expensive, individual businesses and universities purchased them in ever greater quantities. These groups quickly realized that the machines needed to be connected into networks. By the late 1970s and early 1980s, many UNIX sites were trying to link several machines into local area networks.

In late 1977, AT&T added UUCP (UNIX-to-UNIX CP, or file copy) to UNIX as a means of connecting computers over telephone lines (not surprisingly, Bell Labs had many phone lines). UUCP was primarily a way to exchange files over the telephone and was used to transmit electronic mail and network news from one machine to another. UUCP networks don't lend themselves to system administration, however; they're essentially batch process systems, much like the early operating systems. The user queues up a request for a file transfer, and the computer notifies the user on completion of the job.

In the mid-1970s, the U.S. Defense Advanced Research Projects Agency (DARPA) was promoting a set of network protocols. *Protocols* are a set of agreements on how to format messages so that different machines can understand those messages and then hook into networks. To encourage the use of its protocol (called TCP/IP), DARPA decided to make an implementation available at low cost. DARPA arranged for a version of TCP/IP to be written for UNIX, and included it in the 4.2 release of BSD in the summer of 1983.

The TCP/IP protocol is derived from two other protocols: Transmission Control Protocol (TCP) and Internet Protocol (IP). TCP/IP protocols are used within the Internet (and other networks) to connect computers, communications equipment, and programs. Not all computers on the Internet run UNIX, but they all use TCP/IP.

Within a TCP/IP system, data to be transmitted is divided into small packets, which provides several advantages:

- First, communication lines can be shared among many users. Different kinds of packets can be transmitted at the same time, and they will be sorted and recombined when they arrive at their respective destinations.

- Second, data does not have to be sent directly between two computers. Packets are passed between computers until they reach their final destination. Thus, you can send and transmit data between computers even though they are not directly connected.

- Third, not every packet that is sent must follow the same routing path. TCP/IP protocols can, therefore, route packets from one place to another based on the best connection available at that particular instant.

How many protocols does a TCP/IP system support? Today, more than 100 protocols are used to organize computers and communications devices into a network.

Naming Machines

To tell machines apart, they must be given names. (They're given numbers, but they're also given names.) All UNIX computers and printers have names, and UNIX users love to choose clever names, with much the same enthusiasm as truckers pick their CB handles. Often, computers owned by a single group have related names—computers owned by an AT&T group include kandu, namu, and shamu, and were named after the Sea World whales. Cartoon and comic strip characters are popular, such as garfield, gumby, opus, thumper, and zonker, all of which are names of real UNIX computers. Also common are science fiction names (scotty, trantor, and xanth) and classic heroes (porthos and sherlock). Other names provide an interesting insight into their owners' interests in life, such as bikini, doorknob, spam, and yenta.

Other networking approaches were also developed. Both AT&T and Sun Microsystems released networking systems that combined the file systems of all networked machines into a single, huge file system. Both of those systems—RFS (Remote File System) and NFS (Network File System)—remain in use today.

In the early 1980s, the availability of small, inexpensive computers and the entry of UNIX-receptive students into the workforce made the development of work-stations possible and profitable. A *workstation* is a desktop computer, often providing great computing power, that is connected by a network to a larger computer or computers. In a scheme that mixes the advantages of PCs and large computers, workstations can exchange files with larger computers and share processing of complex tasks.

Workstations first became popular for engineers who had to perform intensive computations that slowed down the system for everyone else; when the engineers had their own processors, their work didn't cripple anyone else on the network. Soon, though, everyone was using some form of computation-intensive pro-grams—namely, the programs that make up a GUI.

A *graphical user interface* is an interface that represents parts of the operating system with pictures (called *icons*). The original idea behind the GUI was to cre-ate a user-friendly environment incorporating a consistent metaphor for under-standing operations—for example, a file is represented by a picture of a file folder, the mechanism for deleting a file is represented by a trash can, and so on. Graphical user interfaces are easier to use, not because they are easy to under-stand (clicking a file icon is completely different from opening a file folder) but because they are more consistent. After you have learned to run one program in a GUI environment, you can easily learn to run any other program in the same environment.

UNIX Goes GUI

Graphical user interfaces have been around since the 1970s, and possibly earlier. Most graphical user interfaces derive from work done at Xerox's Palo Alto Research Center. Currently, popular graphical user interfaces can be seen on the Apple Macintosh, in Microsoft's Windows, and in IBM's OS/2.

In the early 1980s, graphical user interfaces generated a great deal of interest— the technology of computers was advanced enough to handle the calculations needed to move graphic images around the screen. DEC and MIT collaborated on Project Athena, which incorporated a windowing system based on Stanford University's W windowing system. In the tradition of B and C, the new windowing system was named X, or X Window System.

X is very popular, partly because the source code is in the public domain, and because X Window now runs on many different computers and operating systems, not just UNIX. Unfortunately, X Window provides a way only to display windows, graphics, and text; it doesn't define their appearances. One group that decided to create a standard GUI was the Open Software Foundation, or OSF. Its GUI, Motif, is created using X Window. Another popular GUI is Open Look, available from Sun Microsystems.

UNIX Today

UNIX is now one of the most popular operating systems in the world; UNIX or UNIX look-alikes are available for almost every hardware platform. In 1989, DMR Group (a computer software consulting and services company) surveyed approximately 6,000 UNIX sites and found about 25 brands of UNIX. Of those, they identified six as the top UNIX versions: SunOS, SCO Xenix and SCO V/386 (together), HP-UX, Ultrix, USL System V Release 4.0 (UNIX System Laboratories was a division of AT&T created to handle UNIX), and AIX by IBM.

Since then, the market has shifted again. Both AT&T and the University of California at Berkeley are out of the software business. AT&T sold USL to Novell, a PC networking software company. A number of companies are still producing BSD-derived software; some of them are mentioned in the next section, "Flavors of UNIX and UNIX Look-Alikes."

More important, a recognizable UNIX culture has emerged. Any computer system (or any technological device or system, really) must support two groups of users: users who want to get the job done and don't care how the process works, and users who are passionately interested in the tools. When someone mentions "UNIX culture," the person is usually referring to the latter group. This culture has generated UNIX user groups (USENIX started in 1975 and UniForum in

1980) and a number of vendor organizations—groups of UNIX vendors that have joined to promote the industry or some particular type of UNIX or interface.

The UNIX culture is quite distinctive. Perhaps the best example of UNIX culture (and the most obvious) is Usenet. Usenet, also known as Netnews, is a vast information-sharing network that resembles a huge electronic bulletin board. Unlike most bulletin boards, Usenet has no central manager; each site carrying Netnews articles decides which articles or group topics (called newsgroups) are carried there and passed on to other sites. As represented by Usenet, UNIX culture is anarchic. It's not organized or managed from any central location, and it's varied enough that contradictions are certain to exist. Thus, any attempt to categorize UNIX culture must recognize that it does not apply to all members of this group.

The UNIX culture can be said to harbor a number of distinct biases. It values intelligence and knowledge, especially knowledge of UNIX and how to find information about UNIX. Free access to information and the freedom to spread information are also valued—including freedom of speech and free debate. For any position or opinion, it's possible to find a number of opposing (and sometimes crackpot) positions. In some ways, UNIX culture resembles a giant university (except that everyone who owns a UNIX machine has tenure).

Consider the Free Software Foundation, which is part of UNIX culture. The Free Software Foundation (or FSF) was founded by Richard Stallman, who believes that all software should be free to individuals. (In this context, "free" means that software should be available, not that developers of software shouldn't charge money for their products.) The FSF has set out to provide a comprehensive array of UNIX software under the name GNU (which stands for "GNU's Not UNIX"). Programs are distributed in source form for the cost of the media on which they are distributed. Users have the source code to which they can make changes, and they are actively encouraged to give the software away. Among products available from the FSF are a C compiler, a C++ compiler, a debugger, the emacs editor, and a shell. These products are used by major hardware vendors such as DEC, Hewlett-Packard, and the Open Software Foundation.

Of course, not everyone agrees with Stallman—and that's an important part of UNIX culture, too.

The discussion here has provided only an overview of UNIX's history and culture, and has, admittedly, overlooked many important people and events. For a chatty and more complete history of UNIX, see the book *Life with UNIX*, by Don Libes and Sandy Ressler.

Flavors of UNIX and UNIX Look-Alikes

Given the availability of more than 25 types of UNIX and UNIX look-alikes, how do you tell them apart? How do you determine which systems are compatible? This section describes the major flavors of UNIX and operating systems that resemble UNIX.

UNIX is the only operating system that runs on all sizes of computers, from microcomputers (such as PCs) to mainframes and supercomputers. You can't classify UNIX operating systems (some people refer to them as "Unices" as in the plural of "helix" and "matrix") by platform (although some of the more popular PC-based UNIX systems are discussed here).

The first issue is to distinguish UNIX from non-UNIX operating systems. Traditionally, any product that contained code derived from AT&T source code was considered a true UNIX system, and any product that had never contained AT&T code was designated as a look-alike. (The look-alikes sprang up to avoid paying license fees to AT&T for the use of its source code; because the look-alikes contained no AT&T source, they didn't have to be licensed, but programmers couldn't use the UNIX name on products created from this code.) If a product required an AT&T license, either now or in the past, it could be called a UNIX; otherwise, it's a look-alike. Thus, a product can conform to a UNIX standard yet not be an official UNIX.

This system will change soon: USL has passed the UNIX trademark to the X/Open consortium, a group of software vendors that deal in UNIX. In the future, a standard or a set of tests will be used to certify an operating system as a "UNIX."

The easiest way to categorize different types of UNIX is by ancestry: Most UNIX-like systems closely resemble either AT&T UNIX (System V) or a Berkeley version of UNIX (BSD). If the system contained source code from one of those two types of UNIX at some point, the system is usually called a derivative. For example, DEC's Ultrix operating system is a BSD derivative, whereas SCO UNIX's operating system is a System V derivative. From a user's perspective, however, most important features exist in both systems; the only real differences lie in some command options and the "standard" file-system structure.

AT&T and USL

AT&T no longer sells UNIX, but its name will be associated with UNIX for a long time. AT&T recently sold UNIX System Laboratories to Novell. USL is producing the latest version of UNIX, System V Release 4.2 (shortened to SVR4.2), for all platforms except the PC.

AT&T System V, AT&T's first commercial version of UNIX, was first released in 1983. System V was intended to be AT&T's standard version of UNIX, so the company released a document that described how System V and user software should interact. Any program that behaved in the manner indicated by the System V Interface Definition (SVID) was compatible with System V. Programmers could be confident that, if they used the features spelled out in SVID (and no others), their software would run correctly on any future version of UNIX System V.

SVID merely specifies the manner in which the operating system and user software interact; it says nothing of the internal workings of the program. Thus, a non-UNIX operating system—quite different from UNIX in structure, outward appearance, and internal workings—could technically be compatible with SVID. (In fact, the POSIX standard, which is described later in this chapter, falls into this category.) As System V has been extended, so has SVID. Over the years, AT&T (and later USL) has always added features, but has never changed or removed any system characteristics.

System V Release 4 incorporated many of the features that distinguished System V from BSD. Unlike earlier versions, the latest release, System V Release 4.2 (SVR4.2), makes networking and graphics a standard part of the UNIX package. System V Release 4.2 is also available on a variety of platforms. (Sun's operating systems SunOS 5.0 and Solaris 2.0 closely resemble SVR4.2.) Rather than distribute SVR4.2 for the PC itself, USL entered into a joint venture with Novell to market the PC version as UnixWare.

Berkeley Versions of UNIX

The Computer Systems Research Group (CSRG) of the University of California at Berkeley was the first group to offer a version of UNIX that included *memory paging* (a way to treat the computer as having more memory than it actually does); this feature made the BSD releases of UNIX highly popular. Most of the other features associated with the BSD releases (such as the C shell, the vi editor, job control, dynamically mounted file systems, and fast file systems) have since found their way into the System V releases.

The final release of BSD, 4.4BSD, was released by CSRG, after which the group disbanded. New developments of systems with the BSD name are confined to BSDI, a small independent company producing BSD UNIX for the PC. In addition, a number of interrelated public domain projects, such as 386BSD, FreeBSD, and NetBSD, have focused on BSD UNIX for PCs.

To provide compatibility with both BSD and System V systems, some vendors provided dual-operating system machines—that is, computers that are based on one operating system and that could emulate the other. (Some vendors went further: Some computers sold by Siemens-Nixdorf in Germany provide three operating systems: System V, BSD, and the company's own version of UNIX, SINIX.)

PC Versions of UNIX

Versions of UNIX for the PC have existed since the early 1980s, when Microsoft began selling Xenix for PCs. Xenix was AT&T UNIX Version 7, rewritten in assembly language for the Intel 8088 processor. Because of AT&T's licensing rules at the time, the system could not bear the name UNIX, so Microsoft labeled it as Xenix. (Some people consider Version 7 UNIX to have been the "last true UNIX," and tend to regard Xenix as the "only commercial UNIX.") Today's Xenix differs slightly from "official" UNIX but not at a level that an everyday user would notice. Xenix is currently owned and maintained by the Santa Cruz Operation, or SCO. It runs on machines with an 80386 or more advanced processor. SCO also produces an "official" UNIX, SCO UNIX, for PCs.

Many of the changes and fixes that went into Xenix were reflected in AT&T's UNIX. The merged version of the AT&T program for the PC was called System V/386.

As already mentioned, several versions of BSD or BSD-derived UNIX are offered for the PC, including 386BSD, FreeBSD, NetBSD, and BSDI. The first three of these systems are free but require a certain dedication to programming (much like the earlier UNIX systems). BSDI is a commercial product and includes professional technical support.

UNIX Look-Alikes

A number of other operating systems closely resemble UNIX but are not called UNIX for licensing reasons. Functionally, almost all of these are indistinguishable from UNIX. Examples include Mark Williams Company's Coherent and DEC's Ultrix. Table 1.2 lists selected UNIX look-alikes.

Table 1.2 UNIX Look-Alikes	
Operating System	**Manufacturer**
AIX	IBM
Coherent	Mark Williams Company

(continues)

Table 1.2 Continued	
Operating System	**Manufacturer**
ESIX	Esix Computer
HP-UX	Hewlett-Packard
MPE/iX	Hewlett-Packard
OSF/1	Open Software Foundation
SINIX	Siemens-Nixdorf
Uniplus	Unisoft
UTS	Amdahl
Venix	Venturecom
VMS POSIX	DEC

Of these look-alikes, Hewlett-Packard's MPE/iX and DEC's VMS POSIX deserve special mention because they became UNIX look-alikes through a "back door." That is, they came to resemble UNIX because of international standards.

POSIX, XPG, and Other Standards
Almost since the day UNIX was first created, groups have attempted to create standards defining it. The first comprehensive attempt at a standard description of UNIX was the /usr/group Standard, which was created by /usr/group (later called UniForum) in 1981 and released in 1984. Although this standard was initially ignored by most UNIX vendors, it has since become quite influential in shaping the development of UNIX.

Early in 1982, AT&T released the first edition of the System V Interface Definition (SVID), which has since been revised twice. (The third edition was released in 1989.)

Both the /usr/group effort and the SVID concentrated on defining the interface, independent of the hardware underneath, in order to create a portable environment. With the presence of such a standard, programmers and users can rely on the existence of certain facilities. A shell always exists, for example, and it always has certain features. When you move to a new computer, it's comforting to know that you already know and understand many of the programs available!

The SVID was too closely tied to AT&T for the comfort of other UNIX manufacturers, and the /usr/group standard was neither complete enough nor associated with a recognized standards utility, which hampered its adoption. In 1985, when the Institute of Electrical and Electronics Engineers (IEEE) decided to create a standard for operating systems, it chose the /usr/group standard to be the first draft, however. This standard ultimately became the Portable Operating System Interface (POSIX).

Operating systems are such a broad topic that the POSIX standard has been subdivided into smaller sections. Some of the more important sections are listed in Table 1.3.

Table 1.3 Some Parts of the POSIX Standard	
Standard Number	**Topic**
1003.1	System calls
1003.2	Shell and user interface
1003.3	Testing and verification
1003.4	Real-time extensions
1003.6	Security
1003.7	System administration
1003.8	Networking interfaces

Computer systems sold to the U.S. Government are required to conform with the POSIX standard. Incidentally, the word "conform" is important when referring to the standard: A system that is "POSIX-conformant" meets the standard; a system that is "POSIX-compliant" does not. Both MPE/iX and VMS POSIX are subsystems of the MPE and VMS operating systems that conform to the POSIX standard. Even if you are unfamiliar with the MPE and VMS operating systems, if you know UNIX (more correctly, POSIX), you can work effectively in these POSIX subsystems.

Basically, POSIX-compliance means that applications portability is not guaranteed. Only POSIX-conformant systems are guaranteed applications portability. Thus, POSIX standards or profiles specify both program and user interfaces but not implementations. Different levels of conformance are observed within the

POSIX-conformant systems: Implementation conformant and Application conformant. If you are an experienced UNIX programmer, to write portable POSIX programs, you will have to learn new function interfaces and new concepts.

Another standard frequently encountered is XPG/4, or the X/Open Portability Guide, Version 4, released by the X/Open Group. X/Open was formed in 1984 by five European manufacturers of UNIX-based systems, and now has more than 100 members. The XPG includes all of POSIX and much of the SVID. Furthermore, it addresses some areas that other standards don't, such as window interfaces and relational databases.

Exercises

1. What does UNI stand for in the name UNIX?

2. Define time-sharing. Is UNIX a time-sharing system? Is time-sharing a successful concept?

3. Is UNIX popular with colleges and universities? Why?

4. UNIX is written in a popular programming language. Name the language.

5. What is a shell?

6. What is a utility? Describe the difference between a shell and a utility.

7. Shell + Utility = Application in UNIX. Explain what is meant by this expression.

8. Explain why the file structure in UNIX is hierarchical.

9. Although UNIX is unique, a wide variety of UNIX operating systems exists. Name some of these systems and explain their differences.

2

Getting Started with UNIX

Topics Covered

- Starting the System
- Logging In
- Working with the User Interface
- Changing Passwords
- Logging Out
- Shutting Down the System

32

"The great thing about standards is there are so many of them." This quotation may sound familiar to you, but if not, you can appreciate its humor the more you work with different versions of UNIX. In spite of the differences in UNIX, the one constant you will undoubtedly discover is that each version has virtually identical access procedures. This is not to say that each terminal's screen on all UNIX systems looks the same. Be assured that you will find many GUIs (graphical user interfaces), menus, and shells that can be customized by your local system administrator. The steps to accessing the system, however, are fairly standardized.

Starting the System

Before UNIX can be used, you must gain access to the operating system through a connected terminal. The following are the most common configurations of terminal hardware in UNIX:

- Terminal/minicomputer configuration (see Figure 2.1). UNIX in its original form (circa 1969) ran on a single minicomputer made by the DEC Corporation. Today, UNIX can run on any minicomputer. Dumb terminal/minicomputer configuration is still popular due to the sizable memory and disk capacity of the host. Users sit at dumb terminals connected directly to the minicomputer by cables. This enables users to access the UNIX system's utilities and applications software.

Figure 2.1

A dumb terminal/ minicomputer system.

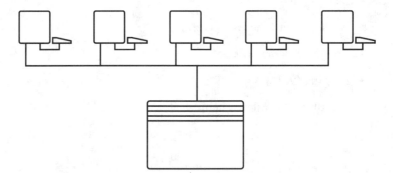

- Stand-alone workstation/minicomputer configuration (see Figure 2.2). Similar in layout to the dumb terminal/minicomputer just described, this configuration was popularized when PCs with greater processing power became more affordable. Although it offered the flexibility to work in local DOS applications stored at each workstation or to switch online and log in to the UNIX operating system on the minicomputer, its main advantage was the capability of a user to continue computer work even when the minicomputer became inoperative.

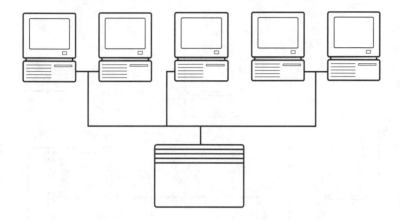

Figure 2.2
A workstation/
minicomputer
system.

- Workstation on LAN (see Figure 2.3). As technology progressed, providing new ways to communicate with each other from computer to computer, *local area networks* (LANs) were used to develop and stimulate user interaction. The result was predictable as LAN technology spread to the workplace. Each workstation requires a special add-on communication board and associated software protocols that enable it to access the network. A single workstation is designated as a *file server*, either *dedicated* (used only as a file server) or *nondedicated* (used as file server and workstation), with the other workstations accessing UNIX utilities and applications from it as needed or working "alone" in local DOS programs. Because of the prohibitive cost of minicomputers and the greater processing power now available in PCs, LANs became the fiscal favorite of corporate computer users.

- PC-based systems (see Figure 2.4). Today, dozens of UNIX variants and products can run on practically any desktop PC with a 386 or higher microprocessor, making it the most powerful and adaptable operating system available. A PC-based system is configured just like the workstation LAN described in this section, except that PCs are used instead of workstations.

2

Figure 2.3
A workstation/
LAN system.

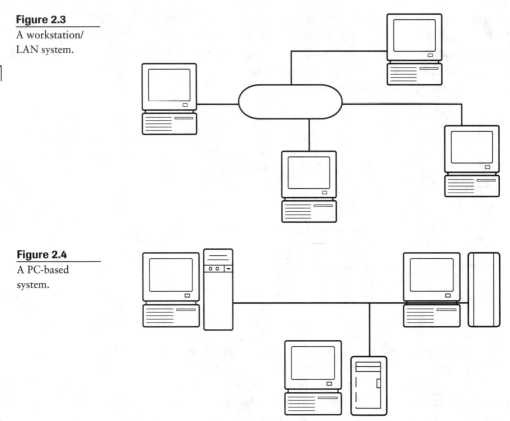

Figure 2.4
A PC-based
system.

- Modem hookups (see Figure 2.5). Many computer users don't have the convenience of any of the system configurations described previously, but they can still access a UNIX system with a modem. The modem merely provides the means for users to communicate with another computer/modem hookup over standard telephone lines. As with PC-based systems, special add-on communications boards and software are required to enable the computers (workstations or PCs) to "talk" with each other. When so configured, PCs, minicomputers, and mainframes can share information and peripheral hardware.

Terminal configurations vary greatly, so these examples are not exclusive. All configurations share a common element in that all must be turned on and hooked into a UNIX system.

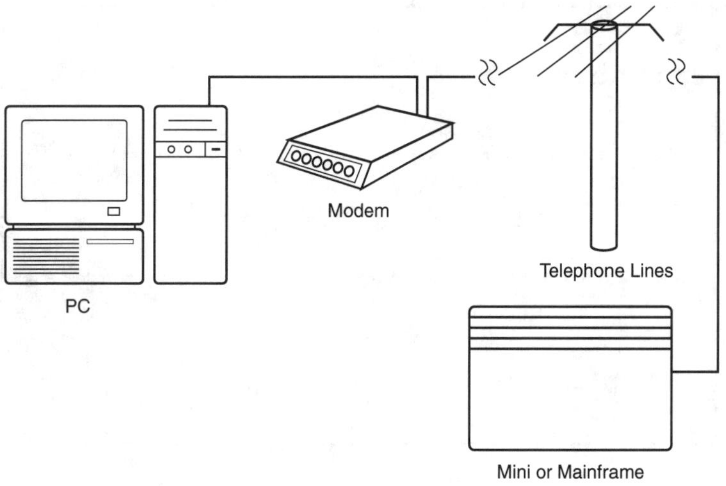

Figure 2.5
Modem access to
UNIX.

Modem

Telephone Lines

PC

Mini or Mainframe

Assume that you are seated in front of a properly configured and functioning UNIX terminal or workstation/PC. At your desktop, you should have at least a keyboard and a *display unit* such as a printer or, more commonly, a *video display unit* (also called VDU, monitor, or display). Both are integral parts of the terminal: one for input (keyboard) and the other for output (VDU or printer). You must be sure that your terminal equipment is turned on.

If you cannot readily determine this, consult the hardware users' manual or contact the system administrator. After you are certain that your terminal is indeed on and functioning normally, you are ready to log in to the UNIX operating system.

Logging In

Accessing the UNIX operating system requires you to have certain information at your disposal. Some system configurations need several items; some are set up to require you to supply only your personal password to gain access. Although the amount of information required varies, the basic steps covered in this section give you access to the UNIX operating system.

To connect your terminal to the UNIX system, you must turn on your terminal, press a key (or combination of keys), or dial a telephone number to connect by way of your modem. If you are unsure, contact your system administrator. As the UNIX system is booted (turned on), it does a number of system checks and reports the status by way of the output unit. Typically, the VDU or printer displays information similar to Figure 2.6.

Figure 2.6

UNIX start-up
display.

```
$
francis


*********************************
*                               *
*      Welcome to QUEs System V  *
*                               *
*********************************


francis!login:_
```

Because UNIX is a "case-sensitive" operating system, always use lowercase characters when entering login information or UNIX commands. Uppercase letters
may be used in password or file names only.

Entering Login Information

Unless you are starting up (booting) the system, the only thing you see on your
display is

```
login: __
```

Some terminals are hooked into more than one computer running the UNIX
operating system. If this is how your system is configured, your login prompt
may be preceded by the computer's name to remind you which system you're
using, as in this example:

```
victor!login: _
```

The cursor is now located where you type your login name. Your system administrator has set up an account just for you on the UNIX system, using your login
name. UNIX keeps a record of each time you (or someone else) use your account. After typing your login name, press Enter.

> **NOTE** *On some systems, the Enter key is called Return. This book uses the
> term Enter for this key.*

The UNIX system responds by asking you for your password, as in this example:

```
login:  gmeghab
Password: __
```

Notice that as you type your password, the screen does not display what you type. This prevents unauthorized access to your account by others who may be watching your screen. (If you make a mistake as you type your password, press Backspace once for each time you entered a character of your password and then attempt to type it again.) When you have typed the password correctly, press Enter. The following display (or one similar) appears:

```
Last login:  Fri Mar 7  08:35:39   on tty02
UNIX System V, Release 4
$ __
```

The dollar sign ($) prompt indicates that UNIX has accepted your access information and is ready for a command. Your system prompt can also be a percent sign (%), a pound sign (#), or something customized by your system administrator. The prompt tells you that you are working in the UNIX shell provided by your particular UNIX operating system.

If, instead of the shell prompt, you are presented with the message

```
Login incorrect
```

you may have simply made a mistake typing your login name or password. Try the access procedure again. Notify your system administrator if repeated attempts prove unsuccessful.

Auto Login Systems

Some terminals provide users immediate access. With these terminals, logins are automatic and passwords are not entered. If you have this kind of system, it allows you to select and use UNIX applications and services immediately. Other terminals do not place you in the UNIX shell, but in a menu-driven display. These systems are discussed in the following sections.

Working with the User Interface

After you've accessed the UNIX system, you have a number of application and utility selections available. These are presented on your screen in a number of ways:

- Some terminals present a menu or listing from which you can select available applications and services.

- Another option you may come across is the UNIX shell. This particular environment requires you to be more familiar with specific UNIX commands and their structures.

The following sections provide more information about each of these options.

Menu-Driven Systems

Menu-driven UNIX systems offer a great degree of personalization and provide the system administrator with an extra measure of security. Your system administrator can customize your menu to allow you access only to those applications and services that you need to perform your job.

Your menu may or may not look the same as the one a coworker is using, even if you both have the same job description. Remember that the system administrator can customize each one, so your name may even be used to identify your menu. Menu selections are normally listed next to a number or letter.

With a menu-driven system, you choose the application you want to run by typing the number or letter and pressing Enter. Again, the number and variety of applications shown on your screen may differ from another user's screen. If you find that you cannot access a program you need, speak to your supervisor or system administrator so that she or he can add it to your menu.

Shell Environments

The UNIX shell is by far the most demanding of the user environments you will come across. It requires you to be familiar with specific UNIX commands and the required structure, or *syntax*, for those commands to be effective.

If you don't have a menu to work from, your UNIX shell prompt is displayed after properly logging into the system. As mentioned earlier, your particular shell prompt is determined by the version of UNIX installed on your computer. It can appear as a dollar sign ($), a percent sign (%), a pound sign (#), or something else customized by your system administrator.

Unlike menus, the UNIX shell does not indicate where you are or where you can go. There are no listings of applications from which to select. Instead, you have just the shell prompt staring back at you from an otherwise empty screen. In short, it's up to you to find out what programs are available and how to run them. This section describes how to do this.

First, find out where you are. At the prompt, type the following command:

```
%pwd
```

Press Enter and a message will display similar to the following:

```
% /home/a_s/gmeghab
```

The pwd command stands for print working directory and indicates where you are located within the UNIX file system.

The computer's files are stored in directories. Directories are similar to the drawers of a file cabinet, each containing specific files of information. To retrieve a certain file, you must open (access) the correct drawer (directory). By using the pwd command, you are told by UNIX which directory you are in. Directories can be further divided into subdirectories. These subdirectories are like folders that store many files within the file drawer. For more details concerning file structure, see Chapter 3, "Understanding the UNIX File System."

The structure of all computer files is hierarchical, or "top down." The main directory, known as the root directory, is indicated by a slash (/). Each of the names that follows the / indicates a directory, a subdirectory, or file. For more information, see Chapter 3.

The final directory displayed is your location in the system, known as the *working directory*. In the current example, UNIX is telling you that you are currently working in the gmeghab subdirectory, which is located in the /home/a_s/ directory.

To access applications or services, or to retrieve and file information, you may find it necessary to switch from one directory to another. (If you don't know which directory the desired application is in or what command is required to make it run, contact the system administrator for assistance.) To switch directories, use the cd command with the name of the directory you want to switch to, as in the following example:

```
$ cd research
```

Press Enter. Now use the pwd command; your display reads as

```
$pwd/home/a_s/gmeghab/research
$ __
```

The cd command stands for "change directory." In your example, UNIX has moved you to the research subdirectory belonging to /home/a_s/gmeghab (assuming the research subdirectory has already been created by you). When you are ready to return to the gmeghab subdirectory, enter the following:

```
$ cd ..
```

UNIX returns you to the gmeghab subdirectory. (The two dots following the cd command tell UNIX to take you to the next higher level of directory or subdirectory in the file system.) Use the pwd command:

```
$ pwd
/home/a_s/gmeghab
$ __
```

These commands assist you in navigating through UNIX.

Changing Passwords

Computer system integrity, or security, is a high priority with any company that uses database files, mass storage, e-mail, or any of the dozens of other utilities and services that exist for electronic data manipulation. You are part of the system's security because you have a password to access your files and applications. Remember that your password is not echoed on-screen. This prevents someone else from gaining unauthorized access to the system or your account. UNIX makes no distinction between *you* typing your login name and password and *someone else* typing your login name and password. If someone else compromises the system using your account, whether or not you knowingly gave them your account information, you are held responsible for any damage.

What can you do to protect yourself? If you follow a few simple guidelines, your password can remain *your* password:

- Passwords can be as many as eight characters long; longer is better.

- Passwords can use letter and number combinations; use both.

- Passwords can use upper- and lowercase letters; use both.

- Passwords can use special characters; use some.

- Passwords can be compromised if written down; memorize your password.

- Passwords can be guessed; don't use common items (birthdays, Social Security numbers, anniversaries, employee number, favorite color, your login name, and so on).

- Passwords can be bypassed; don't let someone else use your account after you've logged in, and make sure you log out correctly (see the later section, "Logging Out," for details).

When you were first introduced to the UNIX system, the system administrator created an account for you, using your login name, and provided you with a password. The password provided is intended to be used temporarily. Your UNIX system may prompt you to change it after logging on the first time, or after a few times, or this decision may be left up to you.

Some UNIX systems require you to change your password at a set interval, usually determined by the system administrator. In this case, you are prompted by the system when it's time to change your password.

If you haven't yet changed your password, change it now. From the shell prompt, type

```
% passwd
```

Press Enter. The system responds with an on-screen prompt similar to the following:

```
% passwd
Changing password for gmeghab
Old password: __
```

Type your old password and press Enter. You are then asked to enter a new password:

```
New password: __
```

Type your new password and press Enter. UNIX asks you to retype your new password for verification, as shown:

```
Retype new password: __
```

In the event you make mistakes as you enter your new password, UNIX prompts you with appropriate error messages, such as

```
You may not re-use the same password.
passwd:  illegal password; try again
```

or

```
passwd:  They don't match; try again
```

or

```
passwd:  They don't match; too many tries; try again later
Password request denied.
Reason:  cannot get new password.
% __
```

The preceding error message is generated when you have failed, after three attempts, to change your password. When this occurs, UNIX ends your password change session and exits back to the UNIX shell prompt. You have to try again later.

Remember, for security purposes, UNIX doesn't display passwords as they are typed. Additionally, when UNIX stores your password, it stores it in a form that cannot be accessed by anyone, even the system administrator. So don't forget your password! The passwd operation may differ from system to system because of the inherent program variants. If you have difficulty changing your password, contact the system administrator for assistance.

2

Logging Out

Leaving the system isn't as simple as turning off the computer or terminal. The UNIX operating system may be involved with many tasks for many users, all happening at the same time. Many UNIX processes run in the background without you ever knowing, such as monitoring system usage, managing peripherals (printers, plotters, and so on), and checking user file permissions. Although most of this doesn't directly affect your logging out, it's an important feature of UNIX that you should understand.

Perhaps the most important aspect of logging off the system is that it ensures that your applications and files have been stopped and closed properly, and that your account is *closed*. This prevents someone else from accessing the system through your account, thus compromising system integrity.

> **TIP** *Log out of your system even when leaving your terminal for just a few minutes!*

Most systems require a single command at the shell prompt to log off, such as

```
% exit
```

or

```
% logout
```

Another alternative is to press Ctrl-d.

Once you have successfully logged off the system, you see the UNIX login message on-screen:

```
login: __
```

It is especially important to log off the UNIX system properly when your company is paying for access time. Don't be the one who doesn't log off properly and then goes home for the weekend! On those systems where the UNIX connection is made by way of a modem, be sure to hang up or otherwise disconnect the modem once you have logged off.

Shutting Down the System

The system administrator is the only one who can shut down the system, and only after all other users have properly logged off—unless you are on a single-user PC-based system. Power is seldom shut off when using a minicomputer or

mainframe computer. Exceptions to this policy might include computer maintenance or extended idle periods. Regardless of the reason, when UNIX is going to
be shut down entirely, the system administrator is responsible for generating a
broadcast message (shown on every active user's screen) similar to this:

```
Broadcast message from root   (tty01)   on francis Wed Dec   7 15:27:00...
The system will be shut down in 60 seconds.
Please log off now.
```

This message is followed by another one immediately before the actual system
shutdown:

```
Broadcast message from root   (tty01)   on francis Wed Dec   7 15:28:00...
The system is being shut down now!
Log off now or risk losing your files.
```

When any of these messages appear on your screen, log off quickly to avoid losing or damaging data. Don't log in again until the system has been shut down
and restarted.

To log off your single-user PC-based system, be sure you have properly closed all
applications and data files and then type the following command:

% shutdown

UNIX initiates the shutdown utility by examining its current state, closing applications and files that are open, and then terminating its processes in an orderly
manner. Once complete, your display looks similar to this:

```
System is down
```

CAUTION! *Only now is it safe to remove system power from the computer and
peripherals. Shutting down UNIX any other way can result in damage
to the file structure of the operating system.*

Exercises

1. What is the meaning of the UNIX command pwd?

2. Is the UNIX cd command similar to the cd command in DOS?

3. In the command cd .., what does the .. stand for?

4. In the command cd ., what does the . stand for?

5. Issue the command cd ~gmeghab and then type **pwd** (*gmeghab* is my name.
   Choose the directory that is under your name.) What is the meaning of ~ in
   this case?

6. At the UNIX prompt, type **cd** ~ and then type **pwd**. What is the directory you are in right now?

7. At the UNIX prompt, type **cd *gmeghab*** (again, choose the directory that is under your name). What was the response of UNIX? What can you say about the cd commands in Questions 5, 6, and 7?

8. Assume that you are in your home directory and you type **cd jwang**; the response of UNIX is

   ```
   /home/a_s/jwang
   ```

   What can you conclude about jwang?

   Type **pwd**.

   What can you conclude about the command cd in general?

9. What is the meaning of a home directory? How do you determine the home directory on your system?

10. What is the difference between shutdown and exit in a UNIX system?

3

Understanding the UNIX File System

Topics Covered

- Disks, Directories, and Files
- How UNIX Treats Files
- The Directory Tree
- File Names and Types
- File Placement
- I-Node Tables
- Piping

Your office file system is probably made up of a combination of desk drawers and filing cabinets. You use your file system by placing documents in manila folders or hanging folders and placing the folders in the filing cabinet. When you want to use one of these files, you look at the labels on each drawer and then open the drawer that pertains to the file you want. You then look at the labels on the hanging folders and pick out the one you are looking for. You open the file and start reading the documents until you find the one you want.

Computers have file systems, too. Instead of filing cabinets, computers have hard disks (see Figure 3.1). Instead of drawers and hanging folders, they have directories.

Figure 3.1

A hard disk drive.

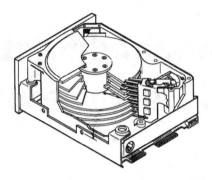

This chapter explores the UNIX file system. By the end of the chapter, you will have a working knowledge of what a file system is, how UNIX treats files, and how the UNIX file system is organized.

Disks, Directories, and Files

The UNIX operating system manages hard disk storage space by *fragmenting* files (breaking them into smaller chunks), and storing them here and there on the disk, wherever unused space exists. UNIX keeps a list of where these file parts are located. It's the same as the warehouse foreman who has shipments broken up and boxes stacked in any available nook or cranny, and then notes each location on a clipboard. Because the boxes are all labeled and their whereabouts known, the entire shipment is easily retrieved and reassembled—just as files are by UNIX. This means that hard disk space is always efficiently used because, as even one tiny sector is freed, UNIX has it immediately available for reuse. Otherwise, the system would soon choke for lack of storage space.

Floppy disks work in the same manner for efficient usage of available space. On a UNIX system, floppies are separate file systems. They must be *mounted* for use and *unmounted* when that floppy is removed and another inserted. Once mounted, the floppy appears as a subdirectory of the root directory. It may then have files written to it or copied from it, and can be otherwise accessed like any other directory on the system. But floppies do not have to be mounted. (See the use of tar and cpio in Chapter 11, "UNIX System Administration.")

Directories on a disk are much like a card catalog at the library. When you want to find a book, you look it up by author or title in the card catalog. The card for the book gives you a number, which identifies the area of the library where that book is located.

Directories work much like the card catalog system. The sectors and blocks of a disk are like the bookshelves. They are the valid locations where files (books) are found. The operating system looks at the directory (card catalog) to see where the file (book) is found. It then reads the location information and can retrieve that file (book).

Directories not only provide the operating system with a location and retrieval mechanism, they also help you to better organize your files. So, directories serve two purposes: They enable you to organize where things are found, and also enable the operating system to find these files easier and faster.

Files are the basic units of UNIX, but they quickly can get out of hand without some sort of management. As a user, you create files whenever you cause a program to save data (redirect output) to the hard disk. Any UNIX user soon has dozens of files. Add in all the other users on the system, and there is the possibility of hundreds of files coming into existence every day! Imagine displaying a list of files on the disk and seeing many thousands of files scroll quickly by. How would you find the one you wanted?

Directories are the answer. The standard analogy is to liken files to file folders and directories to drawers in a file cabinet. But, narrow that analogy even more and imagine those cardboard alphabetical dividers that you see in many file cabinets. Those dividers are equivalent to subdirectories.

Directories and subdirectories are handy slots to categorize and store files. Looking at a few dozen files is far better than searching through several thousand.

UNIX uses a read-ahead/write-behind file access method. This means that data to be written to the disk drives is buffered in memory and written later, when system resources are affected less by the write action. Also, data is read from the disk in larger "chunks" than requested by the application, based on a high

47

3

probability that the extra data is needed in the next read request. This read-ahead/write-behind practice reduces the amount of times the heads of the disks have to move. (Head movement is mechanical and therefore costly in terms of the time it takes to execute the request.)

Because power outages pose a hazard for the data being stored in the buffer, most UNIX systems are protected by an uninterruptible power supply (UPS). There are times, however, when the system halts without having had the system's buffers written to the disk. This situation generates a corrupt file system. Although all the data in the buffers are lost, UNIX provides a utility to justify the file system to a noncorrupted state.

This utility is called fsck, which stands for *file-system check*. It corrects mismatches and enables the file system to be used again. You must have system administrator or superuser privileges to run fsck. There is also a maintenance mode that shuts down the system to other users and allows the check and repair of the file system without chance of interference. Again, special system privileges are required.

The continued use of a corrupted file system leads to further corruption—even for data that may not have been accessed for months. It is important to regularly check the file system with fsck to make sure it is clean.

How UNIX Treats Files

File systems are made up of directories and files, and the operating system uses directories to keep track of where the files that you create are stored. The UNIX file system follows these basic rules, as does any operating system. One thing that separates UNIX from other operating systems, though, is that *everything* in UNIX is a file! Although some operating systems have special notation or references for handling directories and special devices, to UNIX these are all files. The directories that you create on a UNIX system are just files, and you are able to look at them using many of the UNIX file manipulating commands (for example, cat, hd, or dd). Likewise for special devices: disk drives, terminals, or memory.

UNIX sees files as being one of three types (see Table 3.1). An *ordinary file* is the same as a text or program file on a DOS system. Beyond that, UNIX and DOS are not comparable. UNIX sees file directories as simply another kind of file (*directory files*), which can be acted on as any other file. To UNIX, devices are *special files*, which, again, may be manipulated with standard file-handling utilities.

Table 3.1	The Three Types of UNIX Files
File Type	**Description**
Directory file	A file containing names of other files (including other directories)
Special file	A file representing a hardware device

Here's an example to show this difference in the power of UNIX as compared with DOS. On a DOS system, you might have a parallel port (LPT1) and two serial comm ports (COM1 and COM2). You are limited in expanding the system because DOS sees these as specific devices related directly to a fixed name. On many DOS systems, one more parallel port and two more comm ports exhaust the possible names.

A UNIX system, seeing a device as just another file, is not restricted. You can have literally thousands of devices attached, because each device (to UNIX) is simply a file, and the number of files is limited only by storage space.

UNIX also makes no assumptions as to the structure of a file. Many operating systems have special file types for indexing or storing database-type files. Different kernel routines are built into these operating systems for manipulating this type of file. UNIX isn't like this; the applications developer must provide the structure of the files.

Files in UNIX are referred to as *byte streams*. A byte is a string of binary 1s and 0s (the basic or *machine language* that computers use). Instructions consist of 8, 16, 32, 64 or more 1s and 0s, depending on the design of the computer's central processing unit (CPU). This means that when you open a file in UNIX and start reading it, you are given one byte after the other as if it were in a stream of water coming out of a faucet. This simplicity of the file-handling kernel routines keeps the kernel small and optimized.

3

The Directory Tree

The UNIX file system is organized in what is called an upside-down *tree structure*. This means that it is *hierarchical* in nature. The position of the file is important and can be compared with an army. There is one general branching down to several colonels, many majors, many sergeants, and many, many privates. It is called an upside-down tree because, when diagrammed (see Figure 3.2), it resembles a tree with its branches turned upside down. (It is also like a military chain of command or a corporate organizational chart.)

Figure 3.2

The directory structure resembles an upside-down tree.

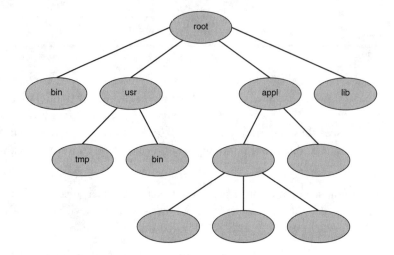

The top directory is referred to as the *root directory*. Notice how each successive directory is located "beneath" the root. This is what gives UNIX its hierarchical structure. Each succeeding directory is a *child* of its *parent* directory. In Figure 3.2, usr is a child of root, and root is the parent of usr. Likewise, tmp is a child of usr, and usr is tmp's parent.

To reference directories use the forward slash (/). Each successive slash takes you lower in the directory structure. For example, to reference the root directory, you specify a single /, as in the following command:

```
%cd /
```

This command changes the directory to the root directory. The following command references the tmp directory found in the usr directory found off the root directory:

```
%cd /usr/tmp
```

These examples use *absolute referencing*. In an absolute reference, the reference is anchored with the preceding slash. Another form of referencing is *relative referencing*. For example, referring to the directory /usr/linda/letters in a command, such as cd /usr/linda/letters, is an example of using absolute addressing (the complete path information is given). Relative referencing is faster because it's not necessary to type all the path information, which could be much longer than this example. If you are in /usr/linda/revisions and you want to go "up and over" to /usr/linda/letters, simply use a relative address in your command and type **cd ../letters**. This tells UNIX to go up one directory level and down to the named directory.

In the command

```
% cd home
~
%
```

home stands for the user's home directory; home is a C shell variable (see Chapter 8, "Shells and Shell Scripts," for more details on C shell variables). The *tilde* symbol (~), which is the response to the UNIX command cd home, is a C shell variable (also Korn shell variable; see Chapter 8 for more details), which means, "consider everything relative to my home directory." So, if there is a research directory in /home/a_s/gmeghab, the command

```
% cd ~/research
```

is equivalent to the command

```
% cd /home/a_s/gmeghab/research
%
```

You could also go "home" by issuing the following command:

```
%cd
%
```

The command

```
% cd ~gmeghab
%
```

also results in checking to see whether gmeghab is recognized as a user with a home directory and taking it home. If the same command were issued and the response was Unknown user: home, this means that the system does not recognize a user called home:

```
% cd ~home
Unknown user: home
%
```

The command cd jwang or cd ~jwang results in the same thing:

```
% cd ~jwang
%
% cd jwang
%
```

There are two forms of relative referencing: One is relative to the current directory, and the other is relative to the parent directory. To reference a directory relative to the current directory, use a dot (.). To reference a directory relative to the parent, use two dots (..).

Figure 3.3 contains two bin directories and two tmp directories. If the present working directory is /usr, then ./bin refers to the bin directory below usr. If the current working directory is the root directory, however, ./bin refers to the bin directory off the root directory.

Figure 3.3
Relative
referencing.

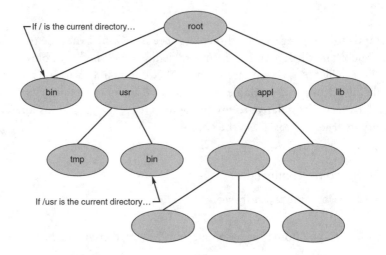

Because /bin is an absolute reference, it always refers to the bin directory off of root. Likewise, if the present working directory was /usr/bin, ../tmp is referring to /usr/tmp. Table 3.2 summarizes absolute and relative referencing.

Table 3.2 Absolute and Relative Referencing	
Syntax for Referencing	**Reference Meaning**
/usr/bin	Absolute
./usr	Relative to current directory
usr/tmp	Relative to current directory (this is also acceptable)
../tmp	Relative to parent directory

You may also chain the double dots to mean the parent of the parent (../../). For example, suppose that the current working directory was /usr/bin and you wanted to move to /appl. Type **cd ../../** and press the Enter key. Each .. took you up one more directory. In this example, you went up to /usr, then up to the root directory, then back down to /appl.

Files follow the same rules as directories (remember that everything is a file in UNIX). To reference the file myfile in the directory /appl/data, you use the command /appl/data/myfile. If you are in the root directory, you can simply type **appl/data/myfile** and omit the slash. If your present working directory is /appl/data, you can type just **myfile**.

File Names and Types

File names are made up of words, numbers, or special symbols. You can, technically, use any characters in your name, but avoid using the following symbols, because they are meaningful to the shell:

   ;   \ $ *   !   ?   ¦   '   "   `   %   (   )   @   ^   [   ]   &   #

Although you can name files using these characters in a word processing or spreadsheet application, they are difficult to deal with from the command line. Do not use space, tab, and backspace for similar reasons.

By convention, most people use either the dot (.) or underscore (_) to separate multiple word files (for example, my_file, or my.file). File names can be as long as 256 characters. In UNIX, the notion of file extension is not as stringent as in DOS. For the most part, UNIX does not think much about a dot except that it is another character that is added to your name. Some applications, however, expect to see a particular letter after the dot (.) or *extension* of a file name. For example, a .c means that the file is a C source file and can be compiled by a C compiler, whereas .p is a Pascal source file, .z is a compressed file, and .tar is an archive file (like ZIP files in DOS). There are other conventions, but these are the most common.

UNIX is case-sensitive. This means that the uppercase letters and the lowercase letters are unique and meaningful. The file names myfile, MYFILE, Myfile, MyFile, and myFile represent five distinct files to the UNIX system, and you can have many more combinations out of the letters *myfile*. This is useful because backup versions of files can be renamed with a different case, therefore differentiating them from the original file. It can also be an inconvenience when mixed case is used. You must type the file name exactly as it appears (uppercase and lowercase) when you want to retrieve it.

53

3

Hidden Files

UNIX can have *hidden files*. These are files that the `ls` command family won't display without a special option. Hidden files are often used by applications to store user-specific setup information. This prevents this information from being deleted or changed accidentally. Table 3.3 provides some examples of hidden files.

Table 3.3 Hidden Files	
File	**Used By**
.wp.set	WordPerfect
.wpc.set	WordPerfect
.l123cnf	Lotus 1-2-3
.profile	Bourne and Korn shell
.login	C shell

You can create your own hidden files as well. Put a dot (.) at the beginning of the file name to hide the file. To see the hidden files in a directory, type the command `ls -a`. The `-a` option shows all files, including the hidden ones.

File Types

UNIX users work with a wide variety of files. The following list expands on the files listed in Table 3.1. Any UNIX file command that gives a "long" listing (shows all information for the file instead of just its name) can be used to determine a file's type. For example, the command `ls -l` causes all information on files in the current directory to be displayed.

- *Regular files* are spreadsheets, word processing documents, executable programs, and so on.

- *Directory files* are the directories on the system that keep track of the list of files available in the current directory and any subdirectories.

- *Block special devices* are the disk drives and file systems themselves (for example, `/dev/fd0` is a special device file that references a type of floppy disk drive to the system).

- *Character special devices* are the terminals, tape drives, and so on.

- *Named pipes* are files created to write to and read from. They act like a pipe line. See the section, "Piping," at the end of this chapter for a discussion of pipes.

- *Semaphores* are controls for resources. They can be compared with a key to a lock, or a token allowing access to a resource. Typically, processes use semaphores to control access to shared memory.

- *Shared memory files* are locations in memory where two or more processes are talking back and forth, writing information and reading it from this area.

Regular files also come in several "flavors":

- *ASCII text files* are the kinds of files typically created by a text editor such as vi, and that contain readable English characters. Most of the UNIX administrative files are ASCII files.

- *Command text files* are shell scripts. A shell script is a set of stored UNIX commands. These are ASCII text files that are executable.

- *Executable files* are binary files created by a language compiler such as C. These files, unlike text files (except for the occasional string of letters), are mostly nonreadable.

- *Data files* are those files created by applications such as word processing, spreadsheets, or databases.

File Placement

By convention, UNIX places certain files in particular locations (see Figure 3.4). Table 3.4 provides some examples.

Table 3.4 UNIX File Placement Examples	
Location	**Purpose**
/bin or /usr/bin	User-oriented commands
/usr/local/bin	Local user commands
/etc	Administrative commands and files

(continues)

Table 3.4 Continued	
/lib	Area for the C compiler libraries
/tmp or /usr/tmp	Temporary storage
/dev	Special device files

Figure 3.4

Standard directory
structure.

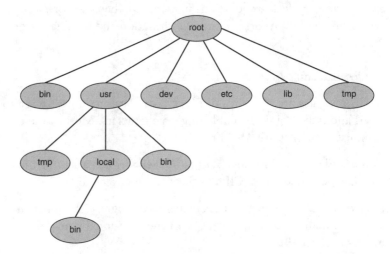

In the early days of UNIX, disk drives were considerably smaller than they are
now. The /usr directory structure (with its redundant names of bin and tmp—
duplicating the root directory's /bin and /tmp) was created to store programs not
needed during the boot process or maintenance mode because they were on a
separate disk drive. Also, /bin is short for binary, /etc stands for et cetera, and
/usr is short for user. /usr is historically the directory structure used to store the
user data. In practice, most applications install their executables and data in the
usr directory (for example, /usr/wp for WordPerfect or /usr/lotus for Lotus
1-2-3).

Most UNIX systems today place the user home accounts right off the /home/
directory (a home account is your base directory, the one you are in when you
log into the machine). The result of this is home accounts such as /home/a_s/
gmeghab, /home/a_s/junji, /home/a_s/dgibson, and /home/a_s/jwang/ for users with
the names *gmeghab*, *junji*, *dgibson*, and *jwang*. This means that, for example,
/home/a_s/ is the directory where users who belong to the School of Arts and
Sciences in a university setting are located.

Users in a business environment will have home directories in their respective divisions, such as /home/acct for users in the accounting department of the company. Users named *sue*, *kris*, *ben*, and *pete*, in an accounting department in a business environment, would have the following accounts: /home/acct/ben, /home/acct/sue, /home/acct/kris, and /home/acct/pete. The rationale for isolating the users is that it allows for easier manipulation of the acct directory as a unit. The same rationale can be applied to the /home/a_s/ directory.

Administratively speaking, this can save a lot of time when you need to look for something in a user's home account, or need to update the accounts all at once. You don't have to sift through the mess of every user who has access to your system, but only the division to which those users belong.

I-Node Tables

UNIX uses an *i-node table* to manage files. The i-node table is located on a special spot on the hard disk called the *super block*. The i-node table is a data structure, or record of information, that holds all the attributes (characteristics of a file such as its type, length, name, and date and time created) about all the files on the file system. There is one entry in this table for every unique file on the system. Each directory entry references an i-node number. An *i-node number* is an index to the i-node table. The i-node table tracks the following information:

- *I-node*. The i-node number.

- *Type*. Type of file: directory, character special, block special, pipe, regular, and so on.

- *Permissions*. Read, write, or execute permissions for owner, group, and other.

- *Links*. A count of the directory entries for this information, including the number of references (aliases or other names by which the file is known).

- *Uid*. The identity of the user who owns the file.

- *Gid*. The identity of the group that owns the file.

- *Creation date/time*. When this i-node entry was created. (This isn't the time that the file was created, but when this table entry was created or an aspect of this table was modified.)

- *Access date/time*. The last time the file was opened and looked at in any way.

58

- *Modification time.* The last time the file was modified.

- *Size.* The size of the file in bytes.

- *Location of file on disk.* This is a structure listing the blocks on which the file is located.

Each directory entry references the i-node number and is stored in the first two bytes of the directory entry as a binary number. The remaining 14 bytes are used by the name of the directory entry, that is, the file name.

Piping

Piping is a handy feature of UNIX that allows the output of one process to become the input of another, saving steps for you. For example, if you want to print three files, you can issue three separate print commands, such as `lp chpt.1`, `lp chpt.2`, and `lp chpt.3`.

More efficiently, pipe this into one command by typing `cat chpt.1 chpt.2 chpt.3 ¦ lp`.

The vertical bar (¦) in the previous example is how you tell UNIX to link processes. This command combines and prints the three files.

Here's another example. You want to send a text file, perhaps a report of some kind, to several other users. A quick way is to use the command `cat report.txt ¦ mail linda robin ben brad marvin`. UNIX reads your file to the mail program, which sends it to the recipients specified.

Pipes are worth learning and should become a part of your daily UNIX arsenal of commands. They are excellent little shortcuts for getting your work done faster.

Exercises

1. You are given a file named `random`.

   a. List in a table the information that you would have available on `random`.

   b. What information does the i-node number #24 provide on file `random`?

2. Say that a directory /usr contains a file called tmp. Explain exactly the relationship between the directory /usr and the file tmp in terms of their corresponding i-number. Assume that the i-number of the directory is #100 and the i-number of the file is #24.

3. Do hidden files or files beginning with a dot (for example, .hosts) have a different i-node numbering systems than regular files?

4. Explain what is meant by the number of links that a file has. Why does a directory have two links?

5. From a /home/a_s/gmeghab/research directory listing, you are shown the following lines:

```
%ls -als
drwx------ 5 gmeghab          512   Oct 15  18:04 .
drwxr-xr-x 48 gmeghab  9728   Oct 15   17:56 ..
```

   a. What does the . (one dot) stand for?

   b. What does the .. (two dots) stand for?

   c. How many subdirectories are there in the actual directory?

   d. How many subdirectories are there in /home/a_s/gmeghab?

   e. What command would you use to find how many directories there are in /home/a_s/gmeghab and to count them?

6. Can the same file be known by different names? Explain why. Do you think this is an elegant feature of UNIX?

7. Describe, step by step, how you might have four different file names for the same file in three different subdirectories. As an example, say that you have a directory called research and this directory has three subdirectories: pehng, junji, and myself. You would like to see the file name abstract.tex in myself exist in each directory under a different name. Use the command ln to accomplish that.

8. Understanding the concept of a link is vital to understanding other UNIX commands that manipulate a file: cp (copy), mv (move), and rm (remove). Explain how these commands work from the concept of a link. Use an example in each command to describe the relationship between these three commands and a link.

9. Why doesn't UNIX have a command called erase or delete instead of rm?

60

10. The ln command explained in this chapter concentrates on linking files in the same file system. How would you create a link to a file in a different file system? What happens to the i-node of the file name? Describe with an example the ln command and the details of what happened to the i-node.

11. *(Do not practice this exercise. Answer it theoretically and have your teacher explain why it is dangerous to do it.)* The ln command explained in this chapter basically concentrates on linking files in the same file system. How would you create a link to a directory? What happens to the i-node of the directory? Describe through an example how to use the command ln and the details of what happened to the i-node.

Working with Files and Directories

Topics Covered

- Command-Line Syntax
- Determining the Current Directory
- Listing the Contents of Directories
- Listing the Contents of Files
- Creating Directories or Files
- Using Redirection for Creating Files
- Moving or Renaming Directories or Files
- Copying Directories or Files
- Linking Directories or Files
- Deleting Directories or Files
- Finding Files or Directories
- Classifying Files

Working with a computer file system is like housekeeping—it's necessary, but certainly not glamorous. In completing this work, you look through the contents of files and directories, create directories, move and copy directories and files, and rename or remove directories and files. You may need to change the properties of a file or directory (to designate, for example, who can gain access). Frequently, you need to find a specific file or directory without looking into all of them. If your computer is part of a computer network, you also may need to exchange files with other computers in the network.

This chapter describes how to perform common tasks with files and directories by using the command-line interface. Because files and directories are just special kinds of files under UNIX, many commands work on both files and directories. This chapter includes information, however, on the exceptions to this general rule.

Working from the Command Line

When you work from the command line, learning new commands is more interesting, and you can perform some tasks that are not possible from the desktop. Here are some examples:

- *Gathering files.* The command line is useful when you need to specify files in several directories—for example, when you are deleting intermediate files or when you are trying to consolidate files, such as moving all files that end in .txt into a single directory. The command line also lets you specify more files in one command than you can show on-screen as icons.

- *Repeating actions.* The command line has features for repeating commands or calling up old commands and editing them. For example, you can issue a command to rename all files with a .dos extension to a .txt extension, or delete only the files that haven't been touched in six months, and then easily repeat the same command without retyping.

- *Selecting files.* Several UNIX tools locate files; you can use these tools, for example, to select only those files that haven't been touched in six months or more or only the files that contain the word *avocado*.

The basic file tools are shown in Table 4.1.

Table 4.1 Basic Command-Line File Tools

Task	Command
Show current directory	pwd
Go to new directory	cd
Create a directory	mkdir
Remove empty directory	rmdir
Show directory contents	ls
Show text file contents one screen at a time	more
Copy file or files	cp
Move file or files	mv
Rename a file	mv
Remove file	rm
Remove directory and its contents	rm -r
Find file by text contents	grep
Find file by name or attribute	find

Despite the intimidating appearance of this list, the tools are fairly simple; the power results from their combination.

Command-Line Syntax

This section describes the structure, or *syntax*, of a UNIX command line. A command has three parts that occur in the following order:

```
command options arguments
```

Note the following example:

```
rm -ir notes
```

The following list explains each of the items:

- *command* is the command itself, generally a short word or abbreviation for a word. The command always comes first. In this case, the command is `rm` (for *remove*).

- *options* modify how the command behaves; almost all options begin with a hyphen (`-`). In this example, the `-i` tells `rm` to act interactively by asking for confirmation before deleting each file. The `r` tells `rm` to remove any subdirectories and their contents. You don't have to have options, but when you do, they always come after the command and before the arguments. Also, options can come in any order. Some options have an extra argument; for example, you may have to specify the name of the output file.

  You can group options instead of listing each one separately with a hyphen; for example, the commands `ls -l -F`, `ls -Fl`, and `ls -lF` have the same effect.

- *arguments* are the targets of the command. Arguments always come last. In this case, the `rm` command is acting on the file or directory named `notes`. Not all commands have arguments, and not all commands behave the same way when you omit the arguments.

Some commands (such as `cat`) assume that if you don't specify an input file, you are going to type the input. If you type a command and nothing happens (you don't even get a prompt), the command may be waiting for more input. You can press either Ctrl-c to kill the command or Ctrl-d to end input.

Interrupts

When you are using the command line, you may want to stop or kill a job, or you may need to end input. In these circumstances, you can use signals called interrupts to interrupt the normal processing of a job. These interrupts are the following:

End input (End-of-file)	Ctrl-d
Kill job	Ctrl-c
Pause job	Ctrl-z

You usually can kill a running program with Ctrl-c (just as you can in DOS). But if you are accustomed to a DOS machine, be careful! In DOS, Ctrl-z is the End-of-file character, but on most UNIX machines, Ctrl-d is the End-of-file character. Ctrl-z puts the current job to *sleep*. For instance, suppose that you are sending a mail message and you need to check the status of a particular file: Pressing Ctrl-z puts the current program (the mail program) to sleep and returns you to the command line. You can restart a sleeping job by typing **fg** (foreground) command—suddenly, you are back in mail, just where you left off. (The fg command starts the job you last put to sleep.)

If the command doesn't require any input from you, you can run it in the background with the bg command. Suppose that you've started a big job (for example, converting picture files) and it doesn't require you to type anything, but the job does take up computer time. You can stop the job with Ctrl-z and then run it in the background by typing **bg**. You can now go on giving other commands, and the picture conversion runs without your assistance. (See Chapter 8, "Shells and Shell Scripts," for a more detailed discussion on foreground and background.)

In Chapter 1, "Introduction to the UNIX Operating System," you learned that when you work from the command line, you actually work in a program called the *shell*. The shell interprets your commands and runs the programs. One of the functions of the shell is to expand shell wild-card characters for you. For example, when you type the command ls .*, the ls command never sees the *. Instead, the shell turns that into the list of file names in the directory that starts with a period and gives that list to ls.

If you type an invalid option or command, you get an error message. For example, if you try to use a question mark as an option to cat, you get a message similar to this:

```
$cat -?
No match
```

The error message tells you that the option is illegal because it doesn't match the list of legal options. Some commands, when you type something wrong, show a *usage message*.

4

Usage Messages

To read command usage messages, you must know the conventions they follow. A usage message lists the command, the options, any arguments to options, and which options or arguments are either optional or can't be used with another option. The following descriptions refer to this usage message:

```
cat -usvte [-¦file].
```

(continues)

66

(continued)

- A hyphen (-) indicates the start of the options. Options that can be used together are listed together: You can mix any combination of -usvte. (Some UNIX vendors put their options in alphabetical order, unless the program requires otherwise.)

- A vertical bar indicates options that are mutually exclusive. For example, you can use either a hyphen or a file name with cat but not both.

- Square brackets indicate optional arguments. In this example, you don't have to specify either a hyphen or a file name.

- ... means that the previous argument can be repeated—that is, in cat *file* ..., you can specify more than one file.

Sometimes the output of a command is so long that the output scrolls off the screen. By *piping* the output into the more command, you can read the output one screenful at a time. Use the following command:

```
ls /usr/bin ¦ more
```

To advance by one line in more, press Enter. To advance by one screen, press the spacebar. (If your system doesn't have more, it has a similar program called pg.)

Long-time UNIX users also use the cat program—a program similar to more without page breaks (to be accurate, more is cat with page breaks). The name cat comes from the word *catenate*, which means to join, as a link in a chain. The cat command copies its arguments to standard output (the screen). If you name several files as arguments to cat, the program displays them all as one file. This command is useful for displaying the contents of short files or for joining multiple files into a new file with shell redirection (more on that process later in this chapter).

Determining the Current Directory

Some procedures are necessary when you use the command line that aren't necessary when you work from the desktop. Determining the current directory is one of those procedures; the command-line prompt doesn't normally include the directory. (You can include your current working directory as part of your command-line prompt, but the shell program you use determines how you accomplish that task. Explaining the procedure is beyond the scope of this book.)

To find out what directory is your current working directory, use the command pwd:

```
$ pwd
/home/a_s/gmeghab
```

In this case, the current working directory is /home/a_s/gmeghab.

Use the cd (for *change directory*) command to change your current directory. To go from your current directory to the subdirectory notes, enter the following lines:

```
$ cd notes
$ pwd
/home/a_s/gmeghab/notes
```

You can specify the directory with a relative path name, as in the last example, or you can use a full path name:

```
$ cd /usr/bin
$ pwd
/usr/bin
```

Relative referencing is described in Chapter 3, "Understanding the UNIX File System."

If you don't give an argument, using the cd command alone returns you to your home directory.

Listing the Contents of Directories

The basic command for listing the contents of a directory is ls. Without an argument, ls gives you the contents of the current directory:

```
$cd /
$ ls
bin         cdrom    dev    devices    etc
export      gnu      home   hsfsboot
kadb        kernel   lib    lisp
lost+found  mnt      net    opt        proc
sbin        su       tmp    ufsboot    usr   var   vol
```

The list is sorted alphabetically in columns. Notice that ls doesn't distinguish between types of files. With an argument, ls lists the file only or the contents of that directory:

```
$ ls sbin
autopush  bpgetfile  hostconfig  ifconfig    init      jsh
mount     mountall   rc0         rc1         rc2       rc3       rc5
rc6       rcS        sh          su          sulogin   swapadd
sync      uadmin     umount      unmountall  uname
```

In most cases, when you review the listed contents of a directory, you want to be able to distinguish between directories and files. You can mark the directory contents in two ways, using the ls command or the lc command. Your choice depends on personal preference and availability.

4

You can use the `-F` option with `ls`. With this option, `ls` marks all files that are not text files with a special character. The slash (`/`) indicates a directory, the at sign (`@`) indicates a symbolic link, and the asterisk (`*`) indicates an executable file:

```
$ ls -F
bin@       cdrom/   dev/   devices/   etc/   export/   gnu/        home/
hsfsboot   html/    kadb   kernel/    lib@   lisp/     lost+found/
mnt/       net/     opt/   proc/      sbin/  tmp/      ufsboot
usr/       var/     vol/   stu*
```

In this example, `usr` is one of several directories, `bin` is a link to some other file, and `stu*` is a program.

Several less common file types, such as FIFO files (first-in, first-out files, pronounced "fi-foe"—but usually called "pipes"), and special files also are indicated by `-F`. As a rule, however, you don't see them.

You may want more information about a file than its name, such as its size or the last time it was changed. The `-l` option (for *long list*) displays this information and more. The following is a partial listing of `ls -l` output, on user `junji`'s `home` directory:

```
total 343
-rw-r----   1 junji          5569 Aug  7 16:55 #.cshrc#
-rwxrwxrwx  1 gmeghab         126 Oct 12 12:06 acker2
lrwxrwxrwx  1 gmeghab          32 Oct 12 12:11 acker3 ->
    /home/a_s/gmeghab/research/acker
-rw-------  1 junji          4904 Oct 25  1994 aic
-rw-r--r--  1 junji           237 Aug  7 17:14 calendar
-rw-r--r--  1 junji           901 Apr 29 19:56 remotelogin.1
-rw-r--r--  1 junji           175 Dec 22  1994 result2
-rw-r--r--  1 junji           117 Dec 22  1994 result3
-rw-r--r--  1 junji           196 Dec 22  1994 results
-rw-r--r--  1 junji           537 Jul 28 16:41 texput.log
-rw-r--r--  1 junji          7970 Mar 21  1995 ttt
-rw-r--r--  1 junji            52 Mar 21 14:22 www.notes
-rw-r--r--  1 junji          1609 Oct 19  1994 yifei
```

The first line, `total 343`, is a rough estimate of the listed files in blocks. You can ignore this line. Using the entry for `www.notes` as an example, you can explore what the rest of the example means. First, consider the beginning character of the next-to-last line:

```
-rw-r--r--
```

The hyphen represents the file's properties. The first character is the type of file. The following types of files can be shown:

- `-` Regular data file

- `b` Block special file (such as a disk drive)

c   Character special file (such as a terminal screen)

d   Directory

l   Link to another file or directory

p   Pipe (sometimes called a FIFO)

The next three letters indicate that the owner of the file has read, write, and execute permissions for the file. The three letters that follow those indicate the permissions for the file's group (read and write permissions), and the last three letters are everyone else's permission (read-only).

The next section of the line is

```
1 junji     52
```

This shows the number of links to the file or directory (1), the file's owner (junji), and the size of the file in bytes (52). Links are very small—just a bit larger than needed to store their name. Directories are usually a multiple of 512.

The last section of the line is

```
Mar 21 14:22 www.notes
```

This shows the last time the file was changed (Mar 21 14:22). If a file hasn't been changed in over six months, the time of day changes to the year. This information is followed by the file's name (www.notes). If the file is a soft link, the line also includes a pointer to the real file.

To list the contents of subdirectories, use the -R (for *recursive*) option. The following code fragment is a portion of the output for the directory /home/a_s/ gmeghab/AI4301:

```
% ls -R

NN3
art
lisp
AI4301/NN3:

andersonxor.m    andersonxor.paper    banduxor.m    cbarton xor.m
dlewis_xor.m     eking-xor.m          gmeghabxor.m      jellis-xor.m
report.NN.eking
AI4301/art:
anderson.art     anderson.art%          andersonart.paper
banduroom.art    classroom.eking
classroom.jellis classroomtext.jellis classroomtext.jellis%
dlewis_class.art   dlewis_report
meghabghab.art    report.art.eking
AI4301/lisp:
```

4

```
anderson.lsp      andersonlisp.paper   bandurun         cbarton_lisp.lsp
  dlewis_lisp.
fileseking.lsp    lisp.jellis          lisptext.jellis  report.lsp.eking
```

This example shows that the `/home/a_s/gmeghab/AI4301` has three directories

```
NN3
art
lisp
```

and that each directory has its own files listed with the : separating the name of the directory from the files it contains.

In UNIX, any file that begins with a dot (.) is a hidden file. (Because you don't usually want to see configuration files every time you list the directory, the names of configuration files or directories often start with a dot.) To list hidden files, use the `-a` (for *all*) option:

```
% ls -a

.       ..       .login bin  dev  devices  etc  export  gnu  home  hsfsboot
kadb  kernel
lib  lisp  lost+found  mnt  net  opt  proc  sbin  stu  tmp  ufsboot
usr  var  vol
```

These files are in my root directory (`/`). You might see a different listing in your root directory (`/`).

Listing the Contents of Files

UNIX provides many tools for looking at the contents of a text file. The most obvious is an editor, such as `vi`. But using an editor requires that the information already be in a file and that you use paging commands, which you may not feel like using. The command used most often to read files is `more`. The `more` command displays the specified files but pauses after each screenful (usually 24 lines). To display the next screenful, press the spacebar. To save room, the following example uses the `-n` option to display the first four lines of text (pressing the spacebar will display the next four lines):

```
% more -4 grocery.tex

\documentstyle[12pt]{article}
\input{psfig}
\input{/home/a_s/pehng/Teach/Mat466/std.top}
--More--(0%)
```

If you want to skip the first 40 lines of the text but display the 41st through 44th lines of text, use the following variation of the `-n` option:

```
% more -4 +40 grocery.tex
\newcommand{\Iplus}{{\bf I}^{+}}
```

```
\newcommand{\Iminus}{{\bf I}^{-}}
\newcommand{\xsplus}{x_{sj}^{+}}
--More--(6%)
```

Notice the --More-- lines after each of these commands has displayed its output. The percentage in parentheses shows your location in the file.

At the prompt --More--, you can press the spacebar to see the next screenful of text or press q to quit.

You can also use the more command to search the file for regular expressions. A *regular expression* is one or more strings, each of which consists of letters, characters, numbers, and special symbols. A delimiter character usually marks the beginning and the end of a regular expression. Any character can be used as a delimiter as long as the same character is used at both ends of the regular expression. For example, /usr/ is a regular expression, and the / is the delimiter. Some UNIX utilities, such as grep, do not use a delimiter.

Searching for Simple Strings

You can use the more command to search for text within a file. Simply type a slash (/) followed by the text you're looking for, and then press Enter.

For example, to search for the word binary, type /binary. Sometimes you don't know whether a word is capitalized. A good trick is to leave off the first letter of the search. If you type /inary, it will match binary as well as Binary.

Creating Directories or Files

To create a directory, you can use only one command, mkdir, but to create a file, you can choose from several commands and techniques, depending on what you want in the file.

To create a directory with mkdir, name the directory as the argument:

```
% mkdir biographies
```

This command assumes that you are in your home directory and that your user name is a_s.(/home/a_s/gmeghab).

4

To create directories inside the newly created directory biographies, an explicit reference to the directory name has to be made:

```
$ mkdir /home/a_s/gmeghab/biographies/comedians /home/a_s/gmeghab/
biographies/politicians
```

This command creates the subdirectories comedians and politicians in the biographies directory.

To create several directories, specify all of them. Suppose that you are in the comedians directory and want to create subdirectories for the Marx Brothers, starting with Groucho. Use the following command:

```
mkdir marx marx/groucho
```

mkdir creates the directory marx first and then (within that directory) creates the directory groucho. If you put these arguments in the reverse order, the mkdir fails because mkdir generally creates only one directory level at a time. It can't create groucho in marx if marx doesn't exist. (Some UNIX versions have the -p option for mkdir, which can create intermediate directories if they don't already exist. Check your system.)

In fact, if you wanted, you could create directories for all the Marx Brothers in this way:

```
mkdir marx marx/groucho marx/chico marx/harpo marx/zeppo marx/gummo
```

You can choose from among a number of ways to create files from the command line. An editor is probably the easiest choice if you just want to create a text file.

Using Redirection for Creating Files

If you need a text file that contains only a line or two, redirecting the output of cat is an easy way to accomplish this task:

```
cat > call.txt
```

The cat command takes input (from the keyboard, if you don't name a file) and sends it to standard output; > call.txt sends the standard output to the file call.txt. For this example, add the following text, press Enter, and then press Ctrl-d:

```
Heyyyy, Abbott!
```

The Ctrl-d ends input to cat. If you pressed Ctrl-d before you pressed Enter, the file call.txt contains the text you typed, but there's no end-of-line character there to mark the end of the line.

You can add the output to an existing file (append) by using >> instead of >. To add the line Who's on first? to call.txt, use the following commands, pressing Enter after each line and pressing Ctrl-d after the second time you press Enter:

```
cat >> call.txt
Who's on first?
```

When you look at the contents of call.txt, it contains the following:

```
$ cat call.txt
Heyyyy, Abbott!
Who's on first?
```

Moving or Renaming Directories or Files

To move a file, use the mv command. You can move one file or directory into another location, or a group of files and directories into another directory. You also use mv to rename files because renaming a file is simply moving it to another name in the same directory.

Suppose that you are working in your home directory on your biographies of politicians. You have the directory named nixon, and you want to move it into the directory /biographies/politicians. Enter the following command:

mv nixon /biographies/politicians

This command also moves any subdirectories in nixon.

To move a file into your current directory, use a period as the destination directory. The command

```
mv /usr/home/chris/grocery.list .
```

moves /usr/home/chris/grocery.list into your current directory.

You can move more than one file and directory at a time if you move them all to the same destination. For example, the following command moves all the listed files into the postscript directory:

```
mv cover.ps toc.ps index.ps /Papers/finished/postscript
```

CAUTION! *Make sure that the destination directory already exists and is a directory! If the destination isn't a directory, the mv command starts going through the arguments one at a time, moving them to the target file. First, the command moves cover.ps to the file /Papers/ finished/postscript, then toc.ps, and so on. The resulting postscript file in the /Papers/finished directory is actually the index.ps file with a new name.*

4

To rename a directory or file, just move it to the new name:

```
mv call.txt catchphrases.txt
```

At some point, you may want to change the file extension on many files at once. Do not try to rename a group of files by using this command:

```
mv *.doc *.txt
```

This command does not change all the files with the doc extension to the txt extension. The command doesn't produce the result you want because mv just moves each file to the last name in the list. You can rename a group of files, but it involves a little bit of shell programming, which is beyond the scope of this chapter. (Refer to Chapter 8 on shells to learn how to write shell scripts.)

Copying Directories or Files

You already know one way to copy a file: You can use cat and redirection. The command cat diary.jan > diary.feb, for example, copies the file diary.jan to the file diary.feb. Such a procedure doesn't work, however, with a directory. The true copy command is cp. This command copies files and directories. The cp command behaves very much like the mv command, except that cp doesn't copy subdirectories automatically.

Suppose that you are about to make some drastic changes to your grocery list and you don't want to lose the original. Protect yourself by working on a copy of the file. You can create the copy by using the following command:

```
cp grocery.list food.list
```

Unlike mv, cp doesn't copy subdirectories unless you use the -R option, as in

```
cp -R /home/chris/project /home/leslie/project
```

You don't have to specify the subdirectories.

Linking Directories or Files

The ln command creates links between files. As described earlier, there are two types of links: hard and soft (also called symbolic links). By default, ln creates hard links; if you add the -s option, ln creates soft links. Not all systems have both kinds of links. Older System V UNIX systems have only hard links; newer System V versions of UNIX (SVR 4.0 and later) support both hard and soft links.

Some programs change their behavior with their name. For instance, grep and egrep are usually the same program file, but it behaves one way when named grep and another way when named egrep. Links are used to give the file its second name.

You can also use a link to shorten typing, by linking a file with a long path name to your current directory. For example, if you want to run the file /usr/local/scripts/startup.ksh from your home directory without typing the entire name, you can create a link to it in your home directory:

```
ln -s Startup /usr/local/scripts/startup.ksh
```

You remove a link in the same way you remove a regular file. In fact, when you remove a file with rm, you are just removing a hard link to the file; when no more hard links remain, the file is deleted. If you remove a file that has a soft link associated with it, the file is removed as well as all the soft links pointing to it.

Deleting Directories or Files

Two commands remove directories and files: rmdir and rm. Use the rmdir command only for removing empty directories. The rm command is used primarily for files (although it can remove directories too).

To remove an empty directory, specify the name of the directory in the command:

```
rmdir marx/karl
```

If the directory isn't empty, you get an error message. Incidentally, it's perfectly legal to remove your current working directory—just don't try to do any work there after the directory is gone. Leave your current (nonexistent) directory with cd.

> **NOTE** *If you think that your directory is empty but you still get an error message that the directory is not empty, some hidden files are in that directory. Remember that you have to use the -a option with the ls command to see the hidden files.*

To remove files, use the rm command:

```
rm list
```

To remove all the files in a directory, use the asterisk wild card for the file name:

```
rm *
```

4

CAUTION! *Wild cards and the rm command make a dangerous combination. You can easily destroy months of work by typing a command like rm *. And remember with rm, you can't get the files back!*

This is one reason why you shouldn't spend all your time as the superuser. It's just an inconvenience if an average user deletes an important directory, but it's a disaster for the superuser. The superuser has permission to delete everything on the system.

You can remove any file that you own, even if you have set it to read-only. Here is the reasoning: You own it, so you can make it writable if you want. (When you are acting as the superuser, you can delete any file. This privilege carries risks, so most people with superuser privileges don't log in as the superuser unless they have a specific task in mind.)

If you don't own the file, you can remove it only if you have write permission. The owner has to give you write permission. (For more information on permissions and modes, see Chapter 5, "Understanding Permissions and Other System Information.")

When you try to delete a read-only file that you own, rm asks whether you want to delete the file:

```
$ rm clients
clients: 444 mode. Remove (y/n)
```

You remove the file by typing **y**; any other response leaves the file intact.

If you don't want to be prompted for read-only files, the -f (force) option removes the files without prompting.

To delete nonempty directories, use the -r (recursive) option with the rm command. Suppose that you have decided you are tired of politics and want to delete /biographies/politicians, along with all the directories and files within it. You probably have some read-only files there, so you must force the deletion by using the -f option with the -r option:

```
rm -rf /biographies/politicians
```

Deleting Hard-to-Delete Files and Directories

Sometimes you get a file or directory that you can't seem to delete. In most cases, the file or directory has a funny character in its name. You may have a file name that starts with a hyphen, such as -quiet, and rm keeps responding that there is no option -q. The name may include a nonprinting character. If rm reports that it can't find the file, even though an ls shows it in the directory, the file name is likely to contain a nonprinting character. (Files that come from Macintosh and DOS systems are particularly susceptible to this. Some methods of transferring DOS files leave a DOS end-of-line character in the file name.)

The easiest way to delete the file is with the -i (interactive) option to rm. Follow these steps:

1. Type **rm -i ** * and press Enter. The asterisk indicates that the command interactively deletes all files.

rm presents the name of the first file in the directory with a message like
```
Remove file clients (y/n)?
```

2. If this is the file you want deleted, answer y; otherwise, answer n.

3. Repeat step 1 for all files in the directory, answering y or n as appropriate.

If the directory has so many files that it would take too long to cycle through them all, you can try constructing a wild-card pattern that matches only the file you want to delete. The easiest way to accomplish this task is to add an asterisk to the end of the file name to match any nonprinting characters attached at the end:

```
rm picture.gif*
```

If the file name contains a shell wild card, such as a question mark, you can delete the file by putting apostrophes around it. Apostrophes around an argument are a way of telling the shell to treat the text within *literally*, ignoring any wild cards. For example, if you accidentally create the file work?proj, you can remove it with the following command:

```
rm 'work?proj'
```

Recovering Deleted Directories or Files

In short, you can't recover deleted directories or files from the command line. Normally, when you delete a file, it's gone (although you may be able to get it back from a backup).

Utilities are available, however, that let you recover removed files. (MIT's Project Athena made public a set of utilities called delete, undelete, expunge, and purge. You may be able to get a copy.) True UNIX gurus frown on such a setup. They believe that if you get used to being able to recover files, sooner or later you will be working on a system without the wastebasket and delete something critical. They think it is far better to learn caution from the very beginning.

Finding Files or Directories

UNIX offers several tools for finding a particular file or directory: grep, egrep, and fgrep search for files containing a particular word or phrase, and find looks for a file with a particular set of attributes such as name or time of modification.

Searching by Content

The commands grep, egrep, and fgrep search through files for words or patterns (specifically regular expressions) and display on-screen the lines of the file that match the pattern. Note the following:

- grep uses regular expressions.

- egrep uses extended regular expressions, which are more sophisticated than the basic regular expressions used by grep.

- fgrep doesn't use regular expressions at all and usually is slower than either grep or egrep; fgrep can, however, search many more files than either of the other two programs.

For example, suppose that you keep a list of phone numbers and a list of business contacts in files named phone and contax, respectively. You need to find the phone number for Chris from the lawyer's office, but you can't remember Chris' last name. You can use grep to display all the lines in the files that contain the name Chris:

```
$ grep Chris phone contax
phone:Christmas Club 488-4923
phone:Chris Connell (Connell Build-It) 487-2508
contax:Amazon Accounting: Chris Ploame 487-6657
contax:Christie, Weston & Ritz 488-0003
contax:Mr. Christie x483
contax:Chris Neff x069
contax:Chris Clearmount (lawyer): Butcher & Cook 672-5947
contax: - Three children: Chris, Ellen, and Jay
```

If you want to search for a pattern that contains a space, surround the entire pattern with quotation marks:

```
$ grep "Chris C" phone contax
phone:Chris Connell (Connell Build-It) 487-2508
contax:Chris Clearmount (lawyer): Butcher & Cook 672-5947
```

Searching by Name

You use the find utility to locate files. The following list contains some typical uses of find:

- *Locating lost files*. You know you wrote a memo to your boss, but you can't remember where you stored it.

- *Locating related files*. Your boss asks to see all the financial statements you worked on this week.

- *Locating files recently modified*. If you are performing an incremental backup from the command line, you may want to know which files have changed today. (Backups are described more fully in Chapter 11, "UNIX System Administration.")

- *Locating files not recently modified.* If you are cleaning up your home directory, you may want to delete files that haven't changed in the last year.

- *Checking file organization.* If your company is cracking down on security, it may want to find all files that have write permission for all users.

To use the find command, you must specify three items:

```
find start criteria action
```

First, you specify the starting directory for the search; find will search all subdirectories. Next, you indicate the search criteria. Last, you indicate what action find is to take. For example, you may want to find all the files with a particular name. The following find command prints (to the screen) the names of all the files that end in .txt, starting with your current directory and searching through all the subdirectories:

```
find . -name "*.txt" -print
```

In this command, the period is your current directory. -name indicates that one of the qualities you are searching for is a particular structure of name. The double quotation marks may be necessary on some UNIX systems to keep the shell from expanding the * into the list of file names in the current directory. If there are no wild cards in the name specification, you don't need double quotation marks on any system. -print tells find to print the name whenever a file matches. (On most systems, you don't have to include the -print, but it's good practice because some versions of find require it.) Here's a sample of find's output on /home/a_s/gmeghab directory:

```
% find . -name "*.txt" -print
/home/a_s/gmeghab/quadratic/SSE.txt
/home/a_s/gmeghab/testing.txt
/home/a_s/gmeghab/active_lists.txt
/home/a_s/gmeghab/public_html/draft-ietf-html-specv3-00.txt
/home/a_s/gmeghab/barrierfun/mu.txt
/home/a_s/gmeghab/research/junji/quadrafiles/xorquad1.txt
/home/a_s/gmeghab/research/junji/quadrafiles/xorlin1.txt
/home/a_s/gmeghab/research/junji/quadrafiles/xorold1.txt
/home/a_s/gmeghab/research/junji/quadrafiles/parquad1.txt
/home/a_s/gmeghab/research/junji/quadrafiles/parlin1.txt
/home/a_s/gmeghab/research/junji/quadrafiles/parold1.txt
```

Searching by Attributes

You can also use find to locate files and directories based on their attributes. Table 4.2 shows some of the criteria you can use with find.

Table 4.2   Criteria for the *find* Command

Attribute	Expression
Belongs to specified group	-group *name*
Belongs to a specified user	-user *username*
Belongs to an unknown owner	-nouser
Has specified permissions	-perm mask
Is a certain size	-size *numberc*
Is a particular type	-type *c*
Newer than named file	-newer *file*
Search only *number* subdirectories down	-level *number*
Time of last modification	-mtime *number*

For example, to locate a file by ownership, use the -user criterion. To find all the files in /usr/project/sunbeam owned by user leslie, use the following command:

```
find /usr/project/sunbeam -user leslie -print
```

To locate a file based on the time it was last modified, use the -mtime criterion. If you want to specify files newer than the specified time, use a minus (-) sign before the number of days; if you want to specify files older than the specified time, use a plus (+) sign. To find all files in the current directory that were modified in the last week (7 days), type

```
find . -mtime -7 -print
```

To find all files in the current directory that were modified more than 3 days ago, type

```
find . -mtime +3 -print
```

You can combine these options. To find all files with names ending in .txt that were modified more than 3 days ago and less than 10 days ago, type

```
find . -name "*.txt" -mtime +3 -mtime -10 -print
```

By default, all these criteria add together (in a logical *and*), and you get only the files that match all the criteria you have specified. Some versions of find offer the -or option, which matches any of the criteria. The following command prints all files that are less than 3 days old or belong to no known user:

```
find . -mtime -3 -or -nouser -print
```

The find command has a number of other features, including the capability to run programs on the files it finds. A full discussion of these features, however, is beyond the scope of this book. See the find manual page for more information.

Classifying Files

UNIX offers a tool to help classify unknown files. The file command looks at the directory entry for a file and tries to determine the file's classification. Note this example:

```
$ file bank.c intro.mm vi.txt
bank.c:    C source code
intro.mm:  nroff, eqn, or tbl text input text
vi.txt:    ascii text
```

This command checks three files: bank.c, intro.mm, and vi.txt. All three are printable text files without control codes:

- bank.c is source code in the C programming language.

- intro.mm is a data file prepared for one of the UNIX text processors—nroff, eqn, or tbl.

- vi.txt is simply ASCII text—a printable text file with nothing else notable about it.

The find command depends on a data file, usually called /etc/magic. The find command recognizes files according to their content, so find differs from system to system.

Exercises

1. The utility grep enables you to search a file for a given pattern and then outputs the result of the search to the screen. The line

   ```
   % grep nut abstract.tex
   ```

   searches for the pattern nut inside the file name abstract.tex.

   Try the following commands on your home directory and describe the results:

   ```
   % ls -als > nuke
   % grep t* nuke
   ```

2. The command `ls -l` lists all files including the link files. Use this command to list only the link files from your home directory. *Hint:* Use the `grep` command described in exercise 1.

3. The command `ls -R` lists the contents of all subdirectories encountered in a given directory. Use the last command to list the contents of all subdirectories included in your home directory.

4. The command `ls -s` lists all files starting with the size in kilobytes in front of the name. What is the command that lists all the files that start with a capital T and their sizes in kilobytes?

5. Build the tree of your home directory based on exercise 3. Is there a UNIX command that is equivalent to the DOS command tree?

6. How are directories different from regular files? Give an example.

7. How are links different from regular files? Give an example.

8. Create a directory called `ai` in your home directory. What command do you use? How would you verify that the directory `ai` was created?

9. What command do you use to copy all the files from your home directory into your new directory created in exercise 8?

10. What command do you use to delete all the contents of the new directory created in exercise 8? What command do you use to delete the directory itself?

11. Rename a file called `.profile` with the file name `.projects`. What command do you use? What command do you use to verify that `.profile` exists?

12. What is the command that lists names that correspond only to directories? What do you add to the command to count the number of directories in your home directory?

5

Understanding Permissions and Other System Information

Topics Covered

- Working with Permissions
- Other File Information

84

In an office, there are often file folders certain people don't have to see or shouldn't see. To protect these files from unauthorized eyes, the drawers of the filing cabinet are locked. UNIX must provide the same kind of security to the files in its file system. The locks in UNIX are called *permissions*. Permissions are used to grant or refuse access privileges to files for particular users.

This chapter also introduces you to other system information and how it is used. Finding both the amount of unused space and how much space is being used are two important tasks in keeping a UNIX system operating efficiently. You also find out about ways to see who else is using the system, and you learn information about the user environment (the way the system responds to you). The system date and time are also discussed.

Working with Permissions

UNIX offers three types of permissions:

- *Read*. The user is allowed to open the file for read purposes.

- *Write*. The user is allowed to modify (write to) the file.

- *Execute*. This is a binary file or shell script file, and the user is allowed to run (execute) this file.

If you have a file whose contents you don't want anyone else to see, you can simply turn off the read permission for the other users on the system. You may also have a file that you want to make sure isn't modified by anyone. To do this, you turn off the write permission for other users. In addition, you may have a transaction log file with many users writing to it, but they shouldn't be able to read it. In that case, you turn on the write permission and turn off the read permission. The execute permission is used when you have created a file for execution and you want to control who can execute this file. Executable files are typically called *programs*.

UNIX enables you to control these three basic permissions—read, write, and execute—for the following three types of users:

- *Owner*. This is the person who first created the file or is the current owner. If it was one of your files, these would be your permissions.

- *Group*. Users in the UNIX system can belong to groups. Groups are a collection of users who share in areas of responsibility and may have to work together on projects.

- *Other*. This is everyone who isn't the owner or in the group. These are the privileges that apply to anyone else on the system.

When requesting access to a file, your user id is compared to that of the file's owner. If they are the same, then the permissions set for the owner are used. If you are not the owner, then your group id is compared to that of the file's group ownership. If they are the same those permissions are used. Otherwise, you have the permissions of the "other" category. For example, suppose you logged into the system as the user benah and you belong to the group admin. The file you want to access is owned by susie in the group admin. Because you are not susie, the permissions pertaining to the user susie don't apply to you. However, you are in the group admin so the permissions set for the group admin do apply to you.

Determining the Current Permissions

Use the ls command with the -l option to find the permissions for a file:

```
$ ls -l show_users
```

Figure 5.1 shows the results of this command.

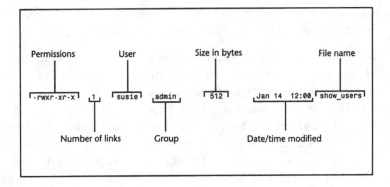

Figure 5.1

The ls -l command displays the permissions for a particular file.

The first hyphen (-) in the list of permissions signifies that this is an ordinary file (a normal text, data, or program file). See Chapter 3, "Understanding the UNIX File System," for a more complete definition of ordinary file. Following this, each set of three characters shows the permissions for the owner, group, and other (see Figure 5.2). In this example, the user is able to read (r), write (w), and execute (x) this file, and the user is in the same group as the owner. Anyone else on the system can read and execute but is not able to modify the file.

5

Figure 5.2
From the permissions list, you can determine who can read, write to, and execute the file.

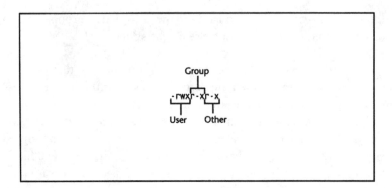

Public Access without Public Permissions

In a multiuser environment files may need to be owned by one user with no privileges to any other user, but these files may have to be manipulated by someone other than the owner of the file. An example of this is when you want to change your password. The password file has to be kept secure and non-modifiable from users. However, good security practice dictates that you change your password frequently, thus in essence changing the password file. When a process runs, it runs under your permissions, so how can you change your password if you can't write to the /etc/passwd file? UNIX has a way.

UNIX solves this type of permissions problem by enabling processes to run thinking they are another user, group, or both. This is accomplished using the SUID (for *set user id*) and SGID (for *set group id*) flags. *Flags* are indicators in the file permissions shown when you perform a long listing (ls -l). Flags are displayed in the permission pattern, for example -rwxrwxrwx (where the hyphen indicates a regular text file and the rwx's mean read, write, and execute permissions respectively for user, group, and other). The SUID and SGID flags are modifiers for the execute permissions flag and show up as an s in the execute positions of a permissions list (instead of an x) when using the ls -l command.

The passwd command, which is used to change your password on a UNIX system, is a good example. It's found in the /bin (or /usr/bin) directory and using ls -l on it reveals the permissions set at -rws--x--x. This means that anyone on the system can execute the command because there is an x or execute permission for user, group, and other. Because the first or user group is set at rws, the user who invoked the command gets his or her password modified because the s permission temporarily changes the owner and group IDs on execution of the command—in this case, just long enough to write the new password to the /etc/passwd file.

The chmod command is used to set up these special types of permissions, and superuser privileges are required to modify the passwd command. The actual syntax is chmod u+s passwd. This assumes execute privileges have already been set. Thus, file permissions of -x-x-x are changed to -rws-x-x.

So, to change your password in UNIX, run the passwd command. The passwd command is owned by root (a special user account with the privileges needed to access every file on the system), but the s flag described causes the program to believe that you are root while it executes. Because root owns the command passwd and the file /etc/passwd and the passwd command is running as if it were root, the command can write to the passwd file. Many of the UNIX administrative commands use this feature as do a significant number of database applications.

Directory Permissions

Directories use the same permissions as files, but the language of read, write, and execute on a directory can be confusing. The following table helps describe how to think of read, write, and execute permissions as they apply to directories.

Permission	Meaning
Read	The user is allowed to list the files in the directory (ls works).
Write	The user is allowed to add items to the directory, to remove them (mkdir, rmdir, rm), and to do work that creates new files such as using an editor program.
Execute	The user is allowed to search this directory—such as using cd to change directories and find to locate which directory a file is in.

Changing Permissions

To change the permissions of a file in UNIX, use the chmod command (for *change mode*). You have two ways to use the chmod command when changing the permissions of a file or directory. One method uses numbers and is called the *absolute method*, and the other uses symbols and is called the *symbolic method*. The absolute method sets the permissions to an absolute state and the symbolic method adds and subtracts permissions.

5

> **NOTE** *Only the owner of the file or the superuser can change the permissions of a file.*

Absolute Method

The absolute method, sometimes called the numeric method, uses a three-digit octal number to store the permissions:

```
%chmod permissioncode name
```

Here is a specific example:

```
%chmod 777 show_users
```

Each permission code is assigned an octal number.

Octal Bit Mask	Meaning/Permission
1	Execute
2	Write
4	Read

These numbers are added together to make the final permission. The position of the number determines whether it applies to the owner (second digit), group (third digit), or other types of users (fourth digit). In the previous example, the value 777 combines all three *bit masks* (1+2+4) for each position, for a total of 7. A bit mask represents a binary string of 1s and 0s, the basic communication of computers at the lowest machine level. Since the octal or base 8 number system has the numbers 0 through 7, with 8 equivalent to 10 in the decimal system, it lends itself well to representing binary strings in an easier to handle format for us humans. The chmod command allows everyone—owner, group, and other—to read, write, and execute this file.

Valid modes for the absolute method are described in the following table:

Mode	Meaning
100	Execute for owner
200	Write for owner
400	Read for owner

Mode	Meaning
010	Execute for group
020	Write for group
040	Read for group
001	Execute for other
002	Write for other
004	Read for other

For example, you can determine the code for a chmod command that changes the permissions on the directory show_users:

1. For the owner to have read, write, and execute permissions, add the following modes:

    100

    200

    400

    - - -

    700

2. For the group to have read and execute permissions but no write permission, add these modes:

    010

    040

    - - -

    050

3. For other to have read and execute permissions but no write permission, add these modes:

    001

    004

5

```
- - -

005
```

4. If you then add these three subtotals, you have the following:

    700 (from #1)

    050 (from #2)

    005 (from #3)

    - - -

    755

Thus, the command is

```
% chmod 755 show_users
```

which means that the owner of show_users has read, write, and execute permissions, the group has read and execute permissions, and other has read and execute permissions.

Assuming that you did not want anyone to have access to your home directory, a chmod like

```
% chmod 700 /home/a_s/gmeghab
```

results in allowing the owner (you) read, write, and execute permissions to your home directory through the 7 in 700, no permissions to the group through the first 0 in 700, and no permissions to other through the second 0 in 700.

Symbolic Method

The absolute method is often best suited when first initializing the permissions after creating the file. There are times when you have to add or subtract a permission to a group of files and can't set them all to the same absolute permission.

For example, suppose a particular user allowed all his files in his home account to be readable by the other type of user. This is a severe breach of security. Therefore, he would want to remove all permissions for the other types of users, without modifying any of the user or group permissions. Because the absolute method would also reset the user and group permissions, you need a method to remove just the other users permissions, leaving all other permissions intact. To do this use the symbolic method. The symbolic method uses symbols to represent the user-type to affect, how to affect the permission, and the permissions to be affected. The command for the example is shown in Figure 5.3.

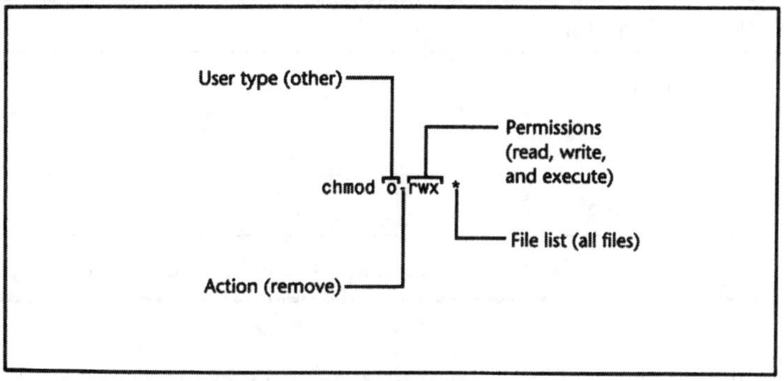

Figure 5.3
An example of a
command using
the symbolic
method.

91

The generic form of the `chmod` command is

```
chmod user-type action permission filelist
```

The following table lists the valid user types.

User Type	Meaning
u	Owner
g	Group
o	Other
a	All

This table describes the valid actions.

Action	Effect
-	Removes permissions
+	Adds permissions
=	Sets the permissions of *files* (where *files* is the file or wild card indicated in the command) to the specified value

This table lists the valid permissions.

5

Permission	Meaning
r	Read
w	Write
x	Execute
s	Sets uid (User id) for users, and sets gid (Group id) for groups

A simple example is `chmod a+rwx` *filename*. This gives read, write, and execute permissions on *filename* to everyone, as in this example:

```
% chmod a+rwx /home/a_s/gmeghab/research
```

So `research` in `/home/a_s/gmeghab` can now be read, written over, and executed by everyone on the system.

More complex usage of `chmod` means that you can mix and match actions with each user type and chain user types with the comma. Note the following example:

```
% chmod ug-w+r+x,o-rwx show_users
```

Here write was removed, and read and execute were added for the user and group. All permissions for other were also removed, meaning that only the owner and his or her group can execute the file.

The preceding command is equivalent to an absolute command:

```
%chmod 550 show_users
%ls -als ¦grep show_users
```

This results in the following:

```
1 dr-xr-wx-- show_users
```

If the `chmod 550 show_users` command is followed by the command

```
% chmod a+s,u+s,g+s,o+s show_users
```

then an `ls -als¦grep show_users` results in

```
1 dr-sr-s-- show_users
```

Consider an example in which = is used in a symbolic method. Assume that you have a directory called `calendar`. First, set `calendar` using the absolute method:

```
%chmod 777 calendar
```

Then `ls -als¦grep calendar` results in

```
drwxrwxrwx calendar
```

In the following example, a relative `chmod` command uses `=`:

```
% chmod go= calendar
```

This `ls -als¦grep calendar` results in

```
drwx------ calendar
```

which means that `go=` sets the group and other permissions to no permissions. The user, being unchanged, keeps the permissions allotted to it with the command `chmod 777 calendar`.

> **NOTE** Shell scripts *are files that are a collection of UNIX commands. These files are opened and read by the shell executing them and must be readable by the users who execute the shell script.*

Default Settings for Permissions

As you create files, the permissions are set according to a default setting. This default setting is controlled by the `umask` command. To use `umask`, give it an argument similar to the `chmod` absolute method. However, where the numbers used in the `chmod` command mean allowed permissions, the numbers you use with `umask` are thought of as the permissions you don't want to allow. For example, the following command sets the default file creation to allow all permissions (this is the opposite logic of `chmod` where 777 indicates the same permissions):

```
umask 000
```

The following command does not allow execution for owner, group, and other:

```
umask 111
```

The following table summarizes the uses of masks.

Mask	Doesn't Allow
1	Execute
2	Write
4	Read
0	None (that is, allows all)

5

umask got its name because you are setting the mask for the creation of files. A mask is something you apply to "cover up" values. For example, when you go to a seminar and the speaker is using an overhead projector, she may have parts of the presentation she doesn't want the audience to see. She will sometimes cover these parts with a piece of paper. In a sense, the paper covering the transparency is a mask. Think of the values you give the command as "the permissions I don't want to allow."

Assume that you want to set the file creation permissions to 077. This command removes the read, write, and execute permissions for members of the group that the file is associated with and everyone else. The owner's permissions are left as the system has specified.

If you change the umask to 066, for example, and create a new directory, morning, then the ls -als¦grep morning results in:

```
1 drwx--x--x morning
```

Setting the Owner and Group of a File

At times, you have to change the owner of a file or its group. There are two commands for this:

- chown changes the owner of the file.

- chgrp changes the group to which the file belongs.

The format for these two commands is the same:

```
#chown frank filename
#chgrp admin filename
```

In this example, the owner of *filename* was changed to frank by the chown command (for *change owner*) and the group was changed to admin by the chgrp (for *change group*) command. Making this type of ownership and group changes requires that you either own the file to begin with or that you have root or superuser privileges.

Other File Information

Occasionally, when you are working with the file system, you want to know how full the file system is. If you are accustomed to working with DOS, you know that DOS's DIR command reports the total number of bytes used by the current directory and how much free space is on the drive. UNIX's ls command doesn't do this. The UNIX ls command was designed to generate lists of files suitable for input to other commands in a pipeline.

Any summary information would confuse the receiving command of the pipe. For generating this same information, two commands, df (for *disk free*) and du (for *disk usage*), were developed.

Command	Reason for Use
bdf	To see how much space on the current file system is free.
du	To see how much space a directory structure is using.

The format of df is

```
bdf options file systems
```

Both bdf and du report information in blocks. Blocks are the smallest storage unit on the file system (the DOS equivalent is an allocation unit). For performance reasons, the file system allocates blocks of the disk for storing data. The typical size of a block is 512 bytes. So a two-block file really consumes 1,024 bytes of disk storage. To obtain the bytes, simply multiply the block count by 512 (or whatever your system's number of bytes per block is).

Reporting Unused Space

If you want to see how much free space is on all the currently mounted file systems type the following:

```
% bdf

Filesystem              kbytes     used    avail  capacity  Mounted on
/dev/dsk/c0t3d0s0        19183    11156     6117     65%     /
/dev/dsk/c0t3d0s7       360607   300767    23780     93%     /usr
/proc                       0        0        0      0%     /proc
fd                          0        0        0      0%     /dev/fd
/dev/dsk/c0t3d0s4        96455    15051    71764     17%     /var
swap                    129008      844   128164      1%     /tmp
/dev/dsk/c0t3d0s6       227263    53957   150586     26%     /opt
/dev/dsk/c0t3d0s5       135847    94212    28055     77%     /usr/openwin
grits:/home/a_s        1952573  1223965   533358     70%     /home/a_s
grits:/home/coba       1952573   146012  1611311      8%     /home/coba
grits:/home/coe        1952573   169645  1587678     10%     /home/coe
grits:/home/con         489702    16932   423800      4%     /home/con
grits:/home/f_a         489702    55272   385460     13%     /home/f_a
grits:/home/other      1952573   267245  1490078     15%     /home/other
grits:/usr/local        489702   114361   326371     26%     /usr/local
grits:/var/spool/mail   489702   329698   111034     75%     /var/spool/mail
```

The results of this command reported that the root file system (/) is 19,183K in size, with 11,156K used and 6,117K free. So the used size says that the root file system (/) is at 65 percent of its capacity. The last column represents the mount point or the pathname for the directory.

Using df -g reports a totally different but related report to the one with the df -k command. The following is a partial df -g report:

```
% df -g

/ (/dev/dsk/c0t3d0s0):
8192 block size
1024 frag size
38366 total blocks
16054 free blocks
12234 available
11328 total files
9851 free files
8388632 filesys id ufs fstype 0x00000004 flag
255 filename length

/proc(/proc):
1024 block size
1024 frag size
0 total blocks
0 free blocks
0 available
1004 total files
934 free files
38010880 filesys id  /proc proc fstype 0x00000000 flag
5 filename length
```

This version of the command reports the block size, which varies from one partition to another. Also if ufs file system type appears, the partition is a local partition and does not need to be mounted. If an nfs file system type appears, the file system is mounted. Mounted partitions report -1 for total files, free files, and filename length, which means that this information is not available on the local machine because the person running the command does not have root privileges on the remote machine. A superuser on the remote machine would receive the correct information that is being replaced with -1 on the local machine. Notice also the frag size, which stands for fragment size. This number is the result of the memory-management type, which could be any of the following:

Paged Memory

Segmented Memory

Paged Segmentation

Segmented Paging

The Sun operating system uses paged segmentation and segmented pages the most. The other information is similar to the one given by the df -k command.

CAUTION! *File systems that grow much beyond 80 percent in used space tend to degrade in performance. Also, as file systems peak to their capacities, it becomes increasingly more likely that the file system will fill up. This can be a severe detriment on operation because UNIX swaps processes on and off the disk to maximize working memory. Watch your file system sizes.*

Reporting Disk Usage

The syntax of du is

```
%du options names
```

The following table contains commonly used options:

Option	Meaning
-s	Causes only a grand total to be displayed if no names are specified.
-a	Causes each file encountered to be displayed with its size in kilobytes.
-r	Only the directories in the currently mounted file system are looked at, other file systems are ignored.
-o	Does not add child directories usage to a parent's total.
-k	Prints allocations in kilobytes.
-d	Does not cross file system boundaries.

If you want to know how much space the current directory is taking up, use the du command. The following example assumes that these directories have read permission for group and other:

```
du
4      ./tmp
4660   ./sco
234    ./c
12     ./pro
2      ./News
2      ./.iq
18     ./.elm
62     ./bin
140    ./docs
182    ./Mail
8      ./ed
30     ./.mvw
5462   .
```

5

Each directory is shown with the size in blocks reported on the left. The last period is the current directory, which is the sum of the preceding numbers plus the sizes of the individual files in the current directory. In this example, the sum of all the subdirectories equals 5,354 blocks, and the total storage of the current directory equals 5,462 blocks, so there are 108 blocks of files not in a subdirectory in the current directory (5,462–5,354).

Finding Out Who's on the System

UNIX is a multiuser system. This means that many other users can be logged into the system and working at the same time. There may be a time when you want to know who these users are, such as when you are looking for a particular person to answer a question immediately instead of later by e-mail. Or you might just be curious to see if Joe has come into work yet. You can find out who is on the system with the who command.

```
who
gmeghab    console    Jul 22 12:15
gmeghab    pts/1         Jul 27 09:17
gmeghab    pts/3         Aug  1 19:14
gmeghab    pts/5         Jul 31 17:13
gmeghab    pts/6         Aug  1 16:24
gmeghab    pts/7         Aug  1 17:15
```

The result of a simple who command (with no options specified) has three columns (see Figure 5.4).

Figure 5.4

The who command provides information about all users currently on the system.

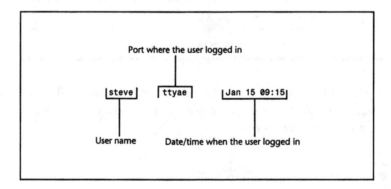

The system keeps track of who has logged in and statistics about what logged in users are doing in the file /etc/utmp. The who command reads this file and reports its information.

The who command can accept several options, and its syntax is as follows:

```
who options utmp-like-file
```

utmp-like-file is an alternate file to read to obtain login information. This is usually named /etc/wtmp. /etc/wtmp is a historical log of what is found in the /etc/utmp file.

The most popular options used with this command are listed in the following table:

Option	Meaning
-a	Reports those users who are currently logged into the system or who logged in and exited since the last time the system was booted. The following columns are reported:
	NAME — The name of the user.
	LINE — The terminal they are logged in to.
	TIME — When they logged in.
	IDLE — The number of minutes since they've typed something in at their terminal. A period indicates there has been some activity in the last minute.
	PID — The process id of the login shell. It is the identification number UNIX assigns in sequence to active processes.
	COMMENTS — System specifics.
-u	Reports those users who are currently logged into the system. The following columns are reported:
	NAME — The name of the user.
	LINE — The terminal they are logged in to.
	TIME — When they logged in.
	IDLE — The number of minutes since they've typed something in at their terminal. A period indicates there has been some activity in the last minute.
	PID — The process id of the login shell. It is the identification number UNIX assigns in sequence to active processes.
-H	Prints the header line, which labels the output with NAME, LINE, TIME, and so forth over the appropriate column.
-q	A quick version of the output. Shows only a list of user names and a count. who -q is a subset of who -u.
-t	Shows when the system date/time last changed. It shows the old and new values.

(continues)

Option	Meaning
-s	This is the default and limits the output to a form like -u but only the following columns are provided: NAME, LINE, and TIME without a header that specifies NAME, LINE, and TIME. The who -s command is equivalent to who -H except for the header line.

The following is an example of who -a:

```
% who -a

NAME        LINE         TIME          IDLE    PID  COMMENTS
   .        system boot  Jul 22 10:31
   .        run-level 3  Jul 22 10:31    3      0  S
rc2             .        Jul 22 10:32  old     50  id=s2 term=0   exit=0
sac         -   .        Jul 22 10:32  old    237  id=  sc
gmeghab     - console    Jul 22 12:15  old    238
zsmon       -   .        Jul 22 10:32  old    240
gmeghab     pts/2        Jul 27 12:49  old    298  id=2/st term=0 exit=0
gmeghab     - pts/3      Aug  1 19:14    .    8783
gmeghab     pts/4        Jul 31 17:13  old   6075  id=4/st term=0 exit=0
gmeghab     - pts/5      Jul 31 17:13  old   7403
gmeghab     - pts/6      Aug  6 18:46  0:02 12711
gmeghab     - pts/7      Aug  1 17:15  old   8433
phighami    pts/8        Aug  3 10:38  old   9862  id=tn10 term=0 exit=0
   (pluto)
```

On the first line of the who -a command, you are reminded when the system was booted. Also the information on gmeghab on the consoles pts/3, pts/5, pts/6, and pts/7 is similar to that of the simple who. But more login sessions have happened at the system level, which are followed by comments that specify the system level of the process, the terminal, and whether it has exited. For example, a user named phighsmi logged in from the machine named pluto to my machine. The date of that login and whether or not the session has ended also appear.

By the same token, a who -q command results in a list of users and the number of users without any additional information:

```
% who -q
gmeghab gmeghab gmeghab gmeghab gmeghab gmeghab
# users=6
```

Idle time in UNIX, as referenced by this command and others, refers to the time that has elapsed since a character was output to the screen. Many administrative books and articles have been printed that talk about forcefully logging out users whose idle time is longer than some predetermined amount of time. These discussions, although well-intended, can't be implemented with a "blanket" approach. The fallacy of this approach returning an accurate measure of idle time is twofold. First, processes can be doing something even though they are not displaying anything. An example is an extremely complex background database query. If you automatically logged this user out, he couldn't complete the query. Second, many modern applications continually update the screen with a system clock or some sort of status. In this case, a user who isn't really doing anything appears active.

> **NOTE** *The `-t` option is extremely useful when trying to determine if the machine has rebooted or not. From an administrative standpoint, this can help distinguish if a system problem was also part of a reboot. For example, suppose that every morning the users are complaining about how something isn't behaving right. You know that a week ago when you rebooted the machine you had the same problem. The `-t` option reports the "old time," which is the time the system displayed just before it shut down. If that time is still from a week ago, then the system hasn't shut down since then! The problem isn't because of a reboot issue.*

A variant of the who command is who am i:

```
% who am i
gmeghab     pts/6        Aug  1 17:15
```

This reports the same information as who, but it is limited to your current login session and only to your own user name. This is useful, for example, if you have several user accounts going at the same time (especially useful on a single-user system) and forget which account is the current one.

Another command similar in syntax to who am i is the command whoami:

```
% whoami
gmeghab
```

The last command is different in purpose from who. It simply states the user's login name.

Exercises

1. Assume that your home directory is readable by the whole world.

   a. What is its actual permissions status?

   b. A colleague wants to use FTP to send files from your home directory to her home directory. Would she be able to do so with the actual permissions set on your home directory? If yes, why?

   c. If the answer to 1b is No, what is the command to make 1b work?

2. What does it mean to have a directory with the following permissions:

```
8   drwxrwxrwx 50   ai   8192   Jul 26   09:08   gmeghab
```

3. Assume that the directory ai has the following permissions:

```
8   drwxrwxrwx 50   ai   8192   Jul 26   09:08   gmeghab
```

a. What command do you use to change the directory ai to a readable and executable directory by you?

b. Assume that the user issued the following command:

```
% chmod 700 ai
```

How are the permissions of the original ai directory changed?

c. Are the results of 3a different from those of 3b?

d. From the results of 3b, can you tell what the 700 stands for?

e. Issue the following command on the ai directory after issuing the chmod command in exercise 3b:

```
% chmod 777 ai.
```

Are the permissions of the ai directory now different from the original ai directory? If yes, why? If no, why?

4. Assume that the only person capable of reading, writing, and executing to your directory is you.

a. What is the actual permissions status of your home directory?

b. What command do you use to find out which group you belong to?

c. What command do you use to make your home directory readable only by the group of people you belong to?

d. What command do you use to make your home directory readable by everyone?

5. What command generated the following listing?

```
NAME          LINE         TIME                      IDLE    PID  COMMENTS
   .          system boot  Oct 22 19:55
   .          run-level 3  Oct 22 19:55               3      0  S
rc2              .          Oct 22 19:56 13:23        48   id=  s2 term=0
exit=0
rc3              .          Oct 22 19:56 13:23        219  id=  s3 term=0
exit=0
sac         -    .          Oct 22 19:56 13:23        237  id=  sc
gmeghab  - console          Oct 22 20:56 12:16        565
zsmon       -    .          Oct 22 19:56 13:23        240
gmeghab  - pts/1            Oct 22 20:57    .         603
gmeghab  - pts/2            Oct 22 20:57 12:21        605
```

```
gmeghab      pts/3          Oct 22 20:56  9:07      352   id=3/st term=0
exit=0
jwang        pts/3          Oct 23 00:11  9:07      775   id=rl10 term=0
exit=0
(grits)
```

   a. What is the information conveyed by the LINE system boot Oct 22 19:55?

   b. What does pts in pts/3 stand for? What can you tell about the users with a LINE type of pts?

   c. There is a line with gmeghab - console. What does console stand for? What is the difference between a LINE type of console and a LINE type of pts?

   d. There is zsmon line with a LINE type of dot (.). Explain the meaning of this line.

6. Describe two different ways of using the du command (you may think of piping it with another command) to find the exact size, in kilobytes, for a subdirectory named lispfiles in your home directory. Your answer should yield this information without displaying information about any other subdirectories.

7. What command do you use to find out the space used, in kilobytes, only by a file named newgraph15.ps? Assume that the file is located in the subdirectory /european/simulation/ in your home directory. (Create the directory european in your home directory and then create a directory called simulation in european. Use vi to create a file newgraph15.ps and make sure you type a few lines into the file.)

Working with Applications

Using the *vi* and *emacs* Editors

Topics Covered

- Introducing *vi*
- Setting the *vi* Environment
- Using the *emacs* Text Editor
- A Survey of Other Editors

In previous chapters, you saw how convenient and advantageous it is to have sequences of commands or shell programs stored in a file. You probably need to create data, e-mail, lists, memos, notes, and reports—and you need a text editor to do these tasks. You may have several editors or word processors available on your UNIX system to help you with those tasks. To put commands or shell programs in a file, however, you need an editor that can save your work in a text file in ASCII format. UNIX comes with a standard text editor called vi that you can use for all but the most complex writing and editing projects.

Your UNIX system may have other text editors; UnixWare offers the graphical Text Editor. Two standard, nongraphical text editors are ed and ex, both line-oriented editors. When you use them, you work with only one line at a time. However, vi and Text Editor are full-screen editors; when you use them, you see a screen's worth of information so that you can make changes or additions in context. This chapter doesn't discuss ed or ex very much because you will find vi easier to use.

emacs is also a popular text editor, used by almost as many people as the users of vi. Although not included with many versions of UNIX, emacs is freely available over the Internet.

You may have other text editors available on your system. Two popular ones are Joe and pico. This chapter closes with a survey of some popular text editors.

Introducing *vi*

UNIX was developed in an environment in which the user's terminal was a teletype or some other slow, hard-copy terminal; video monitors generally were not used. A natural editor for that environment was a *line-oriented editor*—one with which the user sees and works on one line of text at a time. Two line-oriented editors are on UNIX systems today: ed and ex.

In its early days, UNIX was made available to universities essentially for free. Students and faculty at several universities made many contributions to the UNIX working environment. Several notable improvements came out of the University of California at Berkeley. One of these was a *full-screen editor*—one that lets you work with a screen full of information at once rather than use a single line. That full-screen editor is called vi (pronounced vee-eye), which stands for *visual*. The time was right for the transition to screen-oriented work because users were working with video terminals rather than hard-copy devices.

Most likely you're working on a terminal or X-terminal (a terminal capable of displaying graphics) connected to your UNIX computer. Naturally, you expect some sort of full-screen editor. Although vi may not be the perfect editor, you will find it may be the most expedient tool to use in many situations.

> **NOTE** | *This chapter doesn't cover all the features of vi. That would take more space than is available! In fact, there are entire books written just on vi. Instead, you learn the commands to do most editing tasks. If you want to know about the more advanced features of vi and advanced text-editing operations, consult the reference manual supplied with your system. You don't have to become a vi expert to use it.*

What Is *vi*?

The vi editor is probably the most popular, full-screen UNIX text editor. There are even versions available for DOS. Because it is part of the standard UNIX environment, it has been learned and used (to one degree or another) by millions of UNIX users. You find that it starts quickly and can be used for both simple and complex tasks. As you would expect, you use it to enter, modify, or delete text; search or replace text; and copy, cut, and paste blocks of text. You also customize it to match your needs. You can move the cursor to any position on the screen and move through the file you're editing. You use the same methods with any text file, regardless of its contents. All the files vi produces and all the files UNIX commands work with are ASCII or text files.

The vi editor is not a word processor or desktop publishing system. There aren't any menus and virtually no help facilities. Word processing systems usually offer screen and hard-copy formatting and printing such as representing text as bold, italic, or underlined. vi doesn't offer these functions. Other UNIX commands can perform some of these functions (for example, lp can print and nroff can format text). In addition, you may have access to a word processor on your system.

The vi editor operates in two modes. In command mode, your keystrokes are interpreted as commands to vi. Some of the commands you use allow you to save a file, exit vi, move the cursor to different positions in a file, and modify, rearrange, delete, substitute, and search for text. In input or text-entry mode, your keystrokes are accepted as the text of the file you are editing. When vi is in input or text-entry mode, the editor acts as a typewriter. In an editing session, you can freely switch between modes. You have to remember the mode you're using and know how to change modes. Some people find this uncomfortable at first. With a little practice, however, you will find vi extremely convenient for editing UNIX ASCII files.

Understanding the Editing Process

You edit text by either creating new text or modifying existing text. When you create new text, you place the text in a file with an ordinary UNIX file name. When you modify existing text, you use the existing file name to call a copy of the file into the editing session. In either case, as you use the editor, the text is held in the system's memory in a storage area called a *buffer*. Using a buffer prevents you from directly changing the contents of a file until you decide to save the buffer. This is to your benefit if you decide you want to forget the changes you've made and start over.

As you make changes and additions to the text, these edits affect the text in the buffer—not in the file stored on disk. When you are satisfied with your edits, you issue a command to save the text. This command writes the changes to the file on the disk. Only then are the changes permanently made. You can save changes to disk as often as you like. You do not have to exit the editor when you save changes. This chapter shows you that there are several ways to exit the editor; some of those ways write the buffer to the text file on the disk.

The vi editor is said to be interactive because it interacts with you during the editing session. The editor communicates with you by displaying status messages, error messages, or sometimes nothing on-screen (in typical UNIX fashion). The last line on the screen, called the *status line*, holds the messages from UNIX. You also see the changes you make in the text on the screen.

You use the editor to modify, rearrange, delete, substitute, and search for text. You conduct these editing operations while using the editor in command mode. In several instances, a command is a single letter that corresponds to the first letter of an action's name. For example, press i when you want to *insert* a character and r when you want to *replace* a character.

Most commands operate on a single line or a range of lines of text. The lines are numbered from 1 (the top line) to the last line in the buffer. When you add or delete lines, the line numbers adjust automatically. A line's number is its address in the buffer. An address range is simply two addresses or line numbers separated by a comma. If you want to specify the range consisting of the third through the eighth line of the buffer, you use 3,8.

The position of the cursor always indicates your current location in the editing buffer. Some of the commands you issue in command mode affect the character at the cursor position. Unless you move the cursor, changes take place at that position. vi has several commands for moving the cursor through the edit buffer.

vi is a full-screen editor. You give vi commands to move the cursor to different positions in a file, and you see the changes you make as you make them. So vi has to be able to move to and modify the text on your terminal as well as on other terminal types. It knows what terminal you are using and what its video capabilities are by checking the shell variable TERM. UNIX uses the TERM variable to determine your terminal's capabilities, such as underlining, reverse-video, screen-clearing method, function-key assignment, and color capability.

Using *vi*

To start vi, you simply type **vi** at the shell prompt (command line). If you know the name of the file you want to create or edit, you can issue the vi command with the file name as an argument. For example, to create the file myfile with vi, enter **vi myfile**.

When vi becomes active, the terminal screen clears and a tilde character (~) appears on the left side of every screen line, except for the first. The ~ is the empty-buffer line flag. Following is a shortened version of what you will see on your screen (only five lines are listed to save space):

```
~
~
~
~
```

The cursor is at the leftmost position of the first line (represented here as an underline). You will probably see 20 to 22 of the tilde characters at the left of the screen. If that's not the case, check the value of TERM and perhaps talk with your system administrator.

When you see this display, you have successfully started vi; vi is in command mode and waiting for your first command.

> **NOTE** *Unlike most word processing programs,* vi *starts in command mode. Before you start entering text, you must switch to input mode.*

6

Looking at *vi*'s Two Modes

The vi editor operates in two modes: *command mode* and *input mode*. In command mode, vi interprets your keystrokes as commands. There are many vi commands. You can use commands to save a file, exit vi, move the cursor to various positions in a file, or modify, rearrange, delete, substitute, or search for text. If you enter a character as a command but the character is not a command, vi beeps. Don't worry; the beep is an audible indication for you to check what you are doing and correct any errors.

You can enter text in input mode (also called text-entry mode) by either *appending* after the cursor or *inserting* before the cursor. At the beginning of the line, this doesn't make any difference. To go from command mode to input mode, press a to append text after the cursor or press i to insert text in front of the cursor.

Use input mode only for entering text. Most word processing programs start in input mode, but vi doesn't. When you use a word processing program, you enter text, issue a command, and use function keys or normal text keys. vi doesn't work that way: You must go into input mode by pressing a or i before you start entering text and then press Esc to return to command mode.

Creating Your First *vi* File

The best way to learn about vi is to use it. This section gives a step-by-step example of how to create a file using vi. In each step, you see an action to perform and then the necessary keystrokes to complete this action. All you need to be concerned with is complete accuracy. The example takes you through the motions and concepts of using vi to create a file, moving between command and input modes, and saving your results. If you run into difficulties, you can quit and start over by pressing Esc one or two times; then type **:q!** and press Enter. (The ! after the q forces vi to exit without saving your changes. Normally, you exit vi by just typing **:q**.)

1. Start vi. Type **vi** and press Enter. You see the screen full of flush-left tildes.

2. Go into input mode to place characters on the first line. Press the a key. Do not press Enter. Now you can append characters to the first line. (You should not see the character a on the screen.)

3. Add lines of text to the buffer. Type the following three lines, pressing Enter at the end of the first and second lines but not at the end of the third line:

   ```
   Things to do today.
   a. Practice vi.
   b. Sort sales data and print the results.
   ```

   You can use the Backspace key to correct mistakes on the line you are typing so don't worry about being precise. This example is for practice. You learn other ways to make changes in some of the later sections of this chapter.

4. Go from input mode to command mode. Press the Esc key. You can press Esc more than once without changing modes. You will hear a beep from your system if you press Esc when you are already in command mode.

5. Save your buffer in a file called `vipract.1`. Type `:w vipract.1` and press Enter. The characters `:w vipract.1` appear on the bottom line of the screen (the status line). The characters should not appear in the text. The `:w` command writes the buffer to the specified file. This command saves or writes the buffer to the file `vipract.1`.

6. See your action confirmed on the status line. You should see the following on the status line:

```
"vipract.1" [New File] 3 lines, 78 characters
```

This statement confirms that the file `vipract.1` has been created, is a new file, contains three lines and 78 characters. Your display may be different if you didn't type the information exactly as specified.

7. Exit `vi`. Type `:q` and press Enter.

When you type `:q`, you are still in command mode and see these characters on the status line. When you press Enter, however, `vi` terminates and you return to the login shell prompt.

Here are some things to remember about `vi`:

- `vi` starts in command mode.

- To move from command mode to input mode, press either a (to append text) or i (to insert text).

- You add text when you are in input mode.

- You give commands to `vi` only when you are in command mode.

- To move from input mode to command mode, press Esc.

- You give commands to `vi` to save a file and can quit only when you are in command mode.

Starting *vi* Using an Existing File

To edit or look at a file that already exists in your current directory, type **vi** followed by the file name and press Enter. Try this with the file you created in the preceding section by entering the following command:

```
vi vipract.1
```

6

You see the following display (the number of lines shown here are fewer than you see on your screen):

```
Things to do today.
a. Practice vi.
b. Sort sales data and print the results.
~
~
~
"vipract.1" 3 lines, 78 characters
```

As before, tilde (~) characters appear on the far left of empty lines in the buffer. Look at the status line: It contains the name of the file you are editing and the number of lines and characters.

Exiting *vi*

You can exit or quit vi in several ways. Remember that you must be in command mode to quit vi. To change to command mode, press Esc. (If you are already in command mode when you press Esc, you hear the terminal beep.) Table 6.1 lists the commands you can use to exit vi.

Table 6.1	Ways to Quit or Exit *vi*
Command	**Action**
:q	Exit after making no changes to the buffer or exit after the buffer has been modified and saved to a file.
:q!	Exit and abandon all changes to the buffer since it was last saved to a file.
:wq	Write buffer to the working file and then exit.
:x	Same as :wq.
ZZ	Same as :wq.

As shown in the table, several keystrokes accomplish the same end. To demonstrate, use vi to edit the file vipract.1 created earlier in this chapter. To edit the file, type **vi vipract.1** and press Enter. You see a display similar to the following:

```
Things to do today.
a. Practice vi.
b. Sort sales data and print the results.
~
~
~
```

```
"vipract.1" 3 lines, 78 characters
```

The cursor is indicated by an underline character; when you first open the file, it is under the first character of the file, the T of Things. Because you haven't made any changes to the file since you opened it, you can exit by typing :q and pressing Enter. You see the shell prompt. You can also type :wq to exit the file. If you do so, you will see the following message before the shell prompt reappears:

```
"vipract.1" 3 lines, 78 characters
```

This message appears because *vi* first writes the buffer to the file vipract.1 and then exits.

Start *vi* again with the same file (type **vi vipract.1** and press Enter). You see a display similar to this:

```
Things to do today.
a. Practice vi.
b. Sort sales data and print the results.
~
~
~
"vipract.1" 3 lines, 78 characters
```

Although *vi* starts you off in command mode, press Esc to be doubly sure. Now press the spacebar enough times so that the cursor moves under the period following today in the first line. To replace that character with an exclamation mark, press r and type !. The first line should now look like this:

```
Things to do today!
```

Because you have changed the buffer, *vi* won't let you exit unless you save the changes or explicitly give a command to quit without saving the changes. If you try to exit *vi* by typing :q, *vi* displays the following message to remind you that you haven't written the file to disk since you changed it:

```
No write since last change (:quit! overrides)
```

To abandon the changes you have made to the file, quit by typing :q!. To save the changes, quit by typing :wq or any of the other equivalent forms (ZZ or :x).

CAUTION! *Use the* :q! *command sparingly. When you enter* :q!*, all the changes you have made to the file are lost.*

6

TIP *vi doesn't keep backup copies of files. After you type* :wq *and press Enter, the original file is modified and can't be restored to its original state. You must make your own backup copies of vi files.*

Undoing a Command

In vi, you can undo your most recent action or change to the buffer as long as you haven't saved that change to the disk file. To do this from command mode, press u to undo the most recent change you made to the file. Suppose that you have inadvertently deleted a line of text, changed something you shouldn't have, or added some text incorrectly. Press Esc to change to command mode and then press u. Things are back to the way they were before the command changed the buffer. Just remember that the undo command can undo only the latest action. Also, you can't use the undo command to undo writing something to a file.

Here is an example to demonstrate the use of the undo command. Start vi again with the file vipract.1: type **vi vipract.1** and press Enter. You see a display similar to this:

```
Things to do today!
a. Practice vi.
b. Sort sales data and print the results.
~
~
~
"vipract.1" 3 lines, 78 characters
```

To add the phrase for 60 minutes between vi and the period on the second line, move to the second line by pressing Enter. The cursor now appears under the first character of the second line. Now move the cursor to the period after the i in vi by pressing the spacebar until the cursor moves to that location. Insert the phrase for 60 minutes by pressing i to give the input command and then typing the characters of the phrase. Press Esc to return to command mode. Your screen should look like the following:

```
Things to do today!
a. Practice vi for 60 minutes.
b. Sort sales data and print the results.
~
~
~
```

Is 60 minutes a good idea? Maybe not. To undo the change to the second line, make sure that you're in command mode (press Esc) and then press u. The second line of the file now looks like this:

```
a. Practice vi.
```

Then again, maybe it was a good idea to practice for 60 minutes. Press u again (you're already in command mode) and you see the phrase for 60 minutes reappear. Will you or won't you practice for that long? You decide. Use the undo command to undo the change as many times as you want. Even if you decide to leave the buffer in its original form, vi assumes that the buffer has changed and you must exit with either :q! (abandon changes) or :wq (save the changes).

116

If you decide to save the file with the changes, save it to another file. Type **:w** **vipract.2** and press Enter.

You can use the Backspace key to correct mistakes you make while typing a single line. Unfortunately, as you backspace, you erase all the characters you go back over.

Writing Files and Saving the Buffer

You have seen how to write the buffer to a file and quit *vi*. Sometimes, however, you want to save the buffer to a file without quitting *vi*. Be sure to save the file regularly during an editing session. If the system goes down because of a crash or power failure, you may lose any recent work. To save the buffer, use the :w (for *write*) command from command mode. There are some variations to the steps you follow to save a file. The form of the write command you use depends on the case. There are four distinct ones. The following sections describe these cases. Table 6.2 lists the variations of the write command.

Before you issue the write command, press Esc to make sure that you are in command mode, if you are not already there. If you are already in command mode, you hear a harmless beep.

Table 6.2 Commands to Save or Write a File	
Command	**Action**
:w	Writes buffer to the file *vi* is editing.
:w *filename*	Writes buffer to the named file.
:w! *filename*	Forces *vi* to overwrite the existing named file.

> **TIP** *Save the changes you are making to a file regularly. Use the :w command frequently (at least every 15 minutes) during an editing session. You never know when the system might go down.*

Saving a New File

If you started *vi* without specifying a file name, you must provide a file name if you want to save the file to disk. The write command you issue in this case has the following format:

    :w *filename*

This command writes the buffer to the file `filename`. If the command is successful, you see the name of the file and the number of lines and characters in the file. If you specify the name of an existing file, an appropriate message appears on the status line:

```
File exits - use "w! filename" to overwrite.
```

This condition is described in "Overwriting an Existing File," later in this chapter.

Saving to the Current File

You may want to save the buffer to the file you are currently editing. For example, if you started *vi* with an existing file, made some changes, and wanted to save the changes to the original file, you can simply enter `:w`. This command saves the buffer to the file with which you are currently working. The status line tells you the name of the file and the number of lines and characters written to the file.

Saving as a New File

You may want to save the buffer to a new file—a file different than the one you originally started with. For example, if you started *vi* with the file `vipract.1`, made some changes, and wanted to save the changes to a new file without losing the original `vipract.1` file, you could save the file as a new file. Type the following form of the write command to save the file with a new file name:

```
:w new_file
```

This form of the write command is essentially the same as the original form described in "Saving a New File," earlier in this chapter. The buffer is written to the file named `new_file`. If the command was successful, you see the name of the file and the number of lines and characters in the file. If you specify the name of an existing file, an appropriate message appears on the status line:

```
File exists - use "w! new_file" to overwrite.
```

The following section explains this scenario.

Overwriting an Existing File

If you try to save the buffer to an existing file different than the one you started with, you must explicitly indicate to *vi* that you want to overwrite or replace the existing file. If you specify an existing file name when you try to save the buffer, *vi* displays the following message:

```
File exists - use "w! new_file" to overwrite.
```

If you really want to save the buffer over the existing file, use this form of the write command:

```
:w! existing_file
```

In this syntax, `existing_file` is the name of the file you want to replace. Be careful. Once you overwrite a file, you can't bring it back to its original form.

Positioning the Cursor

When you edit text, you need to position the cursor where you want to insert additional text, delete text, correct mistakes, change words, or append text to the end of the existing text. The commands you enter in command mode to select the spot you want are called *cursor-positioning commands*.

The Arrow Keys

You can use the arrow keys on many, but not all, systems to position the cursor. It's easy to see whether the arrow keys work. Start `vi` with an existing file and see what effects the arrow keys have. You may also be able to use the Page Up and Page Down keys.

Enter the following command to create a new file called `vipract.3` that contains a list of the files and directories in the directory `usr`. You can use this file to experiment with cursor-positioning commands.

```
ls /user > vipract.3
```

After the file is created, start `vi` with the `vipract.3` file (type **vi vipract.3** and press Enter). Now try using the arrow keys and the Page Up and Page Down keys to move around the editing buffer. If the keys appear to work well, you may want to use those keys for cursor positioning.

It may be the case that, although it appears that the cursor-positioning keys work, they are introducing strange characters into the file. To check whether the keys are entering characters instead of just moving the cursor, press Esc to be sure that you are in command mode and then enter **:q**. If `vi` allows you to quit and doesn't complain that the file was modified, everything is fine.

 TIP | *In* vi, *you can clear the screen of spurious or unusual characters by pressing Ctrl-l.*

6

Other Cursor-Movement Keys

There are other ways to position the cursor in `vi` without using the arrow keys. You should become familiar with these methods in case you can't or don't want to use the arrow keys. This section also shows you some ways to position the cursor more efficiently than using the arrow keys.

When vi was developed, many terminals did not have arrow keys. Other keys were and still are used to position the cursor. Figure 6.1 shows how the h, j, k, and l keys can position the cursor. Why those keys? They are in a convenient position for touch-typists.

Figure 6.1

Keyboard cursor-movement keys are in a convenient location for touch-typists.

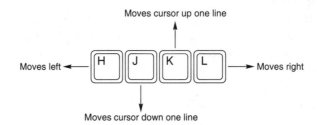

It takes a little practice to get comfortable with these keys, but some experienced vi users prefer these keys over the arrow keys.

Here are some other keys that move the cursor:

- Press the spacebar to move the cursor to the right one position.

- Press Enter or + to move to the beginning of the next line. Note that using the j key to go down one line preserves your position in the line.

- Press the minus sign (–) to move to the beginning of the previous line. Note that using the k key to go up one line preserves your position in the line.

- Press 0 (zero) to move to the beginning of a line.

- Press $ (the dollar sign) to move to the end of a line.

Some vi commands allow you to position the cursor relative to words on a line. A word is defined as a sequence of characters separated from other characters by spaces or usual punctuation symbols such as ., ?, ,, and -. These commands are listed in Table 6.3.

Table 6.3 Commands to Position the Cursor Relative to a Word

Command	Action
w	Moves forward one word.
b	Moves to the beginning of the current word.

Command	Action
e	Moves to the end of the current word.
W	Similar to w except it moves forward by blank-delimited words including punctuation (see Figure 6.2).
B	Similar to b except it moves backward by blank-delimited words including punctuation (see Figure 6.2).

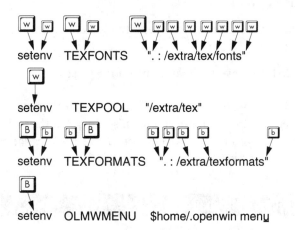

Figure 6.2
Use the keys b, B, w, and W to move the cursor by words.

The following example demonstrates some of these actions. Start vi and open the viprаct.1 file by typing **vi viprаct.1** and pressing Enter. Now use any of the cursor-positioning commands just described to move the cursor, indicated by an underline character, to the t in the word *data* on the third line of the file. The third line looks like this:

```
Sort sales data and print the results.
```

To move to the beginning of the next word, press w. The cursor is now positioned under the a of the word and. To move to the end of that word, press e. The cursor is now positioned under the d in and. To move to the beginning of that word, press b. The cursor is now positioned under the a in the word and again.

You can move forward several words to the beginning of another word by typing a whole number before pressing w. To move the cursor from its current position (under the a of the word and) to the beginning of the word three words forward (under the r of the word results), press 3-w.

Likewise, you can move backward four words by pressing 4-b. You can move forward to the end of the second word by pressing 2-e.

6

You can also use this whole-number technique with the keys h, j, k, l, +, and –. Press 1-5-j to position the cursor down 15 lines. If there aren't 15 lines left in the buffer, you hear a beep and the cursor stays where it is.

Big-Movement Keys

You can quickly move the cursor to the top, middle, or bottom of the screen. In each case, the cursor appears at the beginning of the line.

- Press H (Shift-h) to move to the first line of the screen. This is sometimes called the home position.

- Press M (Shift-m) to move to the line in the middle of the lines currently displayed on the screen.

- Press L (Shift-l) to move to the last line on the screen.

If you want to move through a file a screen at a time, which is more efficient than pressing Enter or j 23 times, use commands that scroll through a file. The command Ctrl-f moves you forward one screen. Table 6.4 uses the caret character (^) to indicate the Ctrl key.

Table 6.4 Scrolling through the Buffer	
Keystroke	**Action**
^f	Moves forward one screen.
^b	Moves backward one screen.

To move quickly to the last line of the file or buffer, press G (Shift-g). To move to the first line of the file, press 1-G (Shift-g). In fact, to move to a specific line in the buffer, type the line number before you press G. To move to line 35 of the file, press 3-5-Shift-g.

> **TIP** *Take a little time to practice positioning the cursor using the commands described in these last few sections. Remember that you must be in command mode for the cursor-positioning commands to work. Press Esc before you issue a cursor-positioning command.*

Adding Text

To add text to the editing buffer, you must go from command mode to input mode. Any usual text characters you type are then added to the buffer. If you press Enter while you are in input mode, vi pens, or adds, a line to the buffer. Before you start adding text, position the cursor at the location you want to add text. Press a to go to input mode and append text after the cursor position. Press i to go to input mode and insert text in front of the cursor position. When you are done adding text, press Esc to go back to command mode.

Here are some examples. The position of the cursor is represented by an underline character. For each case, both a before view and an after view are shown.

- Example showing the use of i to add text.

    Before: `This report is important.`

    Press i to insert text in front of the word important, and type <space>**very**<space> and press Esc.

    After: `This report is very_important.`

    Note that the cursor is positioned under the last character you added (in this case, the space).

- Example showing the use of a (the append command) to add text.

    Before: `This report is important.`

    Press a to append text after the word is, and type <space>**very** and press Esc.

    After: `This report is very important.`

    Note again that the cursor is positioned under the last character you added (in this case, the y in very).

When you want to append text at the end of a line, you can position the cursor at the end of a line and press a. Alternatively, you can position the cursor anywhere in the line and press A (Shift-a) to position the cursor at the end of the line. A puts you in input mode, and allows you to append text—all with one command. Likewise, you can move to the beginning of the current line and insert text at the beginning of a line by pressing I (Shift-i).

To add a line of text below or above the current line, you use o or O, respectively. Each opens a line in the buffer and allows you to add text. In the following two examples, you add a line to some existing text:

6

- Example showing the use of o to insert lines below the current line.

  Before: `All jobs complete`

               `please call`

               `if you have any questions.`

- The cursor is on the second line. Press o to add a line or lines below that line. Now type the following lines:

  Lee Nashua
  555-1837

  Press Esc.

  After: `All jobs complete`

               `please call`

               `Lee Nashua`

               `555-1837`

               `if you have any questions.`

- Example showing the use of O to insert lines above the current line.

  Before: `All jobs complete`

               `please call`

               `if you have any questions.`

  The cursor is on the third line. Press O (Shift-o) to add a line or lines above that line. Now type the following lines:

  Lee Nashua
  555-1837

  Press Esc.

  After: `All jobs complete`

               `please call`

               `Lee Nashua`

               `555-1837`

               `if you have any questions.`

In both cases, when you press Esc, the cursor is positioned under the last character you type (the 7 in the phone number). Although you added only two lines, you can add more lines by pressing Enter at the end of each line; you can add only one line by not pressing Enter at all.

Table 6.5 summarizes the commands for adding text. Remember that you have to be in command mode to add text. Press Esc to be sure that you are in command mode.

Table 6.5 Commands to Add Text	
Keystroke	**Action**
a	Appends text after the cursor position.
A (Shift-a)	Appends text to the end of the current line.
i	Inserts text in front of the cursor position.
I (Shift-i)	Inserts text at the beginning of the current line.
o	Opens a line below the current line to add text.
O (Shift-o)	Opens a line above the current line to add text.

Deleting Text

Making corrections or modifications to a file may involve deleting text. You must be in command mode to delete characters. If you are in input mode when you type the delete-character commands, the letters of the commands appear as characters in the buffer file. If that should happen, press Esc to go to command mode and press u to undo the mistake.

With vi, you can delete a character, a word, a number of consecutive words, all the text to the end of a line, or an entire line. Because vi is a visual editor, the characters, words, and lines are removed from the screen as you delete them. Table 6.6 lists the delete commands and describes their actions. They all take effect from the current cursor position. Move the cursor to the character, word, or line you want to change and then issue the desired delete command. Practice using them to see their effect. You will find they are helpful in making corrections to files.

Table 6.6	Commands to Delete Text
Keystroke	**Action**
x	Deletes character at cursor position.
d-w	Deletes from the cursor position in the current word to the beginning of the next word.
d-$	Deletes from the cursor position to the end of the line.
D (Shift-d)	Same as d-$: deletes the remainder of the current line.
d-d	Deletes the entire current line, regardless of cursor position in the line.

All these commands can be applied to several objects—characters, words, or lines—by typing a whole number before the command. This whole-number technique was introduced earlier in this chapter in the section on positioning the cursor. Here are some examples:

- Press 4-x to delete four characters

- Press 3-d-w to delete three words

- Press 8-d-d to delete eight entire lines

You can also specify a range of lines to delete. You do that by pressing the colon, typing the two line numbers you want to delete (inclusive) separated by a comma, pressing d, and pressing Enter. To delete lines 12 through 36 (inclusive), type `:12,36d` and press Enter.

When you delete two or more lines, the status line states how many lines were deleted. Remember that you can press u to undo the deletion.

> **TIP** *To have* vi *display line numbers, press Esc to make sure that you are in command mode. Type* `:se number`, *and press Enter. To turn off the line numbers, type* `:se nonumber` *and press Enter.*

Changing and Replacing Text

Another editing task you are often faced with is changing text or replacing one text string with another. The change commands in vi allow you to change a word or the remainder of a line. In effect, you are replacing one word or the remainder of a line with another. You use the replace commands to replace or change a single character or sequence of characters. Table 6.7 summarizes the change and replace commands.

The changes take place relative to the position of the cursor. You must be in command mode before you can use these commands. Position the cursor at the location in the buffer file you want to correct and press Esc. Because vi is visual, the changes are made to the buffer as you execute the commands. Each of these commands puts you into input mode. When you use r to replace a single character, you must press Esc to finish making changes and return to command mode.

Table 6.7   The Change and Replace Commands

Keystroke	Action
r	Replaces a single character.
R (Shift-r)	Replaces a sequence of characters.
c-w	Changes the current word from the cursor position to the end of the word.
c-e	Changes the current word from the cursor position to the end of the word (same as c-e).
c-b	Changes the current word from the beginning of the word to the character before the cursor position.
c-$	Changes a line from the cursor position to the end of the line.
C (Shift-c)	Changes a line from the cursor position to the end of the line (same as c-$).
c-c	Changes the entire line.

To change several words, use a whole number (representing the number of words to change) before pressing c-w.

Here are some examples of how to use the change and replace commands.

- Example showing the use of c-e to change to the end of the word.

  Before: `The report demonstraits thw,strengths of are apporach.`

  The cursor is located at the point in the incorrectly spelled word at which corrections are to begin. To change the spelling, press c-e, type **tes**, and press Esc.

  After: `The report demonstrates thw,strengths of are apporach.`

- Example showing the use of R (Shift-r) to replace a sequence of characters.

  Before: `The report demonstrates thw,strengths of are apporach.`

  The cursor is located at the point in the incorrectly spelled word at which you want to start replacing characters. To correct thw, to the<space>, press R, type **e<space>**, and press Esc.

  After: `The report demonstrates the_strengths of are apporach.`

- Example showing the use of c-w to change text, beginning with the current word and continuing for two words.

  Before: `The report demonstrates the strengths of are apporach.`

  The cursor is positioned under the letter of the word where you want to begin changes. To fix the last two words on the line, press 2-c-w, type **our approach,** and press Esc.

  After: `The report demonstrates the strengths of our approach.`

Remember to press Esc after you make changes to the lines to go back to command mode.

Searching

Finding a word, a phrase, or a number in a file can be difficult if you have to read through each line yourself. Like most editors and word processors, vi has a command that allows you to search for a string of characters. You can search forward or backward from your current position in the buffer. You can also continue searching. vi starts searching from the beginning of the buffer file when it reaches the end and vice versa. The commands for searching are summarized in Table 6.8. In each case, vi searches for the string you specify, in the direction you specify, and positions the cursor at the beginning of the string.

Table 6.8	The Search Commands
Command	**Action**
/*string*	Searches forward through the buffer for string.
?*string*	Searches backward through the buffer for string.
n	Searches again in the current direction.
N (Shift-n)	Searches again in the opposite direction.

When you type the search command, it appears on the status line. To search forward for the string `sales > 100K` in a file, first make sure that you are in command mode and then enter the following:

```
/sales > 100K
```

This command appears on the status line. If the string is in the buffer, `vi` positions the cursor under the first s in the word `sales`. If the string is not in the buffer, `vi` displays the message `Pattern not found` on the status line. To search for another occurrence of the string, press n. `vi` either positions the cursor under the next occurrence of the string or, if there is no further occurrence, the cursor does not move.

Copying, Cutting, and Pasting

When you delete or cut characters, words, lines, or a portion of a line, the deleted object is saved in what is called the *general-purpose buffer*. The name isn't too important. What is important is that you can put or paste the contents of that buffer anywhere in the text you're editing. You do that with the command p or P. The p command pastes the object to the right of or after the cursor position. The P command pastes the object to the left of or before the cursor.

Here are some examples of cutting and pasting text:

- Example showing the use of p to paste the contents of the general-purpose buffer after the cursor.

  Before: `Carefully carry these out instructions.`

  Delete the characters out<space> by pressing d-w. Now move the cursor to the space after the y in `carry` and press p.

  After: `Carefully carry out these instructions.`

- Example showing the use of P to paste the contents of the general-purpose buffer in front of the cursor.

Before: `Carefully carry these out instructions.`

Delete the characters `these<space>` by pressing d-w. Now move the cursor to the first i in `instructions` and press P.

After: `Carefully carry out these_instructions.`

> *TIP* **To change the order of two characters, position the cursor under the first character and press x-p. Try it to change the word** tow **to the word** two.

The preceding examples showed you how to paste after deleting text, but you don't have to delete before you can paste. You can use an operation called *yank,* which is the same as the copy operation in some word processors. The forms of the yank command are similar to the forms of the delete command. The idea is that you yank, or copy, a portion of text and then paste it somewhere else using the p or P command. Table 6.9 lists some of the yank commands. Notice that most of the yank commands use the lowercase letter y.

Table 6.9 The Yank (or Copy) Commands	
Keystroke	**Action**
y-w	Yanks from the cursor position in the current word to the beginning of the next word.
y-$	Yanks from the cursor position to the end of the line.
Y (Shift-y)	Same as y-$: yanks the remainder of the current line.
y-y	Yanks the entire current line.

All these commands can be applied to several objects—characters, words, or lines—by typing a whole number before the command.

To copy a sequence of four lines to another portion of the text, follow these steps:

1. Position the cursor at the beginning of the first of the four lines.

2. Press 4-y-y to yank from the cursor to the end of the line four times. The buffer (what you see on the screen) is unchanged.

3. Position the cursor elsewhere in the text.

4. Press p to paste the yanked lines below the line holding the cursor.

Repeating Commands

Not only does vi keep the text just deleted or yanked for future use, it also stores the last command you used for future use. You can repeat the last command that changed the buffer by pressing the period.

Suppose that you have completed a report but think it would be a good idea to add this text at key points in the report:

```
*************** Please comment ******
*************** On this section ******
```

To insert these lines, follow these steps:

1. Position the cursor in the buffer file where you want to place these lines the first time.

2. Insert the lines by pressing o to open a line and typing the two lines of asterisks and text.

3. Press Esc to be sure that you are in command mode.

4. As often as necessary, position the cursor to another section of the report and press the period to insert these same two lines.

Setting the *vi* Environment

The vi editor has several options you may or may not choose to use. Some of these options can be set on a system-wide basis by the system administrator. You can customize your environment with a number of options that are in effect whenever you start vi. Table 6.10 summarizes all the environment options you can set for vi. When setting environment options (as described in the next section) you can use either the abbreviation shown in the first column of the table or the full name of the option used in the second column.

131

6

Table 6.10 Environment Options for *vi*

Abbreviated Option	Function
ai	The autoindent option indents each line to the same level as the one above. Useful for writing programs. The default is autoindent off.
ap	The autoprint option prints the current line to the screen when the line is changed. The default is autoprint on.
eb	The errorbells option causes the computer to beep when you introduce a command error. The default is errorbells off.
nu	The number option displays line numbers when editing a file. The default is number off.
redraw	The redraw option keeps the screen up-to-date as changes occur, which means that redraw is on by default. If you want this option off, just issue a set command such as: set noredraw.
report	The report option sets the size of an editing change that results in a message on the status line. For example, report=3 triggers a message when you delete three lines but not when less than three lines are deleted. The default is report=5.
sm	The showmatch option shows a matching open parenthesis when the closing parenthesis is entered. This option is mainly useful for programmers writing code. The default is showmatch off.
smd	The showmode option displays INPUT, REPLACE, or CHANGE on the right side of the status line when the associated command is given. The default is showmode off.
warn	The warn option displays a warning message when an attempt is made to exit vi if the buffer has been changed and not saved to a disk file. The default is warn on.
wm=*n*	The wrapmargin option defines the right margin. In the syntax of this command, *n* is a whole number. If *n* is greater than 0, the command forces a carriage return so that no word is *n* or less characters from the right margin.

Abbreviated Option	Function
	For example, wm=5 instructs vi to wrap the line when a character occurs within five characters of the end of the line. Turn this option off by specifying wm=0. The default is wm=0 (off).
ws	The word search (called wrapscan on some systems) option wraps from the eof (end-of-file) character to the bof (beginning-of-file) character during a search. Default is word search on.

Using *set* to See and Set Options

To see the options currently set for your system, type :**set** and press Enter while in command mode in vi. The options currently set for this session of vi are displayed on the status line. The options displayed with the set command vary depending on the options set by default and by your particular implementation of vi. The following is an example of what you might see when you issue the set command:

```
:autoprint errorbells redraw report=1 showmatch showmode term=sun-cmd
    wrapmargin=5
```

> **NOTE** *Issuing the* set *command with no arguments results in a display of only the user-set options. You can abbreviate the set command as* se *or use* set *in full. To set a number of options on the same line, use the* se *command and separate the options with a space, as in the following example:*
>
> ```
>     :se ap eb redraw report=1 sm smd warn wm=5 ws
> ```
>
> *or use*
>
> ```
>     :set ap eb redraw report=1 sm smd warn wm=5 ws
> ```
>
> *Notice that the first character is the colon character. It has special meaning to* vi. *That is, when in the command mode, typing a colon moves the cursor to the bottom line, allowing you to type a* vi *command.*

To see the list of all possible options and their settings, type :**set all** and press Enter. The options and their settings from Table 6.10 appear.

Setting the *showmode* Option

One of the most often used options is the showmode option. To learn about the showmode option, start vi again with the vipract.1 file.

When vi executes, you see the text from your first vi session on the screen. In your first session, you may have noticed that there was no way to determine whether you were in input mode when you entered the text for this file. You can instruct vi to inform you when you are in input mode by using the showmode option. When showmode is on, whenever you are in input mode, the mode displays in the lower corner of the screen.

When you set the showmode option, vi displays whatever type of input mode it is in: regular INPUT MODE, APPEND MODE, REPLACE 1 CHAR mode, and so on. To set showmode in vi, press Esc to be sure that you are in command mode and then enter :set showmode. Now go to input mode (press i). You should see the message INPUT MODE on the status line. Press Esc to go back to command mode. You may want to see what happens when you give the commands to replace or change text.

To confirm that the showmode option is set, type the following commands:

```
:set showmode?
```

press Enter and type

```
showmode
```

Setting Toggle Options

Any option that doesn't take a number argument is like a toggle switch. It can be turned on or off. As you learned in the preceding section, you set the showmode option as follows:

```
:se showmode
```

To turn off the showmode option, you simply add no in front of the option:

```
:se noshowmode
```

Changing Options for Every *vi* Session

Setting an option during a vi session sets that option only for the current session. You can customize your vi sessions by putting the set commands in a file named .exrc in your home directory. To see whether such a file exists, type the following commands:

```
cd
vi .exrc
```

The first command takes you to your home directory. The second starts vi using the file .exrc. If the file exists, it appears on the vi screen. If the file doesn't exist, vi lets you know it's a new file. The set commands in the .exrc file start with the word set without a colon. The following line sets the options number and showmode:

```
set number showmode
```

The options you set and the values you give to some options depend on your preferences and the type of editing you will be doing. Experiment with some options or talk with more experienced users, such as your system administrator, about vi options.

Using the *emacs* Text Editor

The name emacs stands for *EditorMACroS*. The emacs editor is one of the most popular UNIX text editors and is used by almost as many users as vi. A full version of emacs is very large, taking up several megabytes of disk space. It is a powerful, full-featured editor and has been extended to be used for more than text editing. In some installations, you can use emacs to edit files, keep a calendar, work with e-mail, manage files, read Usenet or network news, create outlines, use it as a calculator, and so on. In some sense, emacs is a working environment that contains a text editor.

The emacs editor was created by Richard Stallman. The source code for emacs is available for free. Richard Stallman is a founder and proponent of the Free Software Foundation and the GNU project. Stallman believes strongly that all software should be free and that computer systems should be open for use by anyone. The fact that emacs is freely available matches his philosophy. Anyone can take it for his or her own use. Users are also encouraged to make modifications and share those changes with others.

The emacs editor is modeless; it doesn't have the two modes that vi has. For this reason, anything you type is put into the file buffer. To give the editor commands to save files, search for text, delete text, and so on, you must use other keys. In emacs, you use control characters (usually Ctrl-x and Ctrl-c) and the Esc key.

To start emacs, type **emacs** and press Enter. A screen with some initial instructions and a status line at the bottom appears. emacs has online Help facilities for learning about the keystrokes. If emacs is available on your system, ask for some documentation or talk with a local expert.

The complete GNU emacs system is large, but it can be customized to match your local environment. Some smaller versions of emacs that are readily available are FreEmacs, by Russell Nelson, and MicroEmacs, originally by Dave Conroy. Some commercial versions of emacs are also available. Which of these you use depends on local policies and constraints. Because emacs is so popular, there is a large support network of emacs users.

Creating Your First *emacs* File

Type **emacs** and press Enter. You get a screen that looks like the following:

```
GNU Emacs 19.25.1 of Wed Aug  3 1994 on gumbo (sparc-sun-solaris2.3)
Copyright  1994 Free Software Foundation, Inc.

Type C-h for help; C-x u to undo changes.   ('C-' means use CTRL key.)
To kill the Emacs job, type C-x C-c.
Type C-h t for a tutorial on using Emacs.
Type C-h i to enter Info, which you can use to read GNU documentation.

GNU Emacs comes with ABSOLUTELY NO WARRANTY; type C-h C-w for full
details.
You may give out copies of Emacs; type C-h C-c to see the conditions.
Type C-h C-d for information on getting the latest version.

----Emacs: *scratch*         (Lisp Interaction)--All-------------------
------------------------------------------
For information about the GNU Project and its goals, type C-h C-p.
```

The C- in C-h stands for Ctrl. Press Ctrl-h key to see the online Help manual. You can scroll the online Help by pressing the spacebar.

To view a full-fledged tutorial on emacs, press Ctrl-h. This key combination lets you view the next screen in the tutorial. To save a document, press Ctrl-x followed by Ctrl-s. You are then prompted for a file name.

Starting *emacs* Using an Existing File

If you have a file that needs modification, type **emacs** and press Enter. Then press Ctrl-x, Ctrl-f and you are prompted for a file name for emacs to open. (The name of the last file you saved appears on-screen.)

Table 6.11 shows some of the most commonly used keys for moving the cursor around in a file.

Table 6.11	Cursor Movement in *emacs*
Keys	**Cursor Movement**
Ctrl-f	One character forward
Ctrl-b	One character backward
Ctrl-e	End of line
Ctrl-a	Beginning of line
Ctrl-x,]	Next page
Ctrl-x, [	Previous page

Exiting *emacs*

If you press Ctrl-x, Ctrl-c, you exit from your document and emacs. If you changed the text, you are prompted to save the file before you exit. In this case, you are presented with a variety of choices: y, n, !...q, C-r, C-h. To save your changes, answer yes. Otherwise, answer no. If you answer no, you are asked whether you still want to exit. Answer yes to exit or no to continue editing your document. If you would like help at this point, press Ctrl-h.

Undoing and Repeating a Command

What if the last changes of your file have to be undone? It's as easy to undo changes in emacs as it is in vi. Suppose that you added a line in your document and you are not satisfied with the way the sentence reads. Ctrl-x u will remove the last sentence you added. In general, Ctrl-x u will undo the last editing change you made.

What if there is a sentence from another file that you want to insert in several places in your file? Ctrl-x *n* (*n* is a number) will insert the line *n* number of times.

Splitting Windows and Saving the Buffer

Suppose that you are writing a book and you are contemplating two different versions of a chapter. Obviously, you would like to see the major differences between these two chapters simultaneously. You can do that in emacs by having both chapters occupy two different windows and scrolling back and forth between them.

6

You start emacs and use Ctrl-x, Ctrl-f to read one of the versions in the first window. (You do not have to tell the computer which window to go to.) Ctrl-x 2 opens a second window so that you can see the second version of that same chapter. You can scroll back and forth between windows by just pressing Ctrl-x o. You can use Ctrl-x, Ctrl-s to save changes if any are made to the files. Ctrl-x 2 splits one of the actual windows into two windows. Three windows can now be viewed. It is also possible to have vertical as well as horizontal windows. When is the last time you heard of a text editor that will let you have horizontal and vertical windows? Ctrl-x 3 creates a vertical window. Ctrl-x o lets you jump between the horizontal and vertical windows. You can eliminate all the windows and keep just one by pressing Ctrl-x 1.

Inserting an Existing File into Another File

If you want to include another file in your current file, how would you go about it? Is it as easy as in vi? Ctrl-x i enables you to insert an existing file into your current one.

Deleting Text

Deleting text is easy. Ctrl-d deletes one character forward, and Del deletes one character backward. Ctrl-k deletes everything to the end of line. A *meta*-d (where *meta* is usually an Esc key) deletes the next word and *meta*-Del deletes the previous word.

To delete the next sentence, press *meta*-k. To delete the previous sentence, press Ctrl-x Del.

Deleting text from emacs is as easy as it is from vi. *Meta*-\ deletes a tab or space at the cursor position. Ctrl-x h and then Ctrl-w wipes out an entire paragraph. To yank back what you just deleted, press Ctrl-y.

Changing and Replacing Text

To search for a word in your document, press Ctrl-s. A prompt is displayed. Enter the word you want to search for. After emacs has found it, the cursor is positioned at the end of the word. If the word is not in the text, you will hear a beep signaling that the word was not found.

If you are at the end of your document and you want to perform a search, use Ctrl-r. This tells emacs to search backward through your document.

If you want every occurrence of a word to be replaced by another word, use C-h f, for getting help on a function. When you press C-h f, you are prompted for a function name. Type **replace**. emacs then displays no match, and you have to press the Tab key to get out. As soon as the Tab key is pressed, emacs lists all the possible functions that start with *replace*.

Here are possible completions:

replace-buffer-in-windows	replace-dehighlight
replace-buffer-in-windows	replace-match
replace-highlight	replace-string
replace-regexp	

The *replace* you are looking for is replace-string. Type **replace-string** to get the following help:

```
"Replace occurrences of FROM-STRING with TO-STRING.
```

To use the replace-string function, press *meta*-x (Esc-x), followed by a replace-string, and press Enter. The computer prompts you for a replace-string. Type

```
replace string:alpha
replace with:beta
```

In this example, the word alpha is replaced with the word beta.

Copying, Yanking, and Pasting

Marking an area or a page that needs to be copied, moved, or deleted is a simple task. Start by setting bookmarks on what to mark. Click the left mouse button at the beginning of the text to be marked. Move the mouse cursor to the end of that paragraph and click the middle mouse button. Now the text is marked and appears in boldface.

Next click the right mouse button and select Copy from the Term pane. Move the mouse to where you want the marked paragraph copied, and select Paste from the Term pane. A copy of the selected text is inserted at the mouse cursor.

To move text to a new location, highlight the text and press Ctrl-x r m. Use Paste to insert the text at the mouse cursor.

To delete a block of text, highlight it but use Ctrl-w.

Setting the *emacs* Environment

You can change the default settings that emacs uses by saving them to a file that emacs reads when it starts. For example, if you want the color of the foreground set to red, the default font set to Helvetica, a dummy variable (named stupid) set

to 20, and the color of the cursor set to blue, save the following to a file called ~/
.*username*-emacs, where .*username* is your login name:

```
(set-foreground-color red)
(set-default-font Helvetica)
(set-default stupid 20)
(set-cursor-color blue)
```

This file is then read automatically when you start an emacs session.

A Survey of Other Editors

You may have other text editors available on your UNIX system. Some are commercial and others are available free on the Internet or from other sources. Editors other than vi have been created because some users are uncomfortable with the two-mode (command and input) operation of vi. Some users are familiar with editors available on other systems and want to use the features of those editors when they move to UNIX. You should be aware of or familiar with some of these editors to match your working environment or personal tastes. However, as an experienced UNIX user, you should have some familiarity with vi or emacs.

A few dozen text editors are available for UNIX systems. This chapter mentions only two: Joe (Joe's Own Editor) and pico.

The editors discussed are examples of some types of text editors available on UNIX systems. You may find that other editors are in use and popular on your system. Apologies to those who feel slighted that their favorite editor isn't mentioned here.

Looking at *Joe*

Joe's Own Editor, or Joe, is a full-screen editor developed and maintained by Joseph H. Allen. It is available by anonymous FTP on the Internet. The Joe editor is a small, modeless editor. You specify commands with keystrokes similar to those in the popular DOS editor, WordStar (Joe is particularly popular with users who come from a DOS environment). It has online Help and all the features you expect. It works only if you have an ANSI or VT100 terminal type.

NOTE | **Anonymous FTP is a special service that allows users to download files from a server without a password.**

To start Joe, type **Joe** and press Enter. You see an essentially blank screen with some status information. To get help, press Ctrl-k-h. The top 10 lines or so of the screen show all the necessary control-key combinations necessary to accomplish your work.

Looking at *pico*

The pico editor was developed at the University of Washington. Although it can be used on its own, it is part of the large Pine mail system. The term pico stands for *PIne COmposer*. Like emacs and Joe, pico is a modeless editor. When you start it, you are in input mode. You use control characters to move around the screen or perform other functions.

To start pico, type **pico** and press Enter. You see a screen that allows you to enter text. You also see the following brief help at the bottom of the screen:

```
^G Get Help ^O Writeout ^R Read File ^Y Prev Page ^K Del Line ^C Cur Pos
^X Exit      ^J Justify  ^W Where Is  ^V Next Page ^U Undel Lin ^T To
     Spell
```

The pico editor is good for those bothered by the two modes of vi. It isn't as powerful as vi or emacs, but it is good for many editing tasks.

Exercises

1. If you are in vi, what do you type to enter input mode? To enter command mode?

2. If you are in vi and at the beginning of the file, what command do you type to jump to the end of the line? To jump to the end of the paragraph? To jump to the end of the document?

3. If you are in vi and at the beginning of a word, what command do you type to reverse the first two letters of the word? To append a letter to the end of a word?

4. Assuming the cursor is at the end of the word vict, what command do you type to add the letter e to vict to make the word evict? Add a line below the current line? Add a line before the current line? Replace the c in evict with b? Replace ic in evict with ice?

5. You are in vi and want to replace every occurrence of DOS with UOS. What command do you use?

6. You have opened a file named yahoo within vi. What command do you use to insert an existing file called WebCrawler at the end of the second paragraph in yahoo?

7. What command do you use to move an entire paragraph from a file called yahoo and insert it into a second file called WebCrawler?

8. Formulate your own strategy to learn the vi commands. What would you suggest to a friend who has never used vi but is familiar with other word processors like WordPerfect and Word? Describe some of the major differences between vi and other word processors with which you are familiar.

9. Redo exercises 1 through 7 using the emacs editor.

7

Electronic Mail

Topics Covered

- What Is Electronic Mail?
- Working with E-mail from the Command Line

In Chapter 1, "Introduction to the UNIX Operating System," you learned that UNIX was developed in an environment that encouraged sharing, cooperation, and the exchange of ideas and information. As the UNIX market expanded, this philosophy of sharing was one of the features that attracted new users to UNIX. This chapter looks at electronic mail, which lets you exchange messages, data, and programs with your colleagues and friends, whether they work on your computer or anywhere in the world.

If electronic mail is simply mail sent through the computer, why is it so important? What are its advantages, its limitations? What do the funny characters in someone's e-mail address mean? With electronic mail, a little understanding goes a long way.

Many mail programs are available for UNIX. Two mail programs that come with most versions of UNIX are `mail` and `mailx`. All of them let you perform essentially the same tasks: send mail, read mail, send replies to mail, save mail to files, and configure your mail.

E-mail is tightly tied with networking—after all, if your computer doesn't connect with any other computers, your mail service is limited to other users on your own computer. The network doesn't have to be a huge international network. It could be a small UUCP network among three different offices or an Internet-style network joining all the computers in one building. The type of network connection you use can affect the kind of mail you send, too. If you're sending mail through a UUCP connection, you may have to address your mail differently.

What Is Electronic Mail?

Electronic mail (*e-mail*) is the sending and receiving of messages by computer. E-mail is changing the way the world thinks about exchanging information. It has invaded every area of computing, not just UNIX, and has revolutionized science and business. Scientists across the world are sharing information through e-mail (and related electronic bulletin boards). There are cases where scientists working on the same project never meet—they do all their work through e-mail. Business travelers using laptops can communicate with others in the office or on the road without annoying "phone tag" sessions.

E-mail isn't just text, although that makes up the bulk of it. E-mail messages are normally text data, such as, "Hi, are you free for lunch on Thursday?" but don't have to be. You can send almost any kind of data, such as programs, spreadsheets, databases, and even audio recordings and pictures. Some software organizations use e-mail to update their clients. There are mailing lists for people with similar interests. People can receive mail messages dedicated to sailing, jokes, international standards, or almost anything else you can imagine. There are even e-mail magazines that are distributed electronically.

Billions of e-mail messages every year are delivered cheaply and quickly—in most cases, virtually instantaneously. These messages are sent not only on UNIX systems but also through local area networks, mainframe networks, and commercial services such as MCI Mail. Postal services in North America are watching warily as e-mail handles a growing number of messages formerly sent by first-class mail. (Many European postal services already have jurisdiction over computer networks and charge a license fee for access or modem time.) Most major companies have already discovered the advantages of e-mail.

Advantages of Electronic Mail

Why are so many people using e-mail? The following are some reasons that make sense from a corporate standpoint:

- *Low cost.* Electronic mail is an extremely cost-effective way to move information, especially when it must be moved quickly. A three-page letter can cost $15 to ship overnight or about $5 to telex. The same letter can be sent by electronic mail for a few cents locally or for about $1 long distance.

- *Speed.* Electronic mail can be delivered almost as fast as the wire can carry it.

- *Flexibility.* Because all the messages are just computer files, you have much more control over how you use the information. If you receive a copy of a spreadsheet by fax and you want to play with the data, you must enter the spreadsheet into your computer. If you receive the same spreadsheet by e-mail, it's already on your computer, ready to use. You have control over what to do with the information—you can print it, edit it, incorporate it into a report you are preparing, or use it as input data for some other program.

- *Waste reduction.* Electronic mail reduces the clutter of paper in the modern office, not to mention saving many trees.

The following are some more personal reasons:

- *Ease of use.* It's easy to send an e-mail message, and it doesn't take hours of explanation before you grasp the basics. You don't have to retype it three times, find an envelope, go to the corner to buy a stamp, and then find a mailbox.

7

- *Rapidity*. If you're working on a project and you have a question for a coworker, it's easy to dash off a quick e-mail note rather than search for the coworker and ask immediately.

- *Maintenance record*. Because all the messages are files, you can automatically maintain a record of communications with someone else. And because most mail messages are just text files, you can use all the UNIX text tools to search the messages and extract information.

- *Patience*. E-mail waits until you read it. It doesn't have the jangling urgency of a phone call; if you don't read it as soon as it arrives, you will still have the message.

This is a persuasive list of reasons for electronic mail.

Limits of Electronic Mail

The following are the disadvantages and limits to electronic mail:

- *Hardware requirements*. You have to be at a computer to read or print e-mail.

- *Text only*. Some mail programs now handle multimedia, but the majority of older software handles only text. If you're sending binary files, you may have to convert them to a text format before you send them. UNIX offers the tools uuencode and uudecode to transform binary files into text and back again.

- *Impermanence*. Your saved mail messages can be altered in all the ways that UNIX offers, including text changes and outright deletion.

- *Size*. Some older UUCP mail-handling software is restricted to messages of 64K or less. If your mail is traveling via UUCP and you aren't certain of the sites that will transport your mail, you should restrict mail messages to 60K or less. This restriction is becoming rare, though, because most e-mail is now sent via Internet-style connections that don't have the 64K limit.

Some of the advantages can be disadvantages if you're careless:

- *Haste*. Because e-mail is so easy to use, it's also easy to send a message that you later regret.

- *Lack of emotional context*. Without the extra cues of voice, posture, and expression, it's easy to misunderstand what someone really means in a message. Jokes, sarcasm, and irony are particularly easy to miss. Combined with the hastiness of e-mail, this problem can result in misunderstandings and hurt feelings.

- *Lack of privacy.* Once a message is sent, it is too late to ask the receiver not to read it.

- *Lack of security.* Anybody can send a user a message without the user knowing the true author of the message. If you use the ftp command to send a message, you could send an ugly message to a user, and the user might think that Joe Smith is sending him the message although it is you.

None of these reasons are worth giving up e-mail; they're minor annoyances only. Most of them can be corrected by simple politeness and some extra care in wording when you're dashing off that message.

Structure of a Mail Message

An e-mail message is structured very much like a paper letter—there is addressing information and salutatory material, like the return address and the date, and there is the actual message. Sometimes, there is also a "signature" at the bottom. Figure 7.1 shows a sample e-mail message.

```
From herd!north!kris
Received: by nose (HDB UUCP); Sun,  3 Oct 93 11:33 EST
Received: from north by herd id <AA03654>;
Sun, 3 Oct 93 08:00:32
From: Kris Kringle <kris@yule.com>
Message-Id: <199310030700.AA21386>
Subject: Upcoming Christmas Season
Date: Sun, 3 Oct 1993 07:00:34 (UMT)
To: nose!rudy donner@herd.com

Rudy & Don—

Christmas is almost three months off and I'm still
worried about Prancer. Frankly, he's packed on a lot of
weight since last year when he and Dancer split up.  I
know I'm not really one to talk, but guys, we've got an
image to maintain. How will it look, the sleigh heading
through the sky with seven tiny reindeer and one blimp?
I've got NORAD woes as it is.

Please, guys, you're friends of his. Talk to him. I
know you've been naughty this year; here's a chance to
make it up.

Kris
— —
kris@yule.com
Kris Kringle, Inc.
Gifts and Deliveries
```

Figure 7.1

A sample e-mail message.

7

When you look at a mail message like the one in Figure 7.1, you will notice three parts: the *header*, the *body*, and the *signature*. The header at the top of the message is the envelope; the body is the actual message; the signature comes at the end.

The header describes information about the sender, the message, and the recipient. The first few lines describe the route the message took, who sent the message, the date it was sent, the subject, and to whom it was sent. The first line is always From followed by a space. The header ends with a blank line.

Some common header lines include the following:

To: The recipient(s) of the message.

Date: The date the message was sent.

From: The person who sent the message.

Cc: The people who were mailed copies of the message. Generally, you mail to the people who should respond, and send carbon copies to people who need to be kept informed but don't have to respond.

Bcc: The people who were mailed *blind copies*—their names are hidden from the other recipients. You use blind carbon copies when you want to keep someone informed without the other participants knowing.

The actual body of the message can be any length. It can contain any text. With most mail programs, you can't directly include nonprintable characters, although newer programs let you *attach* binary files (such as pictures, programs, data files, and sound recordings) to create multimedia messages.

The signature is the four lines at the bottom, beginning with the line of dashes; it's optional. An e-mail signature is a short blurb about yourself that some mail programs tack onto the end of the message. The signature usually includes your name, your e-mail address, and maybe your postal address. Often, a person puts a quip or a quotation in his signature. Some people get carried away with signature files, including huge ASCII drawings and extensive song lyrics; this is considered impolite. A signature of three or four lines is usually enough. If your signature is longer than most of your messages, it's too long.

Addressing a Mail Message

Every mail message, like every postal message, has an address that tells the mail software where the message is to go. The address indicates who gets the message and what machine that person is on. If the machine is far away, you may also have to indicate where that machine is. You don't have to understand addressing to start sending mail; most people tell you what their e-mail address is, and you can just send it. The type of address you use depends on how you're sending the mail and how smart your mail software is.

If you're sending mail to a person who has an account on your machine, it's easy—her address is her login identification. To send mail to the superuser identification, you never need any more of an address than root. But when you're sending mail to another machine, address formats come into play.

There are two main styles of mail addressing, UUCP and Internet, for the two main types of networks that handle mail. *UUCP addressing* is like passing a note in class—you have to describe everyone who passes the message along. *Internet addressing* is like sending a letter—the address includes the person who gets the message and where he is. Most sites use Internet addressing, but UUCP addressing is still common, especially with smaller machines and local networks.

E-mail offers two facilities for making addresses easier to use. You can send one message to several people by putting all their addresses in the message address, and you can create short forms for mail addresses, called *aliases*.

UUCP Addressing
A UUCP address looks like the following:

    thor!anansi!jordan

The last name in the line is the login identification of the recipient. The rest of the line is the path the message must take to get there. Your machine must give the message to thor, and thor must give the message to anansi (the machine that jordan's account is on). Each machine's name is separated from the rest by exclamation points. Sometimes exclamation points are called *bangs*, so a UUCP address path is also called a *bang path*. Of course, thor!anansi!jordan is just an example; some bang paths are much longer (ten names, possibly more), and some are shorter. If your machine can call anansi directly, it makes sense to use the address anansi!jordan.

UUCP paths can get very long—you might have to pass a message through eight or ten sites before it reaches its destination—and if you change machines, the path can change. If you're sending mail to jordan from someone else's machine, the address might be inanna!bubastis!anansi!jordan because the message has to travel a different route to get to the destination. Because it can be difficult to keep track of an entire address route, there are several ways to get around it. The most common is to give the mail program the user's login name and machine and let it figure out the rest. After all, you don't care how the message gets there, as long as it *does* get there. That's the idea behind Internet addressing.

7

Internet Addressing

An address for Internet mail looks like this:

```
kris@yule.com
```

You read this as "kris at yule-dot-com." `kris` is the user, and `yule.com` is the address of the machine. The part before the dot is the machine's name (`yule`), and the rest is where the machine is, its *domain*. The machine named `yule` is part of the set of computers in the `com` domain, just as your house is part of the set of houses on your street. A domain is just a grouping of computers. There are a limited number of top-level domains—think of them as the countries in the Internet world. Table 7.1 lists the domains. Internet addressing is sometimes called *domain addressing*.

Table 7.1	Nongeographic Internet Domains
Domain	**Members**
com	Commercial sites
edu	Educational sites
gov	Government sites
mil	Military sites
net	Internet sites that are administrative in some form
org	Organizations, usually nonprofit

There are also domains for each country—for example, an address ending in `.ca` is for a site in Canada, and one ending in `.nl` is for a site in the Netherlands.

Some domains (especially the geographic ones) are so big that they also have *subdomains*. For example, `unix.amherst.edu` is the machine `unix` in the subdomain `amherst` of the `edu` domain.

Gateways

If your message is going across two different kinds of networks, you may have to change the address format. A machine that connects two networks is a *gateway machine*. For example, if your machine accepts mail from one machine via UUCP and another via Internet connections, your machine is a gateway machine. Whether you will have to know about gateways depends on your mail software and how your mail system is configured. Some mail software keeps track of

UUCP and Internet addresses or is smart enough to give mail with unknown addresses to another site that keeps track of them all.

In the network shown in Figure 7.2, thor is a gateway machine; it has a UUCP connection to anansi and Internet connections with the rest of the Internet. Suppose that you're on anansi. To send mail from anansi to kelly on thor, the address is thor!kelly. (Most UUCP sites don't know about domains; if you type kelly@thor, though, the mail program might change that to thor!kelly for you.)

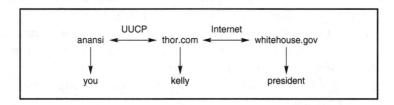

Figure 7.2
A simple network.

What if you want to send mail to somewhere on the Internet, say president@whitehouse.gov? The address, thor!president@whitehouse.gov may or may not work (depending on your mail program); it may interpret the address as whitehouse.gov!thor!president, which is returned because the mail software doesn't know where whitehouse.gov is.

Instead, replace the address character for the destination network with a percent sign (%):

    thor!president%whitehouse.gov

The percent sign doesn't work for all gateways, but it works for many of them.

Obviously, there are more than two kinds of networks and more than two kinds of address characters (there are networks that use a colon, for example). Every gateway can be different.

Aliases

You may not want to keep typing and retyping the same addresses repeatedly, especially if you're using long UUCP addresses. To minimize retyping, UNIX e-mail offers aliases.

An *alias* is a short form for an address or a group of addresses. You might decide to make kelly short for thor!kelly. Whenever you send mail to kelly, the mail software treats the address as if you had typed thor!kelly. Or if you routinely send mail to everyone in your work group, you might decide to create an alias for the group so that typing workgroup is the same as typing anna, bob, chris, dana, ed, or francine.

7

When you create an alias, be sure there are no accounts on your system that use that alias as a login identification. If you already have a user `kelly` on your system and you make the name `kelly` an alias for `thor!kelly`, it will be very difficult to send mail to the `kelly` on your system.

Working with E-mail from the Command Line

All UNIX systems have some kind of mail programs, usually `mail` (the original mail program) or `mailx`. This section discusses `mailx`, which has a few more features than `mail` but is very similar to it. Basically, you can apply all features described for `mailx` and use it for `mail` except for a mail summary and the capability to open a text editor. The `mailx` program is also part of the POSIX.2 standard. (The POSIX.2 standard was briefly described in Chapter 1, "Introduction to the UNIX Operating System.")

From the command line, you can use `mailx` as you would any other UNIX tool. You don't have to use it interactively; you can include `mailx` in shell programs to notify you by mail when they're finished, to automate sending files and reports, and to mail the output of programs directly to other users.

The `mailx` program has two modes: *send mode* and *read mode*. Send mode is used for sending mail. Read mode is for checking your mailbox; reading messages; replying to messages; and printing, saving, and deleting mail. If you start `mailx` with an address or addresses as arguments, it automatically starts in send mode. If you start it without an address on the command line, `mailx` starts in read mode.

In read mode, you can configure `mailx` by using `set` commands. The `set` commands last only until you leave the `mailx` session. Any configuration commands described here can be put in a `mailx` configuration file in your home directory so that they take effect every time you run `mailx`.

Sending Mail

To send mail, type **mailx** and an address. The `mailx` program enters send mode so that you can enter your message. The `mailx` program's send mode is primitive: You can type the lines and backspace over errors on the current line, there's no word wrap, and you can't go back to a previous line to fix it. You can modify the message by using the send mode commands. All send mode commands start on a new line and begin with a tilde (~). To issue a command in send mode, press Enter to start a new line, type the command, and then press Enter again. For example, to review a message before you send it, use the ~p command. Start a new line in the message, type

~p

and press Enter.

To send a mail message using mailx, follow these steps:

1. At the command line, type **mailx *address*** and press Enter. mailx prompts you for a subject, which is optional.

2. If you want to enter a subject, do so, and then press Enter.

   mailx enters send mode, using its built-in text option. Type the message and press Enter at the end of each line.

3. When you've finished the message, you can send it or quit without sending it.

   To send the message, start a new line, type ~. (that's "tilde dot"), and press Enter.

   mailx sends the message and exits.

   To quit without saving the message, start a new line, type ~**q**, and press Enter.

   mailx saves the text of the message in a file called dead.letter in your home directory and exits.

> **NOTE** *When you first send a mail message to an Internet host, you may discover that the at character (@) erases the command line. Some terminals are configured so that the @ key is the line-kill character. To change this, use the* stty *command. A common alternative line-erase character is Ctrl-u. Some versions of* stty *allow you to type the Ctrl-u in this example as either Ctrl-u or the character ^ followed by the character U; others require Ctrl-u. Enter the following command:*
>
>   stty kill ^U

Use the send mode commands to change parts of the message before you send it or quit mailx. For example, to change the list of recipients to dana lee sam, type ~**T dana lee sam** and press Enter. This replaces the existing address list with the new one. Remember that all send mode commands must be typed at the beginning of a line. Some useful send mode commands follow:

- To review the message so far, type ~**p** and press Enter.

- To use vi to edit the message, type ~**v** and press Enter.

- To change the subject line of the message, type ~**s** *new subject* and press Enter.

- To read a text file into the message, type ~**r** *filename* and press Enter. Using this command, you can insert any file you've created with vi into a mail message.

- To write the message into a text file (for example, a file named message), type ~**w** **message** and press Enter.

- To get help, type ~**?** and press Enter.

There are several send mode commands that are available only if you entered send mode from read mode (such as when you're replying to a message). The important one is ~m, which inserts the text of an existing message into the current message. This command is useful for quoting the original message in your reply.

Reading Mail

There are three stages to reading mail with mailx: starting mailx, reading the messages, and quitting mailx. You can do more with your mail (reply to messages, save mail, and so on). These topics are discussed later in this chapter.

To read mail, type **mailx** without an address. mailx starts in read mode. (Read mode is also called *command mode.*) If you have no mail waiting, mailx informs you and exits the program.

If you have mail, mailx displays information about the mail in your mailbox. It will look something like this:

```
mailx version 4.2  Type ? for help.
"/var/mail/jay": 3 messages 2 new 1 old
 U  1 thyme!chris       Tue Dec 14 08:42      9/164    Meeting Thursday
    change
>N  2 basil!lee         Wed Dec 15 15:11      8/127    Still up to swimming?
 N  3 sage!ricky        Wed Dec 15 23:16     11/379    Where are X.400 specs?
?
```

The first line identifies the version of mailx you are using. The second line gives the pathname of your system mailbox and the number of messages—in this example, there are three messages, and two are new. Each line after that summarizes a message. Each message is new (N), old (O), or unread (U) and has a number. You use the number to refer to the messages in read mode commands. After the number comes the name of the person who sent the message, the date of the message, its size (in lines/characters), and the subject. In this example, message 2 has a > character beside it—message 2 is the *current message*. If you give a command to `mailx` (like "read") without specifying a particular message number, the command affects the current message.

The question mark on the bottom line means that `mailx` is waiting for a command. All read mode commands are given at the question mark prompt.

The easiest way to read a message is to press Enter, which is synonymous with the n (next) command. The n command displays the current message and changes the current message to the next message in the list. In this way, you can read through all your mail sequentially.

The p (print) command also displays a message on-screen, but doesn't change the current message. To display message number 2, type **p 2** and press Enter.

If you have a message that has more text lines than your screen, the message may scroll off the screen, leaving you looking at the last few lines. `mailx` doesn't know how big your terminal window or screen is. To fix the problem, do the following:

1. At the question mark prompt, type **set crt=24** and press Enter.

   This tells `mailx` that your Terminal window is only 24 lines long. (Most terminals are 25 lines long, but the extra line helps you keep your place in the message.) If your terminal has a higher resolution, set `crt` to a higher number. Use the `set` command while reading mail with `mailx` (or you can insert it in the configuration file).

2. At the question mark prompt, type **set PAGER=more** and press Enter.

   Now `Mail` knows that for messages over 24 lines long, it should use more to display the text.

3. Display the message again.

> **NOTE** The `more` *command is discussed in Chapter 4, "Working with Files and Directories."*
>
> *If you have to set* `crt` *and* `PAGER` *on your system, put the* `set` *commands in your* `.mailrc` *file.*

7

156

To leave `mailx`, you must be at the question mark prompt. Type **q** and press Enter. Any changes you have made to your mailbox (such as messages you've deleted) take place now, and the mail you have read is saved in the file `mbox` in your home directory. If you don't want those changes made, leave `mailx` with the x (exit) command. `mailx` ends without changing either your system mailbox or your `mbox` file.

Replying to a Mail Message

When you reply to a message, `mailx` takes the address from the original message and puts you in send mode. After you've finished sending you have a choice: Do you want your response to go to everyone who saw the original message, or do you just want your response to go to the sender?

- To respond to everyone who got the original message, type **r** and press Enter.

- To respond only to the original sender, type **R** and press Enter.

While you are replying to a message, you may want to include the text of the original message. The send mode command ~m inserts the entire message, with each line indented by a tab character. (You can use ~m only when you enter send mode from read mode.) If you want to use a character or characters other than a tab character to mark attributed lines, set the `indentprefix` variable. Suppose that you wanted each line of the quoted text to start with a greater-than sign and a space. Type **set indentprefix="> "** and press Enter to set the character to a greater-than sign and a space. The quotation marks are necessary to make the space part of the prefix; otherwise, it just uses the first word. For instance, `set indentprefix=sender name>` would *actually* set the prefix to `sender`. To get both words as the marking prefix, you would have to use `set indentprefix="sender name> "`.

If you want to remove extraneous text (like header lines), remember that you can edit the file in `vi` with the ~v command.

Saving Received Mail

On most systems, `mailx` automatically saves mail you have read in a file called `mbox` in your home directory. New messages are inserted at the beginning of the `mbox` file. You can save messages into other files, though. When you save a message to another file, it doesn't get saved in the `mbox` file.

You can save a mail message in a file named after the author's login name, or in a file with an arbitrary name. To save the current message in a file named after the author, type **s** and press Enter. Using message numbers can save a great deal of time when saving files. To save messages 1 through 4 in files named for their authors, type **s 1-4** and press Enter.

Some versions of mailx let you use the asterisk character as a short form for "all messages." To save all messages in this case, you can type **s ***.

To save mail in another file, type **s** *filename* and press Enter. If you want to specify the messages to be saved, the message number goes between the s and the file name: s 2-4 specification.txt.

Saving Outgoing Mail

In send mode, you can save the message you are working on with the ~w command. For instance, to save your message in the file instructions, type **~w instructions** and press Enter. This saves the message (without headers) as it is at that moment; it doesn't send the message. Once the message is saved, you return to the message. You can add more text (although this means that your saved message is now outdated).

You can also configure mailx to save all your outgoing mail in a single file with set record=*filename*. To save all your outgoing mail in the file ~/mailbox/ SentMail.ml, type the following command at the question mark prompt in mailx and press Enter:

```
set record=~/mailbox/SentMail.ml
```

Reading Saved Mail

If you want to read old mail, either from your mbox file or from another file you have saved it in, use the file command. Suppose that you want to review the messages from an e-mail discussion you saved under the name project. At the question mark prompt, type **file project** and press Enter.

The header display changes to show the mail messages in the file project.

The -f option does the same thing from the command line: mailx -f mbox lets you read your saved mail and sort through it.

Printing a Mail Message

To print a mail message, you can either save it to a file and print it as you would any other text message, or you can pipe it directly to the print command.

To pipe message 3 to the print command (usually lpr or lp), type ¦ **3 lpr** at the question mark prompt and press Enter.

Creating or Modifying an Alias

To create or modify an alias, use the `alias` command in the form `alias newname=address(es)`. To use `bucky` as an alias for

```
leviathan!spud!kong!buckminster,
```

use the following command:

```
alias bucky leviathan!spud!kong!buckminster
```

To show the list of existing aliases, use the `alias` command without any arguments:

```
? alias
bog      bog@newt.waterloo.edu
project anna bob chris dana ed francine
```

To delete an alias for the duration of a `mailx` session, use `unalias` at the question mark prompt. For example, to remove the alias `bog`, type **unalias bog** and press Enter.

If you're going to use an alias regularly, put the `alias` command in your `.mailrc` file. (See the following section for details on creating a `.mailrc` file.)

Customizing *mailx*

The effects of any `set` and `alias` commands vanish when you exit `mailx`. You can make these changes permanent by creating a `.mailrc` file in your home directory. This section summarizes the set commands that have already been mentioned and shows an example of `.mailrc` files.

You can also specify the header lines you *don't* want displayed, using the `ignore` command. For instance, if you don't want to see any lines that start with `Received:`, type **ignore Received:** and press Enter.

Table 7.2 shows the customization commands that have been mentioned.

Table 7.2 Customization Commands for *mailx*	
Customization	**Command**
Alias *address* to *aka*	`alias "aka=address"`
List known aliases	`alias`
Turn off alias *aka*	`unalias aka`
Don't show specified headers	`ignore header: header:`

Customization	Command
Number of lines on-screen	set *crt=number*
Prefix included messages with x	set indentprefix=*x*
Run long messages through *prog*	set PAGER=*prog*
Save outgoing mail in *file*	set record=*file*

When you create a .mailrc file, you can put comments in it; just start the line with the comment with a number character (#—also called *pound symbol*, *sharp*, and *hash*). Comment characters are useful if you want to "disable" a command for a day or two but don't want to have to reenter the entire command later.

Figure 7.3 shows a sample .mailrc file.

```
#These are my aliases:
alias bog bog@newt.waterloo.edu
alias project dara lee sam

# Don't want to see these header lines:
ignore Received: Message-Id Status:
# Sometimes I dial in from home,
# and don't want mail scrolling off the screen:
set crt=24
set PAGER=more

# I'd rather prefix quoted messages with "> ",
not tab:
set indentprefix="> "

# Save my outgoing mail in the directory mailbox
in my home
    directory:
set record=~/mailbox/SentMail.ml
```

Figure 7.3

A sample .mailrc file.

Sending and Receiving a Text File

It's easy to send and receive text files with mailx because all mail messages are text files. To send a file while you are in send mode, you can *read* the file into the message by using ~r:

    ~r yandr.summary

The file is made part of the message.

7

Or you can do it with redirection from the command line:

```
mailx chris < yandr.summary
```

This mail message has no subject; you can supply one from the command line with the -s option. There should be no space between the -s and the subject. If the subject text contains spaces, as most subjects do, remember to surround it with quotation marks:

```
mailx -s"This week on Y&R" chris < yandr_summary
```

If you want to be mailed the text output of a program, you can pipe it directly into mailx. The following command mails rudy the contents of the public uucp directory:

```
ls -lR ~uucp ¦ mailx -s"Contents of public UUCP" rudy
```

Sending and Receiving a Binary File

Most mail programs (mailx included) are designed only for printable (ASCII) characters. Unfortunately, many programs you would like to mail contain nonprintable control characters that may crash or confuse the file transfer programs that actually send the mail.

UNIX provides two utilities to turn binary files into printable text and back again: uuencode and uudecode. You should encode files outside mailx.

A typical uuencode command looks like the following:

```
uuencode pic.xwd pic.xwd > picture.uue
```

The first argument is optional—it's the name of the file you want to encode. If you leave it out, uuencode reads standard input, either from the keyboard or from another program. The second argument is the name of the file *after* it's decoded at the destination. The uuencode command writes to standard output, so the encoded information must be put into another file, in this case, picture.uue. (The .uue extension is just a convenience; it's not required.) Now you just have to mail the file picture.uue.

You can mail the encoded output directly, without saving it into a file:

```
uuencode pic.xwd pic.xwd ¦ mailx -s"here's that picture" thor!lee
```

Normally, the name after decoding is the same as the original file name, but it doesn't have to be. For instance, DOS file names can't be longer than 11 characters, so if you're sending a file with a long name to a DOS machine, you might have to shorten the file name:

```
uuencode quarterly_second.1990.wks q_2_1990.wks > q_2_1990.uue
```

A uuencoded file is about a third bigger than the original. The following is a verse of a nursery rhyme, uuencoded:

```
begin 644 jack_horner.txt
M3&ET=&QE($$(A8VL@2&]R;F5R#0I3870@:6X@=&AE(&-O<FYE<@T**16%T:6YG
M(&AI<R!#:')I<W1M87,@<&EE.T*2&4@<'5T('1H:6X@:&ES('1H=6UB#0I!
M;F0@<'5L;&5D(&]U="!A('!L=6T+;86T:&4@<V%I9"P@5VAA="!G;V]D(&)O>2!A
M;2!)#0I!;F0@<V%I9#H@5VAA=\!G;V]D(&)O>2!A;2!)!(2()(2)U
```

end

The words begin and end mark the limits of the encoded text. In the begin line, the 644 is the file permission, and jack_horner.txt is the name for the decoded file.

If the file is really big, you might want to split it into smaller pieces of about 60K each. It just happens that 900 lines of uuencoded text are about 60K. You can use the split command to break the uuencoded file into chunks of a certain size:

```
split -900 bigfile.uue
```

split names the files xaa, xab, and so on. You can do both the encoding and the splitting on a single command line:

```
uuencode bigfile bigfile | split -900 - bigfile.u
```

uuencode sends the file directly to split. The - tells the split command to use standard input for the file instead of a file name, and the bigfile.u tells split to use bigfile.u instead of x in the names of the output files. Now you can mail each of the pieces. Remember the subject line! It's nearly impossible to put uuencoded pieces together in the right order without clues.

To decode a file, use uudecode. If the uuencoded file is just one piece, type the following:

uudecode bigfile.uue

(If the entire uuencoded file is one mail message, you can decode it within mailx with the command | uudecode.)

To decode a split encoded file:

1. Save all the pieces in the right order into a single file.

2. Use a text editor to remove the header lines from the messages. There should be no empty lines between the begin and end lines. (A line with only spaces should be left in—for instance, in the preceding example, the "blank" line before end actually contains one space.)

3. Save the reassembled file and quit the editor.

4. Decode with uudecode.

The *from, biff, xbiff,* and *mesg* Commands

Users find it convenient if they can be beeped when they receive new mail. `biff` is the application that allows a sound to be issued when new e-mail has arrived. `xbiff` is a graphical version of the program. It displays a box with a flag on the side if there is no incoming mail; the flag moves to the straight-up position when new mail has arrived. So both sound and figure can change to alert a user that mail is coming. To use the `biff` command, insert the following line in your `.login` file:

```
biff y
```

If you're working in a graphical environment, you can also use the `xbiff` command. To run `xbif` in the background, type the following command:

```
% xbiff &
```

This causes a mailbox to appear on your screen with the flag originally on the side. With `biff` and `xbiff` running, you have both audio and visual indications to alert you that incoming mail has arrived.

Users also like to be reminded that there is existing mail in their boxes. The `from` command will do exactly that. Whenever you open a C shell, it will list for you the name of the sender and the time and date the mail was sent, as in the following:

```
From owner-spmail@ee.gatech.edu Wed Jul 19 16:28 EDT 1995
From jwang Fri Jul 28 15:30 EDT 1995
From jwang Fri Jul 28 15:38 EDT 1995
From oainn95@bobcat.ent.ohiou.edu Sun Jul 30 15:07 EDT 1995
From eton@america.net Thu Aug  3 20:41 EDT 1995
```

As you can see, there are five messages in the mailbox. Launching the mail command to read the messages usually follows.

The `from` command also permits the content of the mail you are about to receive in your mailbox to be displayed on-screen as you are using the shell. This might clutter the screen, but it enables you to know who is sending you mail and some of its content before it goes to your box.

If you dread receiving mail, you can turn off your machine to incoming mail by using the `mesg` command. Typing the command shows its current status:

```
% mesg
is y
```

The default is y (yes), which allows mail to be delivered to your machine. If you set it to n (no), messages will not be delivered to your machine:

```
% mesg n
```

Including the mesg command in your .login file is not a good idea. Entering mesg occasionally at the command prompt is something you may want to do when you don't want to be disturbed with incoming mail.

The *wall* and *write* Commands

Users on a network can communicate interactively by using the write command. Although e-mail is a good way to send messages, it's certainly not as daring as the write command. The general format of the write command is

```
% write username
"message"
```

write requires that both users are logged in on the same machine. Suppose that two users are normally logged in to two different machines; for example, user gmeghab is logged in on victor and is trying to use write to send a message to user jwang on random. gmeghab should first use the rlogin command to log in to random, and then use the write command to pass a message on from gmeghab to jwang. The message content certainly reflects an urgency or serious matter. Here is the code:

```
% rlogin random
% users
gmeghab jwang
% write jwang
do you mind if you mount my partition on your machine
Ctrl D
```

Ctrl-D is used to end the message.

wall is another serious command that is usually used by network managers to announce a message to everyone on the network such as when a shutdown is about to begin. wall is definitely not a nice, interactive way to communicate between users, but an urgent matter requires urgent communication. Usually, the sender of such a message has to be a superuser to overwrite any mesg n commands issued by users (see the preceding section).

```
% wall filename
```

filename contains the content of the message. If a short message is being sent, it can be typed at the prompt instead of using a file.

Users who usually receive such a message will read something that starts like

```
Broadcast message from root "reminding you to ........"
```

where the .... corresponds to the content of the file name.

7

Other UNIX Mail Programs

Programmers have always been tempted to write better programs than whatever is available, and this is especially true of mail programs. A few other mail programs are described here. These programs may be available at your site:

- mail is the original mail program, so it's available everywhere. It's very much like mailx, but it lacks a few features, such as aliases, a mail summary, and the capability to start an editor such as vi. To end a message, use either Ctrl-d or type a single dot on a line (<Enter>.<Enter>).

- elm (*electronic m*ail) is a free screen-oriented mailer that automatically invokes your editor. Elm is very simple for beginners to use and is highly configurable.

- MH (*Mail Handler*) is a powerful, complex mailer with many features.

- MUSH (*Mail User's Sh*ell) is another powerful, complex mailer. MUSH is a work environment that happens to do all the work of a mail program.

- NMail is part of Hewlett-Packard's AI workstation Software Environment.

- MIME is not a mailer; it's a draft Internet standard for multimedia transmissions. (MIME stands for Multipurpose Internet Mail Extensions.) If you're interested in multimedia mail (including annotations, sound, and graphics), you should consider looking for MIME compatibility.

- ZMail is a distant descendant of MUSH, significantly altered.

If you are looking for an easier mail program than mailx, elm is a good choice, and it's free from many archive sites. *Archive sites* are computers around the country that make a point of collecting free software and making it available to anyone who wants it.

Exercises

1. Assume that you opened your mail through the mail command and not mailx. What command do you use to save a given mail message number, "15," to a file named schememail?

2. Assume that you opened your mail through the mail command and not mailx, and you want to append an existing mail message, number "25," to an already existing file called schememail. What command do you use?

3. Assume that you are part of a worldwide mailing group and you want to

e-mail a file to the whole group. Describe, by specifying the commands, two different ways to e-mail a file called readthis to the group called friends. Give the name of the file that needs to be edited to accommodate the group.

4. You are to communicate to a set of users accessing a file server that the system is to be shut down. Assume that the tools are mail, write, and wall. How do you convey this message using each of the following tools:

   a. mail

   b. wall

   c. write

5. What variable name specifies the mail path on your system? How would you verify its value?

   If you were to change the path, what file do you check for the value of the pathname?

6. What command do you use to watch yourself mail a message to a user?

7. What is the name of the variable that you set in the .mailrc file to watch the mail being delivered to a user?

8. Explain the usefulness of the following variables that can be set or unset in your .mailrc file:

   verbose

   ask

   askcc

   autoprint

   Replyall

Shells and C Programming

Shells and Shell Scripts

Topics Covered

- What Is a Shell?

- Different Kinds of Shells

- Using the C Shell

- Shell Variables and Environment Variables

- C Shell Scripts

- Control Structure Concepts and Corresponding Shell Concepts

What Is a Shell?

A *shell* is a UNIX program that, when given a command, will interpret and execute it and then return either a prompt or an error message and a prompt. For example, a command such as

```
% dir
```

causes the shell to respond with this error message:

```
dir: command not found
%
```

In addition, a shell can execute UNIX tools, programs, and user applications. UNIX was designed so that the shell is separate from the main part of the operating system (OS). The shell acts as if it is protecting the inside of the operating system from the user. Today, there are a number of shells, including the Bourne shell, the Korn shell, and the C shell.

Aside from being a command interpreter, a shell is a programming language with its own specific syntax. A user can write a specific program, called a *script*, and have it interpreted by the shell. Knowing that a user has a choice between different shells, does it really matter which shell you use? No, it doesn't. Boredom with using one shell often leads to discovering different features in another shell; when boredom sets in with that shell, the user moves on to another one, and another one, and so on.

Different Kinds of Shells

Many UNIX users defend the shell they use as if it were a religious argument. While one user insists that any sane person would use only the C shell, another user would give up anything to keep the Korn shell. This section explores the features of each of the three main shells.

The Bourne Shell

The Bourne shell, also known by its sh program name, is the oldest and most used shell today. It is named after the AT&T developer Steven Bourne. The modern version of the old shell is still on every existing UNIX system. To start using the Bourne shell, assuming that your default shell is a C shell, type

```
% sh
```

and the prompt switches to a dollar sign ($).

The general format of a command in the Bourne shell is

```
$ command arg1 arg2 ... argn
```

where *arg1, arg2,..., argn* are the arguments of the command. Not all arguments are required. Some are optional. Some commands execute without arguments, some need a specific number of arguments, and some have a varying number of arguments.

An example of a versatile command is the command ls:

```
$ ls
```

It lists all names in your current directory, including subdirectories. Such a command leaves out all file names that start with a dot (.). Also, the order in which the names are listed is not alphabetical nor in any other particularly useful order.

The ls command with the option -s lists all names in alphabetical order, plus the size of the files in front of the file names:

```
$ ls -s
```

Here is a complete ls with all possible options:

```
$ ls -als
```

To discover all the built-in variables in the Bourne shell, type the command

```
$ set
```

and a listing of all built-in variables will follow. Some of the most important built-in variables and their values are given in the following list. (Values on your system will be different for several of the variables.)

Variable	Value
HOME	/home/a_s/gmeghab
LANG	C
PS1	$
PS2	>
PWD	/bin
TZ	US/Eastern
IFS	=

(continues)

Variable	Value
PATH	(all paths available to user)
SHELL	/bin/csh
TERM	wyse50
OLWMMENU	/home/a_s/gmeghab/.openwin
OPENWINHOME	/usr/openwin
USER	gmeghab

Any of these variables can be changed by using the command

```
$ variable=value
```

To change the TERM variable, for example, issue the command

```
$ TERM=vt100
```

and follow it with

```
$ set
```

The listing will now contain TERM=vt100.

To impress your next-door user, just switch the value of PS1 from $ to % by typing

```
$ PS1=%
```

and the prompt of the shell is now % instead of $.

To print the value of a variable, you can use the echo command. The line

```
$ echo $HOME
```

results in

```
/home/a_s/gmeghab
$
```

Note that, to display the value of a variable with the echo command, you must precede the variable name with a dollar sign ($). If you don't include the dollar sign, the echo command just displays the word. Note this example:

```
$ echo TERM
TERM
$ echo $TERM
vt100
```

As with other shells, a *script* in a Bourne shell corresponds to a file name that contains a sequence of commands that will execute in order. A Bourne shell script is similar to a batch file in the DOS operating system. You can use any text editor or a word processor to create the file or the script with its commands. An example is the following `morning` script file (you can read the contents of the file with the `cat` command):

```
$ cat morning
date
users
who

$ morning
morning:  command not found
$
```

When the `morning` script was executed, it returned an error message. The following `ls` command shows that `morning` does not have execute permissions:

```
$ ls -als morning
-rw-r--r--   1     gmeghab     599 July 17    16:25 morning
```

You can change the permission to execute for the file `morning` by using the `chmod` command:

```
$ chmod 744 morning
-rwx-r--r--   1     gmeghab     599    July 17    16:26morning
```

Now when the `morning` command is run, you get the following result:

```
$ morning
date:
Tue Jul 18 16:51 EDT 1995
users:
gmeghab
who:
gmeghab      console    Jul 17     19:38
gmeghab      pts/1      Jul 17     19:38
gmeghab      pts/2      Jul 18     14:56
gmeghab      pts/3      Jul 18     16:54
```

Not only can scripts execute, but also a sequence of names of scripts (or any commands) can be executed on one command line if you separate the names with semicolons (;). The following example illustrates three scripts executed on one line:

```
$ morning ; afternoon ; evening
```

These names must correspond to executable file names or scripts.

To list all the commands available through the Bourne shell, read the online `sh` manual page by typing

```
$ man sh
```

8

The Korn Shell

Another shell of the Bourne family is the Korn shell, developed in the early 1980s by David Korn. The Korn shell is an upward-compatible extension to the Bourne shell. It was developed with four important new features not offered in the Bourne shell: the history file, job control, aliasing, and a command editor.

If you have a Korn shell running, the program that was executed is named ksh.

The Korn shell defines a number of built-in variables, including those provided by the Bourne shell and some others. To switch from a Bourne shell to a Korn shell, type **ksh**. To see the variables defined, type **set**.

Here are some of the variables relevant only to the Korn shell:

Variable	Use
PS3	The prompt used by the select command
PS4	The prompt used with the trace option
SECONDS	The time in seconds since the shell was launched
TMOUT	The time in seconds to log you out automatically
PPID	Process id

To change any of the values of the built-in variables, use the command *variable=value*. There is one difference between this command and the *command=value* of the Bourne shell:

```
$ print $TERM
wyse50
$ TERM ='vt100'
$ print  $TERM
vt100
$
```

The difference is that you use an apostrophe both before and after the new value—in this case, vt100.

The Korn shell has the command type *command-name*, offering added flexibility over the Bourne shell:

```
$ type print
print is a shell built-in
$ type date
date is a tracked alias for /usr/bin/date
```

The command `time` is of interest in the Korn shell because it explicitly defines real time, user time, and system time, as in the following:

```
$ time
real    0m0.00s
user    0m0.00s
sys     0m0.00
```

You can view the `ksh` manual page for a list of all the commands available in the Korn shell. Type

```
$ man ksh
```

Script files can also run in the Korn shell similarly to such files in the Bourne shell.

The C Shell

The C shell was developed by Bill Joy at the University of California at Berkeley. This shell was designed as an alternative to the Bourne shell. The name of the program that runs the C shell is `csh`.

Like all other shells, the C shell is a command interpreter that offers a built-in programming language. In addition, the C shell offers many advantages over the Bourne shell, including the history feature, aliasing, and job control. The C shell is based on the C programming language, and, as such, is very popular among university programmers, professors, and lab researchers.

Using the C Shell

Given the popularity of the C shell and its de facto existence on every college and university UNIX-based system, a more detailed description of the C Shell is needed here. The following sections explain how to use the features of the C shell.

Alias

Remembering options that you usually use with a given command is hard for beginners. One of the best ways to keep from forgetting them is to use an *alias*. Imagine that you like to use the commands `ls -als` often. Instead of typing the whole thing, you can start the C shell by aliasing your most commonly used commands with easy-to-remember names. You can use the following format:

```
% alias newcommandname oldcommandname options

% alias ll ls -als
% ll
```

8

```
total 1000
.
.
.
```

You then supply a list of all the names in your working directory.

One of the benefits of an alias is shortening a long name for a command:

```
% alias m more
```

Then, when you type

```
% ll ¦m
```

you get a screen-by-screen listing of all file names plus their sizes, dates, and permissions.

Also, if the tool or application is in a different directory, aliasing the name of the command with the existing directory will save typing, as well as trying to remember the exact location of the application. Assume that the program matlab is in the /usr/bin directory, and that to execute matlab, you need to type **matlab**. Aliasing makes life easier:

```
% alias matlab /usr/bin/matlab
% matlab
```

This way, you can launch matlab from any directory.

The C shell is good at reminding you of the list of all existing aliases in a given session. Just type the command **alias**, and the following list appears:

```
%alias
artim      /usr/artim/bin/artim
banner     usr/5bin/banner
clw        rm -rf $home/.wastebasket; mkdir $home/.wastebasket
ll         ls -als
draw       wb -N "crawfish" -t 10 224.2.111.77/101010
gcc        /usr/local/gnu/bin/gcc
home       cd $home
larchie    rlogin -l archie archie.sura.net
laser      lpr -Plaserjet
later      logout
latex      ~/extra/tex/latex
leo        /usr/leotool/leotool
lf         ls -l
look       cat !* ¦ nroff -man ¦ more
lu         grep
marchie    echo "Archie Sever Search"; mail -s "" archie@nic.sura.net
matlab     /usr/matlab/bin/matlab
netscape   /usr/Xbin/netscape
phone      cd phone
pico       /usr/local/pico
play       cd /usr/local/Xbin
```

```
prt        lpr -Psparc4
sourceart  source /usr/artim/artim-world
type       more
undo       /home/ac/pworth/bin/uuconvert
up         cd .
whois      whois -h rs.internic.net
```

If the aliases created during a session are to be used later, the file .cshrc is the place to save all aliases. Otherwise, any alias you create will disappear when the current session is finished.

After you save the aliases in the file .cshrc, using a word processor such as vi, use the source command with the .cshrc file to make the new aliases current and usable immediately:

```
% source .cshrc
```

If, after you have used a given alias, you do not find it interesting or a time-saver, unalias is the way to get rid of the newly created names:

```
% unalias m
% m
command not found
```

Information on Processes

The who command is useful for reporting who is on the system, but sometimes you may want to know what process someone else is running as well. To do this, you can use the whodo command. The most useful example is to find a process id so that you can use the kill command to stop an unwanted process from continuing to run:

```
whodo
Fri Aug 25 16:38:50 EDT 1995
victor
console     gmeghab    19:16
console      9686      0:00 csh
console     11775      0:00 openwin
console     11779      0:00 xinit
console     11781      0:00 sh

pts/2       gmeghab    19:16
console     11797      0:12 cmdtool
pts/2       11815      0:00 csh
pts/2       13085      0:00 whodo
pts/3       gmeghab    19:16
console     11798      0:00 cmdtool
pts/3       11814      0:00 csh
pts/4       jwang      16:34
pts/4       13036      0:00 csh
```

8

At first glance, the output of this command may seem confusing. The first line is simply the current date and time. The second line is the name of the machine that ran whodo. The lines that follow list each user and what that user is running.

Notice that the user, gmeghab, logged in from different device names (pts/2 and pts/3) and has accumulated 19 minutes and 16 seconds of CPU time during this session. He is currently running a whodo command from a C shell (csh). This session has a process id of 11815, and this shell session has accumulated 0:00 seconds of CPU time.

Note also that the user jwang is logged on from device name pt/4. The user jwang is running a csh and is identified with a process id of 13036. jwang has accumulated only 16:34 (minutes and seconds) on the machine.

CPU time is the amount of time that a process has spent executing in the CPU. CPU time is different from real time. *Real time* is the time that has actually passed. (Real time is sometimes called *wall clock time* because it represents the time that has gone by on the clock on the wall.) A process that takes five minutes to run timed by your watch may take only five CPU seconds to run. The CPU time for a process varies based on the amount of work the process needs to accomplished. If it needs to read 100 records one day and 300 the next, then the CPU time increases. The real time varies based on what everyone else on the system is doing. To do the same amount of work when 30 other users are on may take five minutes as opposed to just one second if you are on by yourself. Execution time is very relative to system load.

The whodo command is actually a combination of the who and ps commands. It runs who and ps and then merges the results.

Usually, in day-to-day operations, you have to know what people are doing in case there is some kind of system problem. For example, someone's terminal is locked or, for some reason, everything is running slowly. These are administrative issues that the system administrator must correct to keep the system running efficiently for everyone. who and whodo are used when you just want to know who is on the system out of curiosity, but neither command addresses the actual system problem that may be occurring. The ps command handles this function. ps stands for *process status* and can report on more than just user processes. It is a better tool for diagnosing problems.

Here's what happens when you type the ps command:

```
%ps
  PID    TT        S  TIME COMMAND
 11775 console     S  0:00 /bin/sh /usr/openwin/bin/openwin
 11779 console     S  0:00 /usr/openwin/bin/xinit -- /usr/openwin/bin/X
    :0 -auth /
```

```
11781 console  S  0:00 sh /home/a_s/gmeghab/.xinitrc
11792 console  S  0:00 olwm -3
11817 console  S  0:00 olwmslave
11815 pts/2    S  0:00 /bin/csh
13032 pts/2    O  0:00 ps
11814 pts/3    S  0:00 /bin/csh
```

When you specify the ps command without any options, you get just the process currently running, including any background processes also currently running. Each column of output has one of the following headings:

Heading	Meaning
PID	The process id
TT	The controlling terminal for the process
S	State of the process
TIME	The accumulated CPU time of the process
COMMAND	The name of the command used to spawn this process

Some common options used with this command are listed in Table 8.1.

Table 8.1 Options Used with the *ps* Command	
Option	**Meaning**
-a	Shows frequently requested processes (not just yours)
-u process-id	Gives a listing showing all information relating to the processes running with process id, including user id, process id, start time, terminal, CPU time, and name of command
-x terminal	Enables you to specify a terminal to report on
-e	Gives a listing showing all information relating to the processes, including PID (process id), TTY (terminal), time, and name of command
-f	Gives a limited listing showing all information relating to the processes, including the command ps -f itself, UID, PID, PPID, C, Stime, TTY, Time, COMD (command name)

8

Note that the user jwang is absent from the ps command result. The reason is that a simple ps command or a ps -u will always refer simply to gmeghab and ignore all other users on the server victor. To see everything on jwang, use the following command, which will specify more of what jwang is doing:

```
% ps -u 13036

USER       PID %CPU %MEM   SZ  RSS TT       S    START  TIME COMMAND
jwang    13036  0.0  2.0 1580 1224 pts/4    S 16:34:21  0:00 -csh
```

The process id 13036 was identified from the whodo command. Note the use of the ps command with the -u option and a process id number.

Suppose that the user gmeghab becomes a superuser. (He does this by typing the su command, which changes the prompt to #, as in the following example.) Suppose also that this user wants to find out why some software cannot be restarted on the machine under his user name. As part of the diagnosis of his problem, gmeghab wants to find out what he is running. To do this, he combines the -f and -u options with the ps command:

```
# ps -fu gmeghab

UID       PID    PPID   C     STIME        TTY  TIME      COMD
gmeghab  3503    2983   22    19:23:14     pts/1 0:00      ls -als
gmeghab  3874     327   17    15:08:32     pts/2 0:00      rlogin doc
```

The user gmeghab could have done the same thing without becoming a superuser. By just combining -aux with the ps command, he would have received the following information:

Header	Meaning
UID	The user name running this process.
PPID	The parent process for this process. This is the process that spawned the current process.
C	The processor used for scheduling.
STIME	The time of day the process started executing.

Also, the COMMAND column is listed as COMD. This column now shows the arguments given to the command when it was executed. (The amount of information provided here is limited to about 30 characters. If the actual command line is longer than that, it is truncated.)

The PPID column is useful when tracking down which process has asked what to execute. If you have to kill a runaway process, this field is invaluable because it gives you the number to plug into the `kill` command to terminate the process.

> **NOTE** *When you work with UNIX, there are times when processes have to be killed. Killing a process sends a signal to the process. The process then responds to the signal and stops executing. For example, suppose that the problem was that the mail program, in the preceding example, was hung for some unknown reason. You could kill it with these commands (the process id number you would use would be different):*
>
> ```
> # kill 2983
> # kill -9 3503
> ```

To track the chain of processes, start by looking at the PPID of each process. Next, find that number in the PID column and note its PPID. Keep going up the chain until there are no more related PIDs. In the earlier example, you can see that the parent process (PPID) of the `mail -f mbox` command is the shell `sh`.

Continuing with the task of figuring out why `gmeghab`'s terminal is hung, you could repeat the command to see whether the TIME field has increased. This field increases each time the process receives a slice of CPU time. If the field has increased, you may want to repeat the command to see whether the process is rapidly gaining time. If it is, it could be that the process has gotten into some sort of continuous loop, in which case you would want to kill it. You can determine this because you know that mail does not normally behave this way.

`ps` is a useful tool for diagnosing system problems. The hung terminal is only one example. You would have to determine the specific steps for resolving each system problem encountered.

Process States

The `ps` command reports the current *state* of the process table. It is a "picture" of the process table at a specific point and time. Therefore, the state of processes running can be completely different on each execution of the command.

In previous examples, the `ps` command has been used without a discussion of the role of the process table. The process table is a queue of jobs to be scheduled.

A *queue* is a computer term for a "first-in-first-out" method of handling things. You can think of a queue as being similar to the hamburger bin at your local fast-food restaurant. Hamburgers are placed at the back of the bin and taken off at the front. The hamburgers being served to customers are the ones that have been in the bin the longest. This strategy ensures that a hamburger will not sit in the bin for several hours and risk having a customer get a significantly old hamburger. A queue is a structure that enables the item waiting the longest to be serviced.

Jobs or processes in the process table can be in several states, which are described in Table 8.2.

Table 8.2	Process States
State	**Meaning**
Sleeping (S)	This state is like sleeping at night. You set the alarm clock to wake you up at a particular time and, until that alarm goes off, you do not do anything but sleep!
Running (O)	While in this state, the process is actually doing something. It is similar to your working on a project without having to wait for something.
Runnable (R)	The process is on the run queue.
Blocked (B)	While in this state, the process cannot do anything. It is waiting for something else to complete. Perhaps it is waiting for a user to press a key. This state is similar to you being at work and having to talk to someone about something, but the person is in a meeting. Meanwhile, you are in a blocked state waiting for the meeting to finish.
Idle (I)	The process is being created.
Traced (T)	The process is being stopped by a signal because a parent is tracing it.
SXBRK (X)	The process is waiting for more primary memory.
Zombie (Z)	A process in this state has been terminated and is no longer working.

To check the process states, query the system's process table using the `ps -fl` option:

```
ps -fl
F S  UID    PID   PPID  C  PRI NI  ADDR SZ  WCHAN   STIME     TTY  TIME
   CMD
```

```
1 S gmeghab  12642 12640 0  30  20  601  20  322a8  22:07:35  aa   0:00
  sh
1 R gmeghab  12687 12642 11 55  20  f4e  36          22:18:40  aa   0:00
  ps -fl
```

In the preceding command, the s column shows the process's state. As you can see, the sh process is in a sleeping state. It is sleeping while it waits for the ps -fl command to finish. The ps -fl command is in the run state.

When a process is in the run state, it is vying for processor time. The processes that are not in the run state are not vying for the processor. When the reason they are waiting (blocked or sleeping) is satisfied, they will go to the run state.

The process table was described in this section as a queue and compared to a hamburger bin at a fast-food restaurant. The hamburger bin is a simple queue: You always want the hamburger waiting the longest to be served next. In a process queue, you do not necessarily want it to work that way. Certain processes may have a higher priority than others. The UNIX process queue is referred to as a priority queue.

Process Priorities

Notice the PRI column heading in the example in the preceding section. Processes in UNIX are given a priority number. The lower the number, the higher the priority. Processes are "aged" in the queue by priority. A high-priority process gets the processor more often than a low-priority process. To help ensure that the lower processes are serviced at some time, their priorities are increased as they sit in the queue. UNIX knows whether a process is primarily high priority or low priority by the nice value of the processes. (For lengthy processes, you are not in a hurry to receive, you can use the nice command to lower their priority; by not slowing the system down for other users, you are being "nice.") The nice value is reported in the NI column. In the example, both processes have a nice value of 20, meaning that they have an equal priority from which to work.

Job Control

After you enter the C shell by using the csh command, any command you issue would have a corresponding process number or job number. Assume that you want to use the speller. A check through the online manual using the spell command lists the following:

```
% man s; spell
spell(1)         User Commands
spell(1)         NAME
spell            find spelling errors
SYNOPSIS         spell [ -bvx ] [ +local_file ][ filename]
DESCRIPTION
```

```
spell collects words from the named filenames and looks them up in a
spelling list.  Words that neither occur among nor are derivable (by
applying certain inflections, prefixes,and/or suffixes) from words in
the spelling list are printed on the standard output.  If no filenames
are named, words are collected from the standard input.  Copies of all
output are accumulated in the spellhist file.
OPTIONS
-b                      British spelling is checked. Besides  preferring "cen-
                        tre," "colour," "programme," "speciality," "travelled,"
                        and so forth, this option insists upon -ise in words
                        like "standardise."
-v                      All words not literally in the spelling list  are
                        printed,and plausible derivations from the words in the
                        spelling list are indicated.
-x                      Every plausible stem is displayed, one per  line,with =
                        preceding each word.
+local_file             local_file is the name of a user-provided file that
                        contains a sorted list of words; one per line.  With this
                        option, the user can specify a set of words that are
                        correct spellings (in addition to spell's own spelling
                        list)for each job. Words found in local_file are removed
                        from spell's output.  Use sort(1) to order local_file in
                        ASCII collating sequence. If this ordering is not
                        followed, some entries in local_file may be ignored.
FILES
D_SPELL=/usr/lib/spell/hlist[ab]hashed spelling lists,
American & British
        S_SPELL=/usr/lib/spell/hstop               hashed stop list
        H_SPELL=/var/adm/spellhist                 history file
        /usr/share/lib/dict/words                  master dictionary
SEE ALSO
        sort(1)
spell(1)
User Commands
spell(1)
NOTES
Because copies of all output are accumulated in the spellhist file,
spellhist may grow quite large and require purging. The line
```

This code shows that, to execute a speller, four files will be involved in the operations:

- The hlist, the spelling list file

- The hstop, or the hash stopping list

- The spellhist, or the history file

- The words, or the master dictionary

These files, being part of the spell operation, will have to exist also as processes with id numbers. Here is a simulation of the spell command used in the background of the C shell (the & at the end of the line signals that the job is to be run in the background):

```
victor% spell abstract.tex > idiot &
[1] 1852
victor% sort: warning: missing NEWLINE added at EOF
ps
   PID TT       S  TIME COMMAND
  1854          Z  0:00
   275 console  S  0:00 /bin/sh /usr/openwin/bin/openwin
   279 console  S  0:00 /usr/openwin/bin/xinit -- /usr/openwin/bin/X :0
    -auth /
   281 console  S  0:00 sh /home/a_s/gmeghab/.xinitrc
   289 console  S  0:01 olwm -3
   313 console  S  0:00 olwmslave
   984 pts/1    S  0:00 /bin/csh
  1852 pts/1    S  0:00 /usr/bin/sh /usr/bin/spell abstract.tex
  1853 pts/1    S  0:00 tee -a /var/adm/spellhist
  1855 pts/1    S  0:00 /usr/bin/sh /usr/bin/spell abstract.tex
  1856 pts/1    S  0:00 deroff -w
  1857 pts/1    S  0:00 sort -u +0
  1858 pts/1    S  0:00 sed -e /^[.'].*[.'][ ]*nx[ ]*\/usr\/lib/d -e
    ^[.'].*[.
  1859 pts/1    S  0:00 /usr/lib/spell/spellprog /usr/lib/spell/hstop 1
  1860 pts/1    S  0:00 /usr/lib/spell/spellprog /usr/lib/spell/hlista
    dev/nul
  1861 pts/1    S  0:00 comm -23 - /dev/null
  1862 pts/1    O  0:00 ps
   327 pts/2    S  0:00 /bin/csh
victor% sort: warning: missing NEWLINE added at EOF
Broken Pipe

jobs
[1]  + Running              spell abstract.tex > idiot
victor% ps
   PID TT       S  TIME COMMAND
   275 console  S  0:00 /bin/sh /usr/openwin/bin/openwin
   279 console  S  0:00 /usr/openwin/bin/xinit -- /usr/openwin/bin/X :0
    -auth /
   281 console  S  0:00 sh /home/a_s/gmeghab/.xinitrc
   289 console  S  0:01 olwm -3
   313 console  S  0:00 olwmslave
   984 pts/1    S  0:00 /bin/csh
  1865 pts/1    O  0:00 ps
   327 pts/2    S  0:00 /bin/csh
[1]  + Done                 spell abstract.tex > idiot
victor%
```

Note that [1] 1852 is the job number and the id process number for the speller. Note also that issuing the ps command on the second line revealed all the processes that took place related to the four files mentioned previously, with numbers that are higher than the process id number 1852.

On the third line, the command jobs revealed that one single job was issued and was still running at the time the jobs command was issued with the process id number [1]. All other processes that took place were not jobs but processes forked (begun) by the initial job of the speller.

On the fourth line of the command, another ps was issued. This time, the listing displays, among other things, the following:

```
[1]+ done          spell abstract.tex > idiot &
```

The job [1] was done, and all other related processes have ended and thus are gone from the list.

The same spelling job could have been executed in the foreground. To do so, you issue the same command but without the &. Users can toggle jobs between foreground and background by using the commands bg and fg. To move the spelling job numbered [1] into the foreground, you can use

```
% fg %1
```

Remember to specify the % in front of the job number. In case you do not remember the job number, one of the following equivalent commands can be used:

```
% fg %sp
```

```
% fg %spell
```

Here sp and spell are close strings that remind the C shells about the spell command issued earlier. Because, in this example, one job was running in the background, a simple fg would have been enough to bring the job to the foreground. You can stop a job from running by pressing Ctrl-z. Issuing the bg command would restart the job in the background. When a job is running in the background, you can use the stop command to stop it. Then use fg or bg to restart it.

As the preceding simulation shows, the C shell notifies a user when a job changes state. When the job changed from running to done, a signal was issued to inform the user that the job was done. The notify command plays the same role of notifying a user of whether a job is running, a job is done, or no job is running at this time. If after job [1] is over, you issued the notify command, you see the following:

```
% notify
notify: no current job
%
```

There are several ways to check a job. If you know the job number, for example, number 1, you can type **notify %1**. In the case of the spell command, you can also type **notify %s**.

The C shell warns a user who is trying to exit a shell while a job is still running. If you issued the jobs command after the warning, the user would be allowed to exit, and the job would be terminated.

Variables

As with the other shells, the C shell has its own built-in variables, as well as variables that you can declare and assign values. You use three commands to declare variables in the C shell: set, @, and setenv. Set and @ declare local variables, whereas setenv allows the declaration of variables that can be exported or inherited to all its child processes.

Variable Declaration through *set*

To declare or assign a local variable using set, use

```
% set username
% echo $username
```

so that username is an empty string.

Note the following example:

```
% set username = gmeghab
% echo $username
gmeghab
% set

argv      ()
cdpath    (/home/a_s/gmeghab /home/a_s /home)
cwd       /home/a_s/gmeghab
history   40
home      /home/a_s/gmeghab
ignoreeof
lpath     (/usr/openwin/bin/xview /usr/openwin/bin /usr/local/bin)
mychoice openwin
noclobber
path      (/home/a_s/gmeghab/bin /usr/lang /usr/openwin/bin/xview /usr/
openwin/bin /usr/local/bin /usr/local /usr/local/grits /usr/ucb /usr/bin
/usr/etc /extra/mf /extra/tex /usr/sbin /home/a_s/gmeghab .)
prompt    victor%
savehist 40
shell     /bin/csh
status    0
term      wyse50
user      gmeghab
username gmeghab
```

Thus, username is added to the already existing list of variables maintained in set (see the last line of set). To delete username from the list, use

```
% unset username
% set
```

The command

```
% set colors red
```

sets the variables colors and red as empty, and they still show up when you list the variables with the set command. To delete them from the set list, you have to use the unset command:

```
% unset colors
% unset red
```

A special character (known as a wild card) in the C shell stands for all file names. The special character is *. If you were to list all the names in a given directory without any information, the following command would work:

```
% echo *
```

What would be displayed on-screen is a listing of all names existing in your directory.

You can also read the values of the variables from the keyboard. Although the C shell has no read statement like the one available in the Bourne and Korn shells, there is a way to use the set command to read a value from the keyboard:

```
% set badname = $<
```

The C shell then waits for you to type a value for the variable badname.

Note that variables in a C shell can have a list of strings as values. Such a variable behaves as an array. Just as individual values of an array can be accessed through an index, so can shell variables. The size of an array is usually known, and you can determine the number of individual values of a C shell's variable with $#variable:

```
% echo $#oldname
3
%
```

The following example illustrates a variable named oldfilename that was assigned *. Remember that * corresponds to all names in the actual directory.

```
% ls -als
total 14
1 drwx------   5 gmeghab      512 Aug 27 11:43 .
10 drwxr-xr-x 53 gmeghab     9728 Aug 26 14:39 ..
1 drwxr-xr-x   2 gmeghab      512 Nov 29  1994 NN
1 drwxr-xr-x   2 gmeghab      512 Nov  7  1994 art
1 drwxr-xr-x   2 gmeghab      512 Oct 13  1994 lisp

% set $oldfilename = *
% echo $oldfilename
(NN art lisp)
% echo $oldfilename[1]
NN
%echo $oldfilename[2]
art
```

```
% echo $olfilename[3]
lisp
%echo $oldfilename[4]
subscript out of range
%echo $#oldfilenname
3
%
```

Variable Declaration through @

@ allows the declarations of local variables that will be held in set or in the @ list
because they both hold equivalent lists. However, @ requires assigning only numeric values to the declared variables in the declaration line, in contrast to set,
which does both numeric values and strings. Note this example:

```
% @ name
@ : syntax error
% @ name = fred
@ : expression syntax
% @ name = 5
% echo $name
   5
% @ name = (5 + 7 *3)
% echo $name
        26
```

In the following list, note that username shows up just as it showed up in the
previous set list:

```
% @

argv      ()
cdpath    (/home/a_s/gmeghab /home/a_s /home)
cwd       /home/a_s/gmeghab
history   40
home      /home/a_s/gmeghab
ignoreeof
lpath     (/usr/openwin/bin/xview /usr/openwin/bin /usr/local/bin)
mychoice  openwin
name      26
noclobber
path      (/home/a_s/gmeghab/bin /usr/lang /usr/openwin/bin/xview /usr/
openwin/bin /usr/local/bin /usr/local /usr/local/grits /usr/ucb /usr/bin
/usr/etc /extra/mf /extra/tex /usr/sbin /home/a_s/gmeghab .)
prompt    victor%
savehist  40
shell     /bin/csh
status    0
term      wyse50
user      gmeghab
```

@ allows the evaluation of numeric expressions; set does not. The general format
of expressions used in @ follows the C programming language syntax and is beyond the scope of this book. For more information, refer to a C programming
book.

Shell Variables and Environment Variables

Preexisting C shell variables are kept distinct by the C shell and are of two kinds: environment variables and shell variables. *Environment variables* are usually listed in uppercase letters, whereas *shell variables* are kept in lowercase letters. Environment variables are usually exported to processes invoked by a parent process, whereas shell variables are not. C shell variables are set in the two files .login and .cshrc. A visit to the .cshrc and .login files will explain why this list of built-in variables appears after the user types the command set or the command setenv:

```
% cat .cshrc

setenv MFBASES ".:/extra/mf/bases"
setenv MFPOOL "/extra/mf"
setenv MFINPUTS ".:/extra/mf/inputs"
setenv TEXFONTS ".:/extra/tex/fonts"
setenv TEXINPUTS ".:/extra/tex/inputs"
setenv TEXPOOL "/extra/tex"
setenv TEXFORMATS ".:/extra/tex/formats"
setenv OLWMMENU $home/.openwin-menu
setenv FONTPATH /home/cs/dboyd/PUBLIC/bin/fonts:/usr/openwin/lib/fonts
setenv MANPATH /home/cs/dboyd/PUBLIC/bin/man:/usr/lang/man:/usr/man:/
    usr/openwin/man
setenv HELPPATH /usr/lang/SC1.0/SourceBrowser.info
setenv GKSDIR /usr/lib/gks
#setenv XGLHOME /usr
setenv NNTPSERVER catfish
setenv VISUAL /usr/local/pico
set mychoice=openwin
set lpath = ( /usr/local/bin)
if ( ${?mychoice} != 0 ) then
  if ( ${mychoice} == "openwin" ) then
    set lpath = ( /usr/openwin/bin/xview /usr/openwin/bin $lpath )
  endif
endif
set path = (~/bin /usr/lang $lpath /usr/local /usr/local/grits /usr/ucb
\
\
\
\
/usr/bin /usr/etc /extra/mf /extra/tex   /usr/sbin ~ .)
set cdpath = (~  /home/a_s  /home )
set noclobber
if ($?USER == 0 ¦¦ $?prompt == 0) exit
set history=40
set ignoreeof
set savehist=40
#set prompt="'hostname':$cwd% "
#set prompt="Yo-Mon% "
alias banner     '/usr/5bin/banner'
alias clw        'rm -rf $home/.wastebasket; mkdir $home/.wastebasket'
alias dir        'ls -la'
alias draw       'wb -N "crawfish" -t 10 224.2.111.77/101010'
```

```
alias home         'cd $home'
alias larchie      'rlogin -l archie archie.sura.net'
alias later        logout
alias look         'cat \!* ¦ nroff -man ¦ more'
alias lf           'ls -l'
alias laser        'lpr -Plaserjet'
alias lu           grep
alias leo          '/usr/leotool/leotool'
alias marchie      'echo "Archie Sever Search"; mail -s ""
    archie@nic.sura.net'
alias phone        'cd phone'
alias play         'cd /usr/local/Xbin'
alias pico         '/usr/local/pico'
alias prt          'lpr -Psparc4'
alias type         more
alias undo         '/home/ac/pworth/bin/uuconvert'
alias up           'cd ..'x
alias whois        'whois -h rs.internic.net'
alias matlab       '/usr/matlab/bin/matlab'
alias gcc          '/usr/local/gnu/bin/gcc'
alias artim        '/usr/artim/bin/artim'
alias sourceart    'source /usr/artim/artim-world'
alias latex        '~/extra/tex/latex'
biff y
mesg y
alias netscape     '/usr/Xbin/netscape'


% cat .login

# @(#)Login 1.14 90/11/01 SMI

####################################################################
#          .login file                                            #
#          Read in after the .cshrc file when you log in.         #
#          Not read in for subsequent shells.  For setting up     #
#          terminal and global environment characteristics.       #
####################################################################
#          terminal characteristics for remote terminals:

#          Leave lines for all but your remote terminal commented
#          out (or add a new line if your terminal does not appear).

if ($TERM != "sun") then
#eval 'tset -sQ -m dialup:?925 -m switch:?925 -m dumb:?925 $TERM'
#eval 'tset -sQ -m dialup:?h19 -m switch:?h19 -m dumb:?h19 $TERM'
#eval 'tset -sQ -m dialup:?mac -m switch:?mac -m dumb:?mac $TERM'
#eval 'tset -sQ -m dialup:?vt100 -m switch:?vt100 -m dumb:?vt100 $TERM'
#eval 'tset -sQ -m dialup:?wyse-nk -m switch:?wyse-nk -m dumb:?wyse-nk
    $TERM'
#eval 'tset -sQ -m dialup:?wyse-vp -m switch:?wyse-vp -m dumb:?wyse-vp
    $TERM'
endif
#          general terminal characteristics
#stty -crterase
#stty -tabs
```

8

```
#stty crt
#stty erase '^h'
#stty werase '^?'
#stty kill '^['
#stty new
#           environment variables

#setenv EXINIT 'set sh=/bin/csh sw=4 ai report=2'
#setenv MORE '-c'
#setenv PRINTER lw


#           commands to perform at login

#w          # see who is logged in
#
# If possible, start the windows system.  Give user a chance to bail out
#
if ( 'tty' != "/dev/console" || $TERM != "sun" ) then
exit      # leave user at regular C shell prompt
endif
if ( ${?OPENWINHOME} == 0 ) then
  setenv OPENWINHOME /usr/openwin
endif
set mychoice=openwin
if ( ! -e $OPENWINHOME/bin/openwin ) then
    set mychoice=sunview
endif
echo ""
#click -n     # click -n turns off key click
echo ""
switch( $mychoice )
case    openwin:
    unset mychoice
    echo -n "Starting OpenWindows (type Control-C to interrupt)"
    sleep 5
    $OPENWINHOME/bin/openwin
    clear_colormap    # get rid of annoying colourmap bug
    clear     # get rid of annoying cursor rectangle
    echo -n "Automatically logging out (type Control-C to interrupt)"
    sleep 5
    logout        # logout after leaving windows system
    breaksw
    #
case    sunview:
unset mychoice
    echo -n "Starting SunView (type Control-C to interrupt)"
sleep 5
    # default sunview background looks best with pastels
sunview
clear         # get rid of annoying cursor rectangle
    echo -n "Automatically logging out (type Control-C to interrupt)"
    sleep 5
    logout            # logout after leaving windows system
    breaksw
    #
endsw
```

The command setenv lists all the environment variables. These variables are usually listed in uppercase letters. Refer to the .cshrc file, and you will discover that the first 15 lines of that file set the environment for 15 variables in uppercase. However, the variable OPENWINHOME is set in the .login file. Follow the setenv command's listing to find even more variables that were not set using the setenv command. These other variables are shell variables, which include the following: user, cwd, home, path, prompt, and status. (For a more complete list, see the following output of setenv.) These variables are set by the shell and not by setenv. The latter means that the shell copies the environment variable USER into the shell variable user, CWD into cwd, HOME into home, and so on. Not all shell variables become part of the environment variables; they include only the most common ones.

Here is output from setenv:

```
% setenv

DISPLAY=:0.0
FONTPATH=/home/a_s/dboyd/PUBLIC/bin/fonts:/usr/openwin/lib/fonts
GKSDIR=/usr/lib/gks
HELPPATH=/usr/lang/SC1.0/SourceBrowser.info
HOME=/home/a_s/gmeghab
HZ=100
LANG=C
LOGNAME=gmeghab
MAIL=/var/mail/gmeghab
MANPATH=/home/a_s/dboyd/PUBLIC/bin/man:/usr/lang/man:/usr/man:/usr/
    openwin/man
MFBASES=.:/extra/mf/bases
MFINPUTS=.:/extra/mf/inputs
MFPOOL=/extra/mf
NNTPSERVER=catfish
OLWMMENU=/home/a_s/gmeghab/.openwin-menu
OPENWINHOME=/usr/openwin
PATH=/home/a_s/gmeghab/bin:/usr/lang:/usr/openwin/bin/xview:/usr/
openwin/bin:/usr/local/bin:/usr/local:/usr/local/grits:/usr/ucb:/usr/
bin:/usr/etc:/extra/mf:/extra/tex:/usr/sbin:/home/a_s/gmeghab:.
PWD=/home/a_s/gmeghab
SHELL=/bin/csh
TERM=wyse50
TEXFONTS=.:/extra/tex/fonts
TEXFORMATS=.:/extra/tex/formats
TEXINPUTS=.:/extra/tex/inputs
TEXPOOL=/extra/tex
TZ=US/Eastern
USER=gmeghab
VISUAL=/usr/local/pico
XFILESEARCHPATH=/usr/openwin/lib/locale/%L/%T/%N%S:/usr/openwin/lib/%T
    %N%S
WINDOW_TERMIOS=
```

The most commonly used shell variables are the following:

Variable	Description
$argv	This variable is inherited from the C programming language environment. argv[0] contains the calling program, and argv[1] contains the first command-line argument.
$cdpath	This variable is set in the .cshrc file and takes several path names. In the .cshrc file listed previously, the cdpath is ~ \home\a_s\ \home. This variable influences the way the command cd filename works.
$cwd	The C shell sets this variable to the actual working directory.
$history	This variable controls the size of the history list. In the example showing the .chsrc file, $history is set to a value of 40.
$home	This variable corresponds to the value of the home directory of the user, which is usually referred to as ~.
$ignoreoff	This variable protects logging out accidentally from the shell without specifying the actual set variable. Otherwise, the default is the famous Ctrl-d key sequence. If you try to use the Ctrl-d command when $ignoreoff is set, the response is Use exit to leave the csh. This forces the user to issue an exit command in order to quit the shell.
$mail	This variable is usually a file name where the C shell checks for mail.
$noclobber	The noclobber variable prevents you from accidentally overwriting a file when you are redirecting your output.
$path	This variable is set in the .cshrc file. It contains most directories you might be using, so when you type a command, you do not have to specify the whole path name.
$prompt	This variable also is set in the .cshrc file. Its value varies according to what the user would like to see as a prompt. A variety of popular prompts is shown in Exercises 1 and 2.
$savehist	This variable specifies the number of lines of commands that will be used when you log out. These commands are saved in the .history file.

Variable	Description
$status	This variable contains the value of the exit status of the last command. It is usually set to 0 if the last command was successful; otherwise, it is -1.
$shell	This variable contains the path name for how the shell will execute. In the case of the C shell, it executes as follows: /bin/csh

Not all shell variables are copied or made into existing environment variables. Note this example:

```
% echo $cwd
/home/a_s/gmeghab

% echo $CWD
CWD: undefined variable.
```

Some variables are maintained in the shell without being set anywhere in the .login, .cshrc, .history, and .logout files. These variables are related to process id information. An example is the $$ variable, which reflects the process id number of the actual C shell running. You could verify it by just issuing the command ps -aux, and the process id number will list an id number with a command that reads csh. In the lines

```
% echo $$
13150
```

the number 13150 is the process id of the actual C shell session.

C Shell Scripts

Like the Bourne shell, the C shell can execute a batch file of C shell commands. Using a word processor, you can create a file name that contains C shell commands, and then execute the file name by typing its name at the command line. The file, however, must have the correct permissions, or an error message is displayed:

```
% morning
bad command or filename
```

After checking the permissions with the ls -l command, you see that morning does not have execute permissions. Use the chmod command to make the file executable:

```
% chmod 755 morning
```

8

Executing `morning` will yield

```
% morning
Sat Jul 22 15:01 :40 EDT 1995
gmeghab     console Jul 22 12:15
gmeghab     pts/1 Jul 22 14:56
gmeghab     pts/2 Jul 22 12:15
```

where `morning` contains the following commands:

```
% cat morning
#! bin/csh
date
who
```

The first line is a comment line. It tells the shells that the C shell is being executed. The second line displays the date; the third line asks who is on the system. The reason for having a shell script called `morning` is that these commands are typically run first thing in the morning when you log on to your system.

> **NOTE** *In this section, in reference to the C shell, the words* script *and program* are used interchangeably.

Users would like to write shells not only for executing a sequence of commands, but also when some command is needed that the system might not have. Assume that you have created a new directory and you want to copy all files from an old directory to the new directory, renaming all the old file names with new file names. The C shell provides a rename (`mv`) command that renames one file at a time. If you had a hundred files, you would literally have to issue a hundred `mv` commands. So a shell script is needed. The concept of a *loop* from programming languages is useful here. (Remember that a shell is a programming language.) How do C shell programming concepts, such as loops, fare when compared with programming language concepts, and can they be used to write scripts or programs? The next section answers these questions.

Control Structure Concepts and Corresponding Shell Concepts

A *control structure* is a concept that allows statements in a given language to combine in a variety of ways. There are three different control structures: sequential processing, selective processing, and iterative processing.

Sequential processing is the sequential composition of commands. If two statements in a shell are to be executed sequentially, a semicolon is needed to separate them. The following example declares two local variables in a shell and executes them on one line using a semicolon in between:

```
set oldfilename; set newfilename
```

If there wasn't a semicolon, these two statements would be parsed incorrectly. Alternatively, you could have put them on two consecutive lines.

Selective processing allows a shell statement or command to execute on the condition that the expression evaluates to true. Structures in selective processing can be composed of a simple if statement, an if-else statement, or a case statement.

The *if* Statement

The syntax of a simple if statement in a C shell looks like this:

```
if (expr) command
```

An example of a shell program that contains a simple if statement is as follows:

```
#!/bin/csh
set bad = 0
if ($bad == 0) echo " I am bad"
```

This program declares bad as a new local variable initialized to 0. The if statement then checks to see whether bad has the value 0. If it does, the echo command displays I am bad on-screen.

The *if-else* Statement

An if-else statement in a C shell looks like the following:

```
If (expr) then
commands
else
commands
endif
```

Here is an example of a C shell program that contains a complete if-else statement:

```
#!/bin/csh
set mychoice = openwin
if
      ( $mychoice == openwin)
      #
      unset mychoice
      echo -n "Starting OpenWindows (type Control-C to interrupt)"
      clear          # get rid of annoying cursor rectangle
      echo -n "Automatically logging out (type Control-C to interrupt)"
```

8

```
        #
else
        #
        unset mychoice
        echo -n "Starting SunView (type Control-C to interrupt)"
        # default sunview background looks best with pastels
        clear           # get rid of annoying cursor rectangle
        echo -n "Automatically logging out (type Control-C to interrupt)"
        #
endif
```

The preceding script checks the value of a local variable, namely `mychoice`. If `mychoice` has the value `openwin`, the script will do the following: eliminate the value of `mychoice`; echo `starting Openwindows`; clear the screen; and echo `Automatically logging out (type Control-C to interrupt)`. Otherwise, if the variable `mychoice` has a different value (it could be anything), the script will do the following: eliminate the value of `mychoice`; echo `starting Sunview (type Control-C to interrupt)`; clear the screen; and echo `Automatically logging out (type Control-C to interrupt)`. As a reminder, the words `else` and `endif` must begin at the first character on a line. The `if` must appear alone on its input line or after an `else`.

The *case* Statement

A case statement in a C shell is equivalent to a complete `if-else` statement, but allows easier reading and flexibility of the code. The expression after the `switch` statement is called a *label*.

Following is the syntax of a `case` statement in a C shell:

```
switch (expression)
      case comparasion1:
            commands
            breaksw
      case comparasion2:
            commands
            breaksw

      default:
endsw
```

Here is an example of a C shell program that contains a `switch`:

```
#!/bin/csh
set mychoice = openwin
switch( $mychoice )
case     openwin:
      unset mychoice
         echo -n "Starting OpenWindows (type Control-C to interrupt)"
      clear            # get rid of annoying cursor rectangl
      echo -n "Automatically logging out (type Control-C to interrupt)"
      breaksw
      #
```

```
case      sunview:
     unset mychoice
     echo -n "Starting SunView (type Control-C to interrupt)"
     # default sunview background looks best with pastels
     clear          # get rid of annoying cursor rectangle
     echo -n "Automatically logging out (type Control-C to interrupt)"
     breaksw
     #
endsw
```

The preceding program is just a rewriting of the if-else script. Remember that the breaksw statement stands for "breaks from a switch." It resumes execution after the endsw statement, which is the last line in the shell. After endsw, the script stops.

An *iterative processing* structure corresponds exactly to the concept of a loop. The C shell provides a number of loops:

- foreach loop

- while loop

- repeat loop

The foreach loop is similar to for loops in other programming languages. The classic concept of a loop statement is that the loop will go on as long as the conditional expression evaluates as true.

Following is the syntax of a foreach loop in the C shell:

```
foreach variable (wordlist)
commands
............
end
```

The meaning of the foreach loop is that the variable is set to each possible value (member) in the *wordlist*. The *wordlist* always starts with a parenthesis, followed by a string, and ending with a parenthesis. The commands are executed between the foreach line and the end statement.

Remember the rename script at the beginning of the previous section? Here, a foreach loop will be used to rename all old file names with new file names. Look at the following lines of commands and what they do:

```
#!/bin/csh
set oldfilename; set newfilename
foreach oldfilename (*)
echo $oldfilename
echo "  is the old name and you need to replace with a new filename"
set newfilename = $<
echo $newfilename
```

8

```
mv $oldfilename $newfilename
end
ls -als
```

The second line declares two local variables, oldfilename and newfilename, but with no initial value. The foreach loop starts on the next line and assigns oldfilename to all values of the wordlist, which is * in this case. Remember that, in a C shell, the * stands for all existing file names in a given directory. Thus, oldfilename will have all possible names existing in your directory. The next line will start executing by echoing the value of oldfilename. The value of oldfilename begins with file names that start with an A, if any. If not, the script proceeds to the next one in ASCII order. If there are no files that start with a capital letter, all the file names starting with a lowercase a are considered.

Line 5 displays a general message reminding the user that he or she is renaming the file name. Line 6 reads a file name from the keyboard (see the earlier section on the set command) and assigns the name read from the keyboard to the newfilename variable. Line 7 echoes to the screen the file name that was keyed by the user from the keyboard. Line 8 executes the command mv, which renames oldfilename into newfilename. Then the end statement executes and goes back to check whether there any names in the directory that were not assigned to the variable oldfilename.

The loop continues until all names have been processed or changed into new names. To verify that the names in the directory are new, a listing is displayed on the screen through the ls -als command.

Another type of loop uses the while statement. This loop is equivalent to the foreach loop. The general syntax of a while loop is simple:

```
while (expr)
commands
. . . . . . . . . . . . .
end
```

expr stands for an expression that will be evaluated before executing any of the following commands. If the expression evaluates as true, the commands execute until they reach the end statement, and the expression is evaluated again. If the expression evaluates as false, the command after end will be launched.

To understand the use of a while loop, consider once again the problem of re-naming files in a directory. Assume that the directory had the following file names:

```
% ls -als
```

```
total 14
    1 drwx------  5 gmeghab     512 Aug 27 11:43 .
   10 drwxr-xr-x 53 gmeghab    9728 Aug 26 14:39 ..
    1 drwxr-xr-x  2 gmeghab     512 Nov 29  1994 NN
    1 drwxr-xr-x  2 gmeghab     512 Nov  7  1994 art
    1 drwxr-xr-x  2 gmeghab     512 Oct 13  1994 lisp
```

What follows is the shell script for the while loop:

```
#!/bin/csh
@ i = 1
set oldfilename = *
set newfilename
while (( oldfilename !~ * ) && ($i <= $#oldfilename))
echo $oldfilename[$i]
echo " old filename and will be renamed to "
set newfilename = $<
echo $newfilename
mv $oldfilename[$i] $newfilename
@ i++
end
ls -als
```

Executing the preceding script on a given directory results in the following output:

```
NN
 old filename and will be renamed to
NN1
NN1
art
 old filename and will be renamed to
art1
art1
lisp
  old filename and will be renamed to
lisp1
lisp1
total 14
    1 drwx------  5 gmeghab     512 Aug 27 11:43 .
   10 drwxr-xr-x 53 gmeghab    9728 Aug 26 14:39 ..
    1 drwxr-xr-x  2 gmeghab     512 Nov 29  1994 NN1
    1 drwxr-xr-x  2 gmeghab     512 Nov  7  1994 art1
    1 drwxr-xr-x  2 gmeghab     512 Oct 13  1994 lisp1
victor%
```

A local declaration of a variable i was needed and assigned 1. This time, the variable oldfilename has been assigned *. Recall that * stands for everything. Also, any variable declared behaves like an array that can be indexed. As long as oldfilename has not gone through the entire list, it will continue processing the file names.

8

The while loop contains two parts to be checked; if they evaluate as true, the next commands will be processed. The second part of the while loop compares the value of index i to the size of the array variable oldfilename. Remember that oldfilename in the preceding example had three names in the directory. The $#oldfilename corresponds to 3. The sixth line will display only the first file to be processed from the list of *. The seventh line just echoes a constant comment to the screen. Then newfilename is read from the keyboard. The mv command will rename the first old name into a new name, and the variable i will be incremented to 2. The expression is evaluated again; the oldfilename is changed into a new one, i becomes 3, and so on, until the end, at which point a listing is displayed on the screen.

Note that if the while loop was written with only the first check (oldfilename ~! *), the commands would have executed until the end, and then a subscript out of error range would have resulted.

The final type of loop is the repeat loop. The usefulness of the repeat loop in the C shell is very limited. It is used to execute a one-line statement a number of times. The syntax of the repeat is as follows:

```
repeat count command
```

count is a variable that has already been assigned a value, and command is a single command.

The use of a repeat loop is very limited. As an illustration, however, the preceding example of renaming files in a directory is rewritten here. Generally, it is not advisable to use a repeat loop for implementing the concept of loops because it will do only one command. The C shell provides the foreach and while loops, which are much more versatile. But to see how a repeat loop might be used, look at the following script:

```
#!/bin/csh
@ i = 1
repeat $i name
```

name is the name of a C shell script. The third line of the script shows that you execute name one time. Thus, name will have to correspond to another script file that will do the renaming of all the files. name could be any of the previous scripts that were used to illustrate the implementation of a for loop or while loop concept.

Shell scripts are now typically used by a system administrator to solve daily problems efficiently. Novice users of UNIX might question how this applies to learning UNIX. With time, however, you will discover that whole commands can be chained and new commands can be created to fit your own needs or to solve your particular problems efficiently, as you saw in the example of renaming a whole directory of names.

Exercises

1. Give the set command that would make your prompt look like the following:

   ```
   victor%
   ```

   If the change is to be permanent, which file is to be changed? Give the command that will allow the change of the command to be effective immediately.

2. What is the result of the following command?

   ```
   % set prompt = "'hostname'{'whoami'}{$$}"
   ```

   If the change is to be permanent, which file is to contain the command?

3. Give the result of the following command:

   ```
   % set prompt ="'hostname'{'passwd'}{$$}"
   ```

   Be careful not to execute the command on your machine. How would you fix the problem if you did execute it?

4. List all the Bourne shell variables that correspond to the C shell variables given in this chapter. What would you conclude about both shells?

5. List all the Korn shell variables that correspond to the C shell variables given in this chapter. What would you conclude about both shells?

6. Redo exercises 1, 2, and 3 using the Korn shell.

7. Redo exercises 1, 2, and 3 using the Bourne shell.

8. Rewrite all the C shell scripts in the last section of the chapter, using the Bourne shell.

9. Rewrite all the C shell scripts in the last section of the chapter, using the Korn shell.

9

C Programming in a UNIX Environment

Topics Covered

- What Is C?
- Your First C Program
- Your First C Program under the Microscope
- Types and Variables
- Controlling the Flow of the Program
- Loop the Loop
- Functions: Programs inside Programs
- Where to Go from Here

What Is C?

This chapter is not intended to replace a book on C programming or to be an "advanced" C programming guide. Instead, the chapter is an introduction to writing programs under UNIX using the C programming language. Most of the time, you will find a C compiler included in the UNIX operating system. If you have trouble accessing the C compiler on your system, ask your system administrator to give you access. In this chapter, you concentrate on standard or ANSI C. ANSI stands for American National Standards Institute, which is a governing body of people who decide what elements will be included in the minimum C language.

C is a highly functional language that can be used to build programs. You can use C to create databases, perform intense math calculations, create reports, and so on. C is fun to learn and will give you more control when performing what you need than shell languages like the Bourne and Korn shells. You'll also find that C is a little faster than shell languages.

Your First C Program

Now you are ready to write your first C program. At first, just type the program; you learn a bit later what the parts of the program are—after you run it. (You will need to know how to use the vi or emacs editor to enter your programs. Chapter 6 discusses these editors.)

Here is a little program that will echo your name on the screen. Open a file call name.c with vi or emacs and enter the following at the prompt:

```
vi name.c
```

Then enter the following:

```
#include <stdio.h>
main()
{

  char your_name[ 60+1 ];

  printf( "Enter your name: " );
  scanf( "%s", your_name );
  printf( "Hello %s\n", your_name );

}
```

Next, save and close your file by pressing the Escape key to put you in vi command mode. Enter a colon (:) followed by **wq!**, save, and quit vi:

```
:wq!
```

For a C program to run, it has to be compiled and linked with the UNIX operating system. *Compiling* is the process in which a program called a *compiler* goes through what you typed and makes sure that it is a program. Your program must have a beginning and an end, indicated by the word main() and by braces { }. main() is the head of the household in a C program. From main(), your program will call other nuggets of code to perform the tasks you expect. It's a little like the captain of a ship giving orders to his crew.

Another process that allows a C program to run is *linking*. In UNIX, linking is done automatically for you. Linking is a way of aligning your program with memory and other operating system parameters so that the program can execute properly within UNIX.

In UNIX, the C compiler, which is called cc, has a number of options. Here you use only one option, -o. This option enables you to name your executable to something other than a.out, which is the default name for all programs compiled with cc. It is now time to compile your program.

At the prompt, enter the following and press Enter:

```
cc -o name name.c
```

Then enter **name** and press Enter:

```
% name
Enter your name: Scott
Hello Scott

%
```

Congratulations, you have just successfully written, compiled, and run your first C program.

Your First C Program under the Microscope

Now go back and review how this program works. Look at the first line in the program:

```
#include <stdio.h>
```

This line is in all C programs, so never forget it. In C, you can include other C code in your program to help C know how to handle output, input, errors, and even files. An example of C code that can be included is found in the header file called stdio.h, which stands for *standard input and output.* stdio.h has segments of code that know how to accept input from the keyboard, output text to the screen, and so on. A header file (indicated with the .h extension) is filled with C code, but it is not a complete C program. It is incomplete because all C programs must have a main(), which is the next line in your program:

```
main()
{
```

You learned about main() and the opening brace in the preceding section, so examine the variable declarations next:

```
char your_name[ 60+1 ];
```

A *variable* is basically like your favorite kitchen bowl—it holds something. Different bowls are used for different foods. Likewise, C has different types of variables to hold different kinds of values. In your program, you want the variable to hold your name, which consists of several characters. A character (char) can be a letter, punctuation, or even a number.

A bunch of characters together is called a *string*. You created a string of characters when you typed [60+1] at the end of the variable your_name. This means that your_name can hold 60 characters plus a null character. Null characters are used to end character strings. You could have used [61] and meant the same thing, but you might like to remind yourself that the null character is there. This is strictly personal preference, and you can do what you like because it's your program. You learn about different types of variables later in this chapter.

As you saw earlier, C can write (output) and read (input) information. The next line in your program calls a print function called printf():

```
printf( "Enter your name: " );
```

A *function* is a specialized piece of code that performs a specific task. In this case, printf() specializes in output to the screen. This code is actually defined in stdio.h, which you already included in your program. Another function that you have already used is main(). It is a very special function that the C compiler looks for as the starting point for all C programs.

Functions normally take information passed to them and perform a task using that information. printf() will output the information passed through the argument string "Enter your name: ". (You create functions later in this chapter.) The last function in your program is scanf():

```
scanf( "%s", your_name );
```

The function name is a little vague, but it scans standard input—that is, your keyboard—for information typed. scanf() takes this input and places it in a variable so that you can do something with it.

The "%s" tells scanf() to look for a string of characters to be input from the keyboard and place the string in the variable your_name. Remember, you promised the program that you would type only 60 characters. If you type 62 characters, your program will not execute correctly. You can code into your program a function that checks how many characters were entered and prints an error message indicating that your program can't handle more than 60 characters. You learn about using functions in your program later in this chapter.

The last line before the ending brace simply takes the value in your_name and prints it to the screen or standard output. You were instructed to enter "Hello %s\n" to help format your output to the screen. %s tells printf() to expect the value of your_name to be a string of characters, and \n tells the function to put a carriage return and line feed after it prints.

Note one more part of a C program—the semicolon. In C, a semicolon tells the compiler that you have finished the current line of code. You can tell from your first program that the semicolon is used on most lines of code. Knowing when to use a semicolon might give you a headache. As you read this chapter, you will get a good feeling of when a semicolon is appropriate. Furthermore, you can look at the *C Language Reference Manual* included with most compilers, and when you compile, the compiler will give you a good indication that you forgot a semicolon. You can tell already that a semicolon is not required after #include statements.

Don't throw away your first program—you'll be building more in it.

Types and Variables

Remember that in your first program you declared a variable to hold your name. This variable could hold a name 60 characters long:

```
char your_name[ 60+1 ];
```

The char in front of the variable is called a *type*. Just as there are different kinds of wrenches and screwdrivers, there are different kinds of variables. You learn about different types in the following section.

Data Types

A variable can be instructed to hold just about any kind of value, but what you do with the value is limited by its type. You might want to add together variables made of numbers to see their sum. To distinguish one value from another, you give it a type. Here are some basic types in C:

```
int variable_name;
```

The int type is short for *integer type*. It allows only a whole number or a negative whole number to be stored in its variable. Note the following examples of int values:

```
10, 22, 500, 10000

-1

-250

-15000

float variable_name;
```

The float type is short for *floating-point decimal*. It allows a dollar amount or a real number to be stored in its variable. Here are some examples of float values:

```
10.1, 3.14, 333.555, 0.125

-20.3

-0.128

-1015.14

char variable_name
```

The char type is short for *character*. Only an alphanumeric value can be stored in its variable. You wouldn't use char variables to do any kind of calculation. Note some examples of char values:

```
c, C, Z, a, 1, 3, 9, #, !
```

More types are found in the C language, but to learn C, you just need to understand these three basic types.

Variables

A variable is given a piece of computer memory to hold a value of a given type. The variable your_name was given space in memory (when your program ran) to hold 60 values of type char. There are some restrictions on how you name your variables. Some versions of the UNIX C compiler restrict the length of a variable name to 31 characters. You might want to limit a variable name to 31 just to play it safe, and begin your variable names with the alphabetic characters A to Z or a to z. Some compilers may allow other symbols and numbers to start a variable, so you will have to check the documentation for your version of UNIX.

Arrays

You have already seen an array in your first program; it was called "a string of characters," but it could have been called "an array of characters." An *array* is simply a collection of a single type that is aligned contiguously in memory. To understand how the variable your_name array looks in memory, look at Figure 9.1.

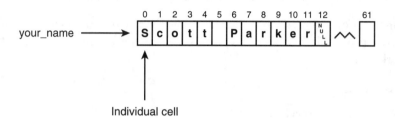

Individual cell

Figure 9.1
The variable
your_name in
memory.

As you can see in Figure 9.1, the array is made up of individual cells of the type char. You can get to each individual cell by giving its cell number in the variable. Do a printf() function that prints only the third cell in the array:

```
printf( "the third cell is: %c\n", your_name[ 2 ] );
```

%c tells printf() to expect a single character from the variable. What about the [2] on the end of your_name? This is how you address individual cells in the array. Why a 2? A C language array starts with 0 (zero) instead of 1. For this reason, 2 is actually the third number when you're counting from 0. Now compile and run the name.c program with the new line inserted. Open name.c with vi or emacs, add the new line, and compile. Here's how your program should look:

```
#include <stdio.h>
main()
{

  char your_name[ 60+1 ];

  printf( "Enter your name: " );
  scanf( "%s", your_name );
  printf( "Hello %s\n", your_name );
  printf( "the third cell is: %c\n", your_name[ 2 ] );
}
```

When you run the program, make sure that you put more than three characters in before you press Enter. Here is my sample output for the program:

```
% name
Enter your name: Scott
Hello Scott
the third cell is: o

%
```

9

You can have an array of integers, characters, real numbers (floats), and so on, and you address them the same way. Multidimensional arrays are arrays *inside* arrays. Such arrays are beyond the scope of this chapter, but you can investigate this topic in a book dedicated to teaching C.

Controlling the Flow of the Program

Sometimes a program needs to make a decision about what to do with the information you provide it. To make this decision, C has special statements that control the flow of a program.

The *if* Statement

The simplest of these special statements is called if...else. The best way to learn how this statement works is to add a simple if statement to your name.c program. Change name.c to look like the following:

```
#include <stdio.h>

main()
{
  char your_name[ 60 ];
  int  ans;

  printf( "Enter your name: " );
  scanf( "%s", your_name );
  printf( "Enter (1)It's Cool Outside or (2)It's Hot Outside: " );
  scanf( "%d", &ans );
  printf( "Hello %s\n", your_name );
  printf( "The third cell has: %c\n", your_name[ 2 ] );

  if ( ans == 1 )
    printf( "You better wear something warm today!\n" );
  else
    printf( "You better find a pool it's going to be hot today!\n" );

}
```

Here is the output from this change:

```
% name
Enter your name: Scott
Enter (1)It's Cool Outside or (2)It's Hot Outside: 1
Hello Scott
The third cell has: o
You better wear something warm today!

% name
Enter your name: Zach
```

```
Enter (1)It's Cool Outside or (2)It's Hot Outside: 2
Hello Zach
The third cell has: c
You better find a pool it's going to be hot today!

%
```

Notice that a semicolon is not needed on the `if` or `else` line. (You can have `if` without the `else`.) Between the `if` and `else` is a logical expression. The evaluation of the logical expression determines the outcome of the `if` statement. In this example, `ans` is the variable that is being evaluated to see whether it is equal (`==`) to `1`. If the evaluation is true, then `You better wear something warm today!` is printed; otherwise, `You better find a pool it's going to be hot today!` is printed. If you were to enter `number one` at the prompt, `You better find a pool it's going to be hot today!` would print because the `if` is looking only for `1`.

Logical Expressions and Other Expressions

Take a short break from the discussion of program flow control to consider *expressions* and how they work. One kind of expression will assign a value to a variable:

```
int var1;

var1 = 16835;
```

Here `var1` is assigned the value of `16835`. The single equal sign is called an *operator*. You can add a number to the value in `var1` in one of two ways:

```
int var1;
var1 = 16835;
var1 = var1 + 10000;
```

or

```
int var1;
var1 = 16835
var1 += 10000;
```

The first method is one you probably remember from elementary school: a = a + b. The second method does the exact same thing but shortens the expression: a += b. Either expression adds `10000` to `16835` and assigns it to `var1`, making it equal to `26835`. There are other types of assignment expressions like the following:

Expression	Same As	Description
a += b	a = a + b	Adds b to a and assigns to a.
a -= b	a = a - b	Subtracts b from a and assigns to a.

(continues)

9

(continued)

Expression	Same As	Description
a /= b	a = a / b	Divides a by b and assigns to a.
a *= b	a = a * b	Multiplies a by b and assigns to a.
a++	a = a + 1	Adds 1 to a and assigns to a.
a--	a = a - 1	Subtracts 1 from a and assigns a.

The last two operators in the table, ++ and --, are called *incremental* operators. You learn more about these operators later in the chapter. There are several other kinds of assignment expressions, but this will do for an introduction.

Another kind of expression is the *logical* expression. These expressions use logical operators. Here are some examples:

Expression	Description
a == b	Does a equal b?
a > b	Is a greater than b?
a < b	Is a less than b?
a >= b	Is a greater than or equal to b?
a <= b	Is a less than or equal to b?
a != b	Is a not equal to b?

Note: It is important that you don't use a single = in a logical expression. Remember that a single = is an assignment operator. This mistake is a common one for beginners or anyone who knows a different computer language.

To evaluate two or more expressions together, C has two other special operators to help perform this operation:

Operator	Example	Description
&&	a == b && c == b	Logical AND: Is a equal to b, and is c equal to b? Both expressions must be true to make the whole expression true.

Operator	Example	Description
¦¦	a < b ¦¦ a < c	Logical OR: Is a less than b, or is a less than c? Only one has to be true to make the whole expression true.

Order of Precedence with Operators

If you were to put a * b + c in a program, would a * b be evaluated and then c added, or would b + c be added and then multiplied by a? Hmmm! This is a problem, but C has a built-in *precedence*, or order of evaluation. Expressions are ranked from left to right:

( ) * / + -	Assignment operators
( ) <= >= > < == != && ||	Logical operators

The use of parentheses enables you, as the programmer, to control the precedence. For example, (a + b) * c is evaluated as a + b with the result multiplied by c. Without the parentheses, b is multiplied by c and then a is added. For logical expressions, it is important to make sure that one expression is evaluated before another. For example, in the expression

```
a > b ¦¦ ( a < c && b < c )
```

the right side of the OR (¦¦) is evaluated first.

A Nested *if...else*

What happens when just one if statement won't do the job? In an earlier example, you saw that you could enter any number except 1 and You better find a pool it's going to be hot today! would be printed. This is not the result you want, however. To prevent this from happening, you can make the following changes to your program:

```
#include <stdio.h>

main()
{
  char your_name[ 60 ];
  int  ans;

  printf( "Enter your name: " );
  scanf( "%s", your_name );
  printf( "Enter (1)It's Cool Outside or (2)It's Hot Outside: " );
  scanf( "%d", &ans );
  printf( "Hello %s\n", your_name );
  printf( "The third cell has: %c\n", your_name[ 2 ] );
```

```
if ( ans == 1 )
  printf( "You better wear something warm today!\n" );
else if ( ans = 2 )
  printf( "You better find a pool it's going to be hot today!\n" );
else
{
  printf( "Oops! You don't really know yet!\n" );
  printf( "Sooo! Turn on the radio and find out!\n" );
}

}
```

First, by adding the extra else if, you have added more control to your program. Now either 1 or 2 is the right answer; if neither is entered, Oops! You don't really know yet! and Sooo! Turn on the radio and find out! are printed. Second, the braces allow you to create blocks of code to be performed in the control of the if statement. You can use if by itself without the else. Here is what to expect when you compile and run the program:

```
% name
Enter your name: Scott
Enter (1)It's Cool Outside or (2)It's Hot Outside: 1
Hello Scott
The third cell has: o
You better wear something warm today!

% name
Enter your name: Zach
Enter (1)It's Cool Outside or (2)It's Hot Outside: 2
Hello Zach
The third cell has: c
You better find a pool it's going to be hot today!

% name
Enter your name: Carolyn
Enter (1)It's Cool Outside or (2)It's Hot Outside: 5
Hello Carolyn
The third cell has: r
Oops! You don't really know yet!
Sooo! Turn on the radio and find out!

%
```

The *switch* Statement

With the nested if...else statement, there is no limit to how far you can nest, but good practice is to use only four levels of nesting. If you nest more than four times, you might consider using the switch statement or restructuring your logical expression:

```
if ( expression )
    ...Do something...
```

```
else if ( expression )
        ...Do something else...
else if ( expression )
        ...Something even different...
else if ( expression )
        ...I'm yawning now...
else
        ...Completely bored stiff...
```

The C language has another solution to this problem: the switch statement. Change your program name.c to include the switch statement:

```
#include <stdio.h>

main()
{
  char your_name[ 60 ];
  int  ans;

  printf( "Enter your name: " );
  scanf( "%s", your_name );
  printf( "Enter (1)Cool (2)Hot (3)Too close to tell
    (4)I don't know: " );
  scanf( "%d", &ans );
  printf( "Hello %s\n", your_name );
  printf( "The third cell has: %c\n", your_name[ 2 ] );

  switch ( ans )
  {
     case 1:  printf( "You better wear something warm today!\n" );
              break;
     case 2:  printf( "You better find a pool it's going to be hot
➥today!\n" );
              break;
     case 3:  printf( "Hey! Your a lot of help!\n" );
              break;
     case 4:  printf( "Okay! Just go back to bed and find out from
➥someone else.\n" );
              break;
     default: printf( "Oops! You don't really know yet!\n" );
              printf( "Sooo! Turn on the radio and find out!\n" );
              break;
  }
}
```

Here is some sample output:

```
% name
Enter your name: Scott
Enter (1)Cool (2)Hot (3)Too close to tell (4)I don't know: 1
Hello Scott
The third cell has: o
You better wear something warm today!

% name
Enter your name: Zach
```

```
Enter (1)Cool (2)Hot (3)Too close to tell (4)I don't know: 2
Hello Zach
The third cell has: c
You better find a pool it's going to be hot today!

% name
Enter your name: Virginia
Enter (1)Cool (2)Hot (3)Too close to tell (4)I don't know: 3
Hello Virginia
The third cell has: r
Hey! You are a lot of help!

% name
Enter your name: Virgil
Enter (1)Cool (2)Hot (3)Too close to tell (4)I don't know: 4
Hello Virgil
The third cell has: r
Okay! Just go back to bed and find out from someone else.

% name
Enter your name: Carolyn
Enter (1)Cool (2)Hot (3)Too close to tell (4)I don't know: 7
Hello Carolyn
The third cell has: r
Oops! You don't really know yet!
Sooo! Turn on the radio and find out!

%
```

There is virtually no limit to the number of case statements you can have in the switch statement. switch makes your program very readable.

> **NOTE** Remember to put a break *statement at the end of each* case *block. If you don't, the program will continue until it gets to another break or to the end of the* switch *block.*

Loop the Loop

It would be silly if you had to run the program name over and over to see how these results change with the input of different information. C has ways of making a program loop. *Looping* basically makes a process run over and over until it terminates.

The *for* Loop

The for loop is easy to implement. It has a beginning and a predetermined end. The basic construction is

```
for ( initial value, logical expression, post loop expression )
{
```

```
    ...do something in here...
}
```

The logical expression is what keeps the loop going. If the expression evaluates as false, the loop stops. Now change your program to loop three times, asking its questions:

```
#include <stdio.h>

main()
{
  char your_name[ 60 ];
  int  ans;
  int  count;

  for ( count = 1; count <= 3; count++ )
  {
    printf( "Enter your name: " );
    scanf( "%s", your_name );
    printf( "Enter (1)Cool (2)Hot (3)Too close to tell
      ➡(4)I don't know: " );
    scanf( "%d", &ans );
    printf( "Hello %s\n", your_name );
    printf( "The third cell has: %c\n", your_name[ 2 ] );

    switch ( ans )
    {
      case 1:  printf( "You better wear something warm today!\n" );
               break;
      case 2:  printf( "You better find a pool it's going to be hot
        today!\n" );
               break;
      case 3:  printf( "Hey! You are a lot of help!\n" );
               break;
      case 4:  printf( "Okay! Just go back to bed and find out from
                   someone else.\n" );
               break;
      default: printf( "Oops! You don't really know yet!\n" );
               printf( "Sooo! Turn on the radio and find out!\n" );
               break;
    }
    printf( "Count is equal to: %d\n\n", count );
  }
}
```

This program loops three times and asks the same questions. The for loop has the initial expression count = 1. The variable count is incremented once after every loop count++ (as the post-loop expression); then the logical expression is evaluated to see whether it loops again. Here is the expected output:

```
% name
Enter your name: Scott
Enter (1)Cool (2)Hot (3)Too close to tell (4)I don't know: 1
Hello Scott
```

```
The third cell has: o
You better wear something warm today!
Count is equal to: 1

Enter your name: Zach
Enter (1)Cool (2)Hot (3)Too close to tell (4)I don't know: 2
Hello Zach
The third cell has: c
You better find a pool it's going to be hot today!
Count is equal to: 2

Enter your name: Virginia
Enter (1)Cool (2)Hot (3)Too close to tell (4)I don't know: 3
Hello Virginia
The third cell has: r
Hey! You are a lot of help!
Count is equal to: 3

%
```

You could have made this loop go forever (an infinite loop) by eliminating the expression from the for loop:

```
for (;;)
{
        ...do something...
}
```

The only way to get out of an infinite loop is to program something to break the loop from within the program, or to interrupt it with Ctrl-c. Don't program like this—it makes a mess. One last point should be made about for loops: It is not wise to change the count variable in the loop itself. This change can lead to unexpected results and makes your program hard to debug.

The *while* Loop

The while loop is a little different from the for loop because the while's logical expression is evaluated before the loop begins:

```
while ( logical expression )
{
    ...do something here...
}
```

Now change your program again to use a while loop instead of a for loop:

```
#include <stdio.h>

main()
{
  char your_name[ 60 ];
  int  ans;
  int  count;
```

```
      count = 1;
      while ( count <= 3 )
      {
        printf( "Enter your name: " );
        scanf( "%s", your_name );
        printf( "Enter (1)Cool (2)Hot (3)Too close to tell
           (4)I don't know: " );
        scanf( "%d", &ans );
        printf( "Hello %s\n", your_name );
        printf( "The third cell has: %c\n", your_name[ 2 ] );

        switch ( ans )
        {
          case 1:  printf( "You better wear something warm today!\n" );
                   break;
          case 2:  printf( "You better find a pool it's going to be hot
                      today!\n" );
                   break;
          case 3:  printf( "Hey! You are a lot of help!\n" );
                   break;
          case 4:  printf( "Okay! Just go back to bed and find out from
                      someone else.\n" );
                   break;
          default: printf( "Oops! You don't really know yet!\n" );
                   printf( "Sooo! Turn on the radio and find out!\n" );
                   break;
        }
        printf( "Count is equal to: %d\n\n", count );
        count++;
      }
    }
```

The output is exactly the same as for the `for` loop. You can manipulate the loop count at any stage in the loop, and as long as the logical expression evaluates as true, the loop continues.

C has a few more loops, but these `for` and `while` are the basic ones. You will find yourself using these two loops most of the time.

Functions: Programs inside Programs

Functions are the real power behind the C language. You have used three functions thus far: `printf()`, `scanf()`, and `main()`. As with these functions and others you write, functions are very specific in purpose. `printf()` prints output on standard output, `scanf()` gets input from standard input, and `main()` is the controlling function of the whole program. To use functions, you need a little background information on global and local variables and on pointers to variables.

Local versus Global Variables

You can declare global variables and local variables. A *global* variable is simply a variable that is available from anywhere in the program. Such a variable is declared outside the program `main()`:

```
#include <stdio.h>
char global_var1;
int global_int1;

function1()
{
    ...do something here...
}

main()
{
    ...do something here...
}
```

In this example, both `function1()` and `main()` can access and make changes to the values in `global_int1` and `global_var1`. This works fine if the program is small and you are the only programmer, but later, other people can write functions that change these variables. Usually, it is better to use a *local* variable and pass the variable to other functions. Here is an example of locally declared variables:

```
#include <stdio.h>

void function1()
{
  int var1;

  var1 = 10;
  printf( "function1's var1 is: %d\n", var1 );
}

main()
{
  int var1;

  var1 = 20;
  printf( "main's var1 is: %d\n", var1 );
  function1();
}
```

The output from this program is

```
main's var1 is: 20
function1's var1 is: 10
```

`var1` is local in both `function1()` and `main()`. Now change the value of `var1` in `function1()` and see how to change local variables:

```
#include <stdio.h>
```

```
void function1( int pass_value )
{
  int var1;

  var1 = pass_value;
  printf( "function1's var1 is: %d\n", var1 );
}

main()
{
  int var1;

  var1 = 20;
  printf( "main's var1 is: %d\n", var1 );
  function1( 40 );
}
```

The expected output is

```
main's var1 is: 20
function1's var1 is: 40
```

Consider another example. Modify function1() to change the value of var1 in main():

```
#include <stdio.h>

void function1( int *pass_value )
{
  int var1;

  var1 = 10;
  printf( "function1's var1 is: %d\n", var1 );
  *pass_value = 150;
}

main()
{
  int var1;

  var1 = 20;
  printf( "main's var1 is: %d\n", var1 );
  function1( &var1 );
  printf( "now ... main's var1 is: %d\n", var1 );
}
```

The expected output is

```
main's var1 is: 20
function1's var1 is: 10
now ... main's var1 is: 150
```

Pointers

In the preceding example, you see some new symbols—the asterisk (*) and the ampersand (&)—in front of the variable being used. A detailed discussion of pointers isn't necessary, but here is the long and the short of how they work. In functions, pointers simply pass the address of where to find the value assigned to a variable. You saw from the output that the value of main()'s var1 had changed to 150. The following code passes the address of where to find the value in var1 to function1():

```
function1( &var1 );
```

In figure 9.2, you can see the value of main()'s var1 at the address of 010102.

Figure 9.2

main()'s var1 in
main memory.

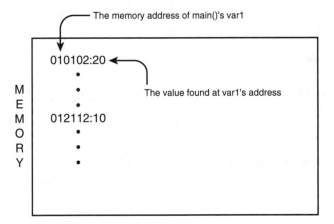

When function1() is called, it gets the actual address of main()'s var1. It can manipulate the value, but you really want to modify the value at the address. To change the value in function1(), you add an asterisk in front of the variable pass_value. Then 150 is the assigned value at the address pointed to by pass_value. If you don't use an asterisk, you are manipulating the address, not the value, and you might get results you don't want.

Putting a Function in Your First Program

Now you are ready to put a function in your first program. Change your name program to match the following:

```c
#include <stdio.h>

void get_your_name( char *some_name )
{
  printf( "Enter your name: " );
  scanf( "%s", some_name );
```

```
    }

    void output_third_cell( char *some_name )
    {
        printf( "The third cell has: %c\n", some_name[ 2 ] );
    }

    main()
    {
      char your_name[ 60 ];
      int  ans;
      int  count;

      count = 1;
      while ( count <= 3 )
      {
        get_your_name( your_name );
        printf( "Enter your name: " );
        scanf( "%s", your_name );
        printf( "Enter (1)Cool (2)Hot (3)Too close to tell
           (4)I don't know: " );
        scanf( "%d", &ans );
        printf( "Hello %s\n", your_name );
        output_third_cell( your_name );

        switch ( ans )
        {
          case 1:  printf( "You better wear something warm today!\n" );
                   break;
          case 2:  printf( "You better find a pool it's going to be hot
                     today!\n" );
                   break;
          case 3:  printf( "Hey! You are a lot of help!\n" );
                   break;
          case 4:  printf( "Okay! Just go back to bed and find out from
                     someone else.\n" );
                   break;
          default: printf( "Oops! You don't really know yet!\n" );
                   printf( "Sooo! Turn on the radio and find out!\n" );
                   break;
        }
        printf( "Count is equal to: %d\n\n", count );
        count++;
      }
    }
```

Output from this program is exactly the same, but you can see two new functions: get_your_name() and output_third_cell(). Both functions print all or part of the value of the variable your_name. The void in front of each function tells the program not to expect a return value.

You can have a function return a value by changing the value in the parameter or argument list. You have already used this method in the last version of the program name, or you can use the return statement:

```
int function2( int var1 )
{
    return( var1 );
}
```

This function will return the value that is passed in var1. It's a useless function, but it illustrates how to return a value. The int in front of function2() tells the program to expect an integer value to be returned:

```
#include <stdio.h>
int function2( int var1 )
{
  return( var1 );
}

main()
{
  int result;

  result = function2( 200 );
  printf( "result is: %d\n", result );
}
```

The expected output is

```
result is: 200
```

Finally, a function can call another function, and a function can be included in the parameter list of functions. The previous example could have been coded with function2() in printf(), thereby eliminating the need to declare the result variable:

```
printf( "result is: %d\n", function2( 200 ));
```

C has many functions that you can call to help manipulate strings, integers, files, system calls, and so on. Functions are one of the features that make C such a powerful and flexible language.

Where to Go from Here

To learn more about C, you can go the library or bookstore and find many books on C programming for beginners and for experts. This chapter only scratches the surface, but it helps you get started in writing C programs quickly and easily without bogging you down with difficult concepts. In this chapter, you learned some basic building blocks of C programming. You are able to declare variables and assign values to them. You can create functions and use them to manipulate variables as well as print them. Most important, you can compile your code and have fun debugging it.

Exercises

1. Write a program that reads your name and reverses it to the screen. You have everything you need to accomplish this task. You need to know that all strings read in with scanf() end with a null character, which is '\0' in C. The following code snippet gives you a hint on how to get started:

   ```
   /* to count the length of a string */

   for ( count=0; string[ count ] != '\0'; count++ );
   ```

   When this loop completes, count will contain the number of characters you typed from the keyboard. To reverse the string, you initialize the for loop so that it prints from the end of string (count). Don't forget how to decrement your counter to zero with --. The printf() has a %c to print single characters from a variable.

2. What is wrong with the following piece of code?

   ```
   #include <stdio.h>

   main()
   {
     int xray;
     int yell;
     int wow;

     wow = -10;
     xray = 1;
     yell = 10;

     if ( yell++ >= 10 && xray = 1 )
        printf( "this isn't obvious\n" );
     if ( wow < xray )
        printf( "got it!\n" );
   }
   ```

3. Modify the name program to continue looping until the word END is entered in your_name. Count the number of times it loops, and output the result to the screen.

4. Write a program that asks the following:

   Your Name

   Your Age

   (1) for Mr. (2) for Mrs. (3) for Miss

Have the program output the following to the screen:

```
Mr. Parker is 31 years old.
```

The age, name, and signatory are processed by you.

5. Write a program that asks for numbers in a loop until 0 is entered, adds the numbers together, and prints the result to the screen.

6. After you complete exercise 5, modify the program to print how many numbers were entered and then to average the numbers.

IV

Networking

10

UNIX Networking

Topics Covered

- Checking Your Network Setup

- Transferring Files

- Remote Login

- Running Remote Applications

- Accessing Remote File Systems Using *mount* and *umount*

- TCP/IP Setup

When you connect your UNIX system to a network, you tap into the true power of the operating system. Built into the UNIX system are powerful networking frameworks for exchanging information with other computers and users, as well as controlling access to your system.

As a first-time UNIX system user, you probably won't be setting up your own network connections. Hopefully, an experienced system administrator has already connected your computer into the local area network (LAN) in your building or set up your modem. If you need to connect to the network yourself, skip to the setup sections at the end of this chapter.

This chapter begins by assuming that you have network connections set up to one or more remote systems. This chapter focuses on the things you can do with UNIX networking. Here are some of the most common ways of using UNIX networking:

- *File transfer.* When you want to copy a file from one system to another system, you can "transfer" that file to the other system. There is a graphical interface, as well as several different commands, for file transfer within the UNIX system.

- *Interactive file transfer.* If you are not sure where a file is, or where you want it to go, you can set up an interactive session with a remote system. During this session, you can poke around the remote and local systems and copy any files across the network (provided your login has permission to do so).

- *Remote login.* You can start up a login session to another UNIX system while you are logged into one UNIX system. This lets you work from the command line on the remote system as though you were on the local system.

- *Accessing remote file systems.* Instead of transferring files between your system and a remote UNIX system, you can get files by connecting part of the remote file system to your file system. In effect, you can move up and down the remote file system tree using standard UNIX commands. You can cd to a directory, list the contents, and copy files, as though the files were on your local system.

Follow the simple procedures at the beginning of this chapter to use the standard networking features that come with UNIX. As you become familiar with those features, you may find yourself wanting, or needing, to do some of the more advanced networking administration functions.

Checking Your Network Setup

Before you try to use the networking features described in this chapter, there are a few things you should find out about your networking setup. In particular, you will want to know how your system is connected to other systems (TCP/IP, modems, direct connections, or other types) and what remote systems you can reach over that network.

Three major networking packages come with UNIX: TCP/IP, Basic Networking Utilities, and Network File System. Each of these packages offers a different way of communicating with remote systems. Find out from your system administrator which of these are supported on your system.

The following are brief descriptions of the networking packages, including what you have to know to use them.

TCP/IP

TCP/IP is the term most commonly used to describe several networking *protocols* (methods of communicating) and *utilities* (networking applications). Developed originally by the U.S. Department of Defense, it is now used by thousands of government, corporate, and university locations to exchange information on the Internet.

Over the years, TCP/IP has become the predominant method of communicating between UNIX systems, both in local area network (LAN) and wide area network (WAN) environments. The TCP/IP package is useful when you have a few computers connected together on a LAN. These computers can work tightly together in *workgroups*. By connecting to a system that has a network connection to the Internet, the power of your system multiplies. You can send files, query databases, and reach users all over the world.

To use most TCP/IP features, you must know the name of the remote system you want to contact. There are two ways to find out to which systems you can connect. First, you can check your Internet Setup window to see a list of those systems your system knows about. Second, you can check the domain name server for system names.

A *domain name server* is a system that keeps a list of many remote systems, as well as the names of other domain name servers. By using domain name service, every system doesn't have to keep its own lists of remote systems. A system can simply query the name server to resolve the addresses of systems it wants to communicate with.

233

10

Assuming your system is set up to use domain name service, you can check the names and addresses of systems known by your domain name server using the `nslookup` command. The `nslookup` command lets you interactively query the name server. Use the following procedure to query the domain name server:

1. At the command line, type **/usr/sbin/nslookup** and press Enter.

2. After you are connected to the server, type **ls** and press Enter. You see a listing of system names and addresses known to your domain name server.

3. Press Ctrl-d to exit `nslookup`.

There are other commands you can use while you are within the `nslookup` command. See the `nslookup`(1M) manual page for further information.

For a description of Internet names and addresses, see the section "TCP/IP Setup" later in this chapter.

Basic Networking Utilities

Each UNIX system has Basic Networking Utilities (BNU) built into it. People who have used UNIX for a long time refer to this package as UUCP, which stands for UNIX-to-UNIX copy. Chapter 7, "Electronic Mail," discusses UUCP addressing for use in electronic mail. Also see the section "Using the *uucp* and *uuto* Commands" later in this chapter for more information.

BNU consists of much more than the `uucp` command for copying files between systems, however. BNU commands let you do remote login, remote execution, send mail, and connect to remote terminals. Most often, you use BNU for serial communications (to use modems, use direct connections, or connect to character terminals).

As with TCP/IP, you have to know the remote system names available to communicate to those systems over BNU connections. At the command line, enter the following to check which systems you can communicate with using BNU connections:

```
uuname
```

The system displays a list of remote systems that are configured for you to communicate with.

Network File System

You can connect to file systems on remote UNIX systems by using the Network File System features (also called *file sharing*). Although the Network File System (NFS) is available on a separate package with some versions of UNIX, it is really more of a network application than a network type.

NFS relies on TCP/IP being installed. When you ask to connect to remote file systems, you use TCP/IP system names and connections set up by TCP/IP to reach the remote systems.

Using NFS to access remote file systems is easy once you have set it up. You simply move up or down the directory structure to find the file you want and then use standard UNIX commands to manipulate the files.

Configuring NFS is described in the section "Accessing Remote File Systems Using *mount* and *umount*" later in this chapter.

Transferring Files

You can copy files from your system to a remote system if you have TCP/IP or BNU set up on your system.

BNU, with the uuto command, gives you the opportunity to copy files to a public directory on a remote system, without requiring any special permissions on the remote system. TCP/IP, with the rcp command, lets you copy files anywhere on a remote system, based on the permission the remote system has set up for you.

Transferring Files

Use the rcp, uucp, or uuto command to transfer files to a remote system. The rcp command works with TCP/IP for transferring files between UNIX systems. The uucp and uuto commands are used with BNU connections. All these commands work in a line-oriented, text-based shell with messages issued back to the user in case of failure.

Using the *rcp* Command

The rcp command stands for remote copy. With rcp, you can copy files from your system to another UNIX system, from another UNIX system to yours, or between two different UNIX systems. The rcp command requires that permissions be set up properly to allow you to write to the remote system, as described in the TCP/IP setup sections.

Figure 10.1 contains examples of the rcp command.

235

10

Figure 10.1

Some examples
of the rcp
command.

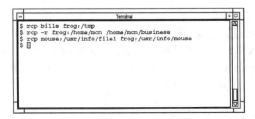

```
Terminal
$ rcp bills frog:/tmp
$ rcp -r frog:/home/mcn /home/mcn/business
$ rcp mouse:/usr/info/file1 frog:/usr/info/mouse
$ ▯
```

- The first example in Figure 10.1 shows how you copy a file called bills (in the current directory) from your system to the /tmp directory on a remote system called frog.

- The second example in Figure 10.1 uses the recursive option (-r) to copy all files, directories, and subdirectories from the directory /home/mcn on the system named frog to the directory /home/mcn/business on your system. As a result, the entire file and directory structure below /home/mcn on frog is reproduced on the local system.

- The third line in Figure 10.1 is an example of how you can copy files between two remote systems. The result is that file1 from the system named mouse is copied to the directory /usr/info/mouse on the remote system named frog.

NOTE *If you got a "Permission Denied" message when you tried rcp, you need to have permissions set up in such a way that you can execute commands on the remote system or remote host. Such permissions are also needed when doing third-party copies. With third-party copies, neither source nor target files are on the current machine. The rcp command does not prompt for passwords. The best way to fix this is to have the remote system's administrator add a login for you (using your same user name), and then add your system name to the .rhost file in your home directory. After that's done, you can write to any part of the system with rcp that you could write to if you had logged into the system directly.*

Notice that you separate the system name and the file name with a colon. You also can add a -p option to pass the date and modification times from the original files to the new files. Otherwise, the current date and time on the remote system are used.

Instead of using simple system names, you can use names in the form *user*@system, where *user* is replaced by a user name on the remote system.

In this way, you can copy files on the remote system as though you were a user other than yourself. Note this example:

```
rcp bills chuck@frog:
```

Here the file `bills` is copied to the remote system `frog` using the permissions of user `chuck` on the remote system. Because there is no file or directory specified after the colon, the file is copied to a point relative to the remote user's home directory (`/home/chuck/bills`).

In this example, `chuck` on the remote system `frog` must allow you to access his login. He does this by adding the line `chuck frog` to the `.rhosts` file in his home directory.

Using the *uucp* and *uuto* Commands

`uucp` and `uuto` are used to copy files to remote systems if you have BNU connections (typically, modems and direct connections). The `uuto` command is simpler to use and provides greater flexibility in where the files are copied from and to.

As with `rcp`, the `uucp` command requires that you set up permissions on the remote system to allow you to write in most remote directories. The `uuto` command, however, lets you copy files to a public directory on any remote system without setting up any special permissions.

Figure 10.2 contains examples for using the `uucp` command.

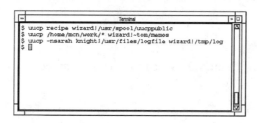

Figure 10.2

Examples of the uucp command.

- In the first example, a file called `recipe` is copied into the `/usr/spool/uucppublic` directory on the system named `wizard`.

- The second example in Figure 10.2 copies all files from the `/home/mcn/work` directory on your system to a directory called `memos` in `tom`'s home directory (probably `/home/tom`) on the system called `wizard`. (A tilde, `~`, in front of a user name means to replace the user's name with the user's home directory.)

- The third example is a file (`/usr/files/logfile`) being transferred to a file (`/tmp/log`) between two remote systems (`knight` and `wizard`). When the file arrives on `wizard`, a mail message tells the user named `sarah` on `wizard` the name of the file that has arrived.

The `uuto` command copies files to a user on a remote system without requiring any additional permissions. With `uuto`, you simply choose what file you want to copy and the name of the user and remote system you want to copy it to.

Figure 10.3 contains an example of the `uuto` command.

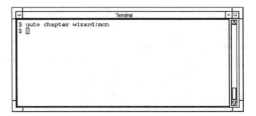

This example copies the file `chapter` to the remote user named `mcn` on the system named `wizard`. The file is copied to the directory `/usr/spool/uucppublic/receive/user/system` on the remote system, where `user` is replaced by the receiving user name (`mcn`), and `system` is replaced by the sending system name. See the following section for information on how to receive files that have been transferred by `uucp` or `uuto` commands.

Receiving Files

After remote files have been transferred to your system, you can pick up those files in one of several ways.

If the file was transferred with the `uuto` command, the file is copied to a public directory. You can pick up a remotely transferred file from public directories in one of two ways. From a Terminal window, do the following:

1. Change to the directory in which you want the file to be copied.

2. Type **uupick** and press Enter. The following output appears:

       From system knight: file log?

3. Type the following:

       m .

The transferred file is moved from the public directory to the current directory. Instead of using a period, you can type the full path of the directory where you want the file to go. You receive one question for each file you have received.

> **NOTE** *When you receive files from a remote system from any of the BNU (uucp) methods, the file permissions are changed to 666 (read and write by everyone). Execute permissions, if they are on, are turned off.*

Interactive File Transfer Using *ftp*

Instead of simply transferring files to a remote system, you can start an interactive session with a remote system, move around through the directory structure, and then move files across that connection in either direction. Use the ftp command to set up an interactive file transfer over Internet connections.

You can reach non-UNIX systems with ftp as well as remote UNIX systems. This is possible because ftp is part of the Internet and not specifically a UNIX command.

> **NOTE** *The cu command, which is used primarily for remote login, can also be used for interactive file transfer in a BNU connection. The cu command is described in the section "Remote Login" later in this chapter.*

After you have set up a connection to a remote system using ftp, you can do many other things across that connection besides transfer files. There are more than 50 commands you can request while you are within ftp. For example, you can run commands, delete files, and change characteristics of the ftp connection.

Figure 10.4 contains an example of an ftp session.

The following is a description of the ftp session in Figure 10.4:

1. Type **ftp wizard** from a Terminal window to start the ftp session.

2. A connection starts up to the remote system (wizard), and you are prompted to log in to the remote system by giving a user name.

   The remote system assumes that you want to log in with your local name on the remote system (mcn, in this case). Press Enter to use mcn.

Figure 10.4

An ftp session.

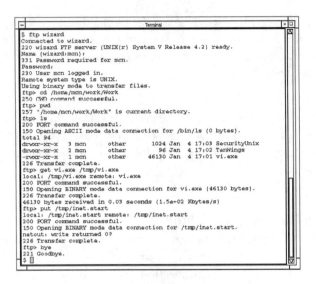

```
$ ftp wizard
Connected to wizard.
220 wizard FTP server (UNIX(r) System V Release 4.2) ready.
Name (wizard:mcn):
331 Password required for mcn.
Password:
230 User mcn logged in.
Remote system type is UNIX.
Using binary mode to transfer files.
ftp> cd /home/mcn/work/Work
250 CWD command successful.
ftp> pwd
257 "/home/mcn/work/Work" is current directory.
ftp> ls
200 PORT command successful.
150 Opening ASCII mode data connection for /bin/ls (0 bytes).
total 94
drwxr-xr-x   3 mcn      other        1024 Jan  4 17:03 SecurityUnix
drwxr-xr-x   2 mcn      other          96 Jan  4 17:02 TenWings
-rwxr-xr-x   1 mcn      other       46130 Jan  4 17:01 vi.exe
226 Transfer complete.
ftp> get vi.exe /tmp/vi.exe
local: /tmp/vi.exe remote: vi.exe
200 PORT command successful.
150 Opening BINARY mode data connection for vi.exe (46130 bytes).
226 Transfer complete.
46130 bytes received in 0.03 seconds (1.5e+02 Kbytes/s)
ftp> put /tmp/inet.start
local: /tmp/inet.start remote: /tmp/inet.start
200 PORT command successful.
150 Opening BINARY mode data connection for /tmp/inet.start.
netout: write returned 0?
226 Transfer complete.
ftp> bye
221 Goodbye.
$
```

3. Type the password for mcn (the password is not displayed as you type).

4. After you are logged in, change to the directory that contains the file you want (cd /home/mcn/work/Work). The system says that you have successfully completed the change working directory (CWD) command.

5. To verify where you are, type **pwd**; then type **ls** to show the contents of the directory.

6. To transfer the file you want (vi.exe) from the current directory on the remote system to the /tmp directory on your system, type **get vi.exe /tmp/vi.exe** and press Enter. ftp tells you that the transfer was successful, indicates the size of the transfer (46,130 bytes), and gives the amount of time for the transfer (0.3 seconds).

7. To transfer a file in the other direction (remote to local), type **put /tmp/inet.start**. This copies the file (startfile) from the /tmp directory on the local system to the current directory on the remote system (/home/mcn/work/Work). Note that if you don't give a directory name, ftp assumes the current directory.

8. To exit ftp, type **bye**. The connection is closed, and you are returned to a shell prompt on the local system.

Remote Login

From your UNIX system, you can also log in to another UNIX system. On the command line, use the `rlogin` or `cu` command to call a remote system, depending on the type of network you are using.

The `rlogin` command (which stands for remote login) lets you log in to remote UNIX systems using a TCP/IP connection. To use the `rlogin` command, open a Terminal window and enter

rlogin *system*

where *system* is replaced by the name of the remote system to which you want to log in. By default, `rlogin` tries to log you in to the remote system using your login name on the local system. So, instead of seeing a login prompt, you simply see the `Password` prompt and are expected to type in the password for your user name on the remote system. Using the `-l` option, you can have `rlogin` try to log in with a different user name.

Here are some examples of the `rlogin` command:

```
$ rlogin cactus -l mcn
$ rlogin cactus.utah.com
```

The first example tries to log in to the system named `cactus` using the login `mcn` as the remote user name. In the second example, a full domain name is used, so you can identify a system that is not in the local domain or known directly by the local domain.

 NOTE | *The* `telnet` *command is another way to log in to a remote system over the Internet. The syntax is primarily the same as it is with* `rlogin`*. Many people use* `telnet` *instead of* `rlogin` *because it is more widely available among systems that use Internet protocols.*

Running Remote Applications

When you use UNIX for networking, not only can you exchange information with remote systems, but you also can share processing power with remote systems. From the command line, you can use `rsh` (with TCP/IP) or `uux` (with BNU).

Remote execution has two major advantages over running an application locally. First, you can take advantage of the processors of other systems on the network.

You might get better performance if the other system is more powerful or less busy than yours. Second, you can take advantage of the remote system's environment. The remote application can easily read and write files from the remote file system and use the remote system's hardware (floppy drives, printers, and so on).

Using the *rsh* Command

Use the rsh command to run a command on a remote system and display its output on your system. You run rsh with options for systems and commands you want to run.

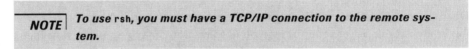

NOTE *To use* rsh, *you must have a TCP/IP connection to the remote system.*

Figure 10.5 shows some examples of rsh commands.

Figure 10.5

Some examples of the rsh command.

- In the first example in Figure 10.5, rsh connects to the system named knight and runs the uname -n command. This shows information relating to the remote system's name, release of system, and system architecture.

- In the second example, rsh runs the date command on knight but runs it as the remote user named hank, instead of using your user name.

Using the *ping* Command to Test Remote Network Connection

The ping command is used to test a remote host connection. If the host responds, ping displays a message indicating that the host is alive. Otherwise, ping displays a message that the host is unreachable. The ping utility uses a particular kind of data packet to send to a remote host and causes the remote host to respond back with a reply. This command verifies that the remote host can be accessible from a machine before time runs out waiting for the packet. The ping command also keeps a log on how well the remote network is operating.

The best way to see `ping` in action is to use the option `ping -s`. For example, the line

```
% ping -s hostname
```

displays, second by second, how the test data was sent and how it was received. No output is produced if no response is received. The `ping` command keeps a log of average round-trip time and data loss statistics, if any.

Here is a partial response to a `ping -s` command sent to the host `goldendog`:

```
% ping  -s  goldendog
64 bytes from goldendog (168.18.130.236): icmp_seq=0. time=4. ms
64 bytes from goldendog (168.18.130.236): icmp_seq=1. time=1. ms
64 bytes from goldendog (168.18.130.236): icmp_seq=2. time=1. ms
64 bytes from goldendog (168.18.130.236): icmp_seq=3. time=1. ms
64 bytes from goldendog (168.18.130.236): icmp_seq=4. time=1. ms
64 bytes from goldendog (168.18.130.236): icmp_seq=5. time=1. ms
64 bytes from goldendog (168.18.130.236): icmp_seq=44. time=1. ms
64 bytes from goldendog (168.18.130.236): icmp_seq=45. time=1. ms

-------------------------------goldendog PING statistics----------
----------------
56 packets transmitted, 56 packets received, 0% packet loss, round-trip
   time(ms) min/avg/max=1/1/2
```

The `ping` command summarized the results with a final line of statistics at the end.

A simple `ping` to a host name in Ohio produced the following:

```
% ping bobcat.ent.ohiou.edu
bobcat.ent.ohiou.edu is alive
```

Accessing Remote File Systems Using *mount* and *umount*

Sharing files among machines on the same network is one of the advantages of UNIX networking. File sharing is built on the Network File System (NFS) facility. NFS is the most popular file-sharing facility used between UNIX systems, and it is also implemented in other systems.

NFS is more flexible, though less intuitive, than the other file-sharing systems. With file sharing, connecting a remote file system is more of an administrative function. Using the `mount` command, you can see what file systems are shared, and by changing your `vfstab`, you can connect the selected file system to any point in your local file system. Connecting a remote file system locally is referred to as *mounting* (the same system term used to describe connecting local file systems).

If, for example, you wanted to share applications among a group of systems, you could mount a directory of applications on a directory called /usr/localapps on each of the systems. Users on each system could add /usr/localapps to their paths so that they could run commands from that directory by simply typing commands from a Terminal window. As applications are added or removed from the directory, all systems immediately get the changes without having to make changes to all the systems.

When you try to mount the remote file system, it is checked to determine whether the remote system will allow your system to mount it. The remote file system can be shared as read-only or read/write, which limits access to the entire file system. After the remote file system is connected, however, the individual user permissions determine whether a user can read or write files to folders in the file system.

Connecting (Mounting) a Remote File System

To find all remote file systems that are actually mounted on your system, use the command mount and press Enter:

```
% mount
#device     device      mount     FS      fsck      mount      mount
#to mount   to fsck     point     type    pass      at boot
   options

/usr on /dev/dsk/c0t3d0s7 read/write/setuid on Sat Jul 22 10:31:26 1995
/proc on /proc read/write/setuid on Sat Jul 22 10:31:26 1995
/dev/fd on fd read/write/setuid on Sat Jul 22 10:31:26 1995
/var on /dev/dsk/c0t3d0s4 read/write/setuid on Sat Jul 22 10:31:26 1995
/tmp on swap read/write on Sat Jul 22 10:31:28 1995
/opt on /dev/dsk/c0t3d0s6 setuid/read/write on Sat Jul 22 10:31:28 1995
/usr/openwin on /dev/dsk/c0t3d0s5 setuid/read/write on Sat Jul 22
   10:31:28 1995
/home/a_s on grits:/home/a_s read/write/remote on Sat Jul 22
   10:31:48 1995
/home/coba on grits:/home/coba read/write/remote on Sat Jul 22
   10:31:48 1995
/home/coe on grits:/home/coe read/write/remote on Sat Jul 22
   10:31:48 1995
/home/con on grits:/home/con read/write/remote on Sat Jul 22
   10:31:48 1995
/home/f_a on grits:/home/f_a read/write/remote on Sat Jul 22
   10:31:49 1995
/home/other on grits:/home/other read/write/remote on Sat Jul 22
   10:31:49 1995
```

To understand the listing, take a quick look at the last line, which indicates the following:

1. /home/other is currently mounted.

2. The mounting device is from `grits:/home/other`.

3. Permissions available are `read/write/remote`.

The `mount` command with no options displays what's in the file `mnttab` (for "mounted table"), which cannot be edited by an editor. If `mount` is invoked with an option, it checks the file `/etc/vfstab` (its name suggests "virtual file system defaults") and supplies the requested information.

The `vfstab` file is a text file that can be edited by a `vi` editor, for example. The following is an example of a `/etc/vfstab` file:

```
% cat vfstab
#device          device         mount            FS      fsck      mount      mount
#to mount        to fsck        point            type    pass      at boot
   options
#

#/dev/dsk/c1d0s2     /dev/rdsk/c1d0s2      /usr              ufs      1
   yes  -
/proc               -                     /proc             proc     -
   no   -
fd                  -                     /dev/fd           fd       -
   no   -
swap                -                     /tmp              tmpfs    -
   yes  -
/dev/dsk/c0t3d0s0   /dev/rdsk/c0t3d0s0    /                 ufs      1
   no   -
/dev/dsk/c0t3d0s7   /dev/rdsk/c0t3d0s7    /usr              ufs      1
   no   -
/dev/dsk/c0t3d0s4   /dev/rdsk/c0t3d0s4    /var              ufs      1
   no   -
/dev/dsk/c0t3d0s6   /dev/rdsk/c0t3d0s6    /opt              ufs      2
   yes  -
/dev/dsk/c0t3d0s5   /dev/rdsk/c0t3d0s5    /usr/openwin      ufs      2
   yes  -
/dev/dsk/c0t3d0s1   -                     -                 swap     -
   no   -
grits:/home/a_s     -                     /home/a_s         nfs      -
   yes  -
grits:/home/coba    -                     /home/coba        nfs      -
   yes  -
grits:/home/coe     -                     /home/coe         nfs      -
   yes  -
grits:/home/con     -                     /home/con         nfs      -
   yes  -
grits:/home/f_a     -                     /home/f_a         nfs      -
   yes  -
grits:/home/other   -                     /home/other       nfs      -
   yes  -
grits:/usr/local    -                     /usr/local        nfs      -
   yes  -
grits:/var/spool/mail -                   /var/spool/mail   nfs      -
   yes  -
```

> **NOTE** *If you look at your own `vfstab` file, it won't be formatted as nicely as this file. In a real `vfstab` file, each field is separated by one tab, and if the information in a field is long, the fields don't line up with each other. The sample file was beautified for clarity.*

The - indicates that a particular field doesn't apply. The last line indicates the following:

1. `grits:/var/spool/mail` is the mounting device: a partition of `grits` that includes only `/var/spool/mail`.

2. The device will be mounted at the mount point `/var/spool/mail`.

3. The `fstype` is `nfs` (Network File System).

4. The directory will be mounted.

5. Any - does not apply.

To effectively mount a partition or a tool called `matlab` from a machine called `gumbo` to your machine, follow these steps:

1. Become a superuser on your machine (issue the command `su` and supply a password).

2. Use the `vi` editor to edit the file `vfsttab` and be in input mode. Then type

   gumbo:/usr/matlab - /usr/matlab - yes

3. Quit `vi` with `:wq`.

4. Quit from being a superuser.

5. Restart your machine.

After rebooting the machine, type **mount** at the prompt, and `mount`'s listing will indicate that `matlab` is now mounted on your machine.

Assume that a user is able to get a remote copy of `matlab` installed directly on his or her machine. The need to keep `matlab` mounted now becomes unnecessary. A `umount` command allows a given file that was shared at a mounting point to cease to exist. The following steps are needed to successfully execute a `umount` command:

1. Become a superuser (using the `su` command).

2. Issue the command

```
# umount matlab
```

The `matlab` tool can no longer be launched from the local machine. But rebooting the local machine will ensure at boot time that `matlab` will be mounted again. To prohibit `matlab` from being mounted when the local machine is rebooted, you need to edit the `vfstab` file, deleting the line previously added.

The same steps to edit `vftsab` for mounting can be repeated for "unmounting":

1. Use the `vi` editor in command mode to delete the last line of the file (the line that talks about `matlab`).

2. Exit `vi` using `:wq`.

3. Quit from being superuser.

4. Boot the machine.

After restarting the machine, the command `mount` lists the partitions without mentioning `matlab`.

TCP/IP Setup

TCP/IP administration can range from simply adding system names and addresses to your system to managing multiple systems across a variety of physical and logical networks.

Before you try to administer your own TCP/IP configuration, however, there are a few simple concepts you should understand. You have to understand system names and network addresses even in the most basic TCP/IP network.

Understanding System Names, Domain Names, and Network Addresses

TCP/IP uses the name you assign your system at installation time as your system name for providing TCP/IP services. If someone wants to send electronic mail to you or run a remote application on your system, that person would use this name to contact you. Each system name also is associated with a four-part IP address.

Using System Names and Domain Names

If you are connected to the Internet, your system name can become part of a larger domain structure that allows systems from anywhere in the world to communicate with you. You can request an Internet domain name from the Network Information Center, 14200 Park Meadow Dr., Suite 200, Chantilly, VA 22021. An example of a domain name you might be assigned is the following:

```
pinky.COM
```

Your domain name in this example is pinky, and the root level domain is COM (which is the commercial domain). Within your domain, you can assign a set of names to the systems you control. For example, system names red, white, and blue in this domain have the following full names:

```
red.pinky.COM
white.pinky.COM
blue.pinky.COM
```

Within your domain (among those three systems), you can use the system name to contact them. To send mail to these systems over the Internet, use the full domain name and attach the destination name. For example, if someone sends mail to a user named chuck on one of your systems, the full name might look like the following:

```
chuck@red.pinky.COM
```

Chapter 7, "Electronic Mail," provides more details on domains.

Setting up domain name service is beyond the scope of this book. See the TCP/IP Administration manual that comes with your UNIX system for information on setting up domain name service.

Understanding Network Addresses

TCP/IP uses a four-part address for identifying each system on the Internet. As with domain names, TCP/IP network addresses are assigned by the Network Information Center to ensure unique addresses throughout the entire Internet.

If you have a small installation (fewer than 254 hosts) at your location, you will probably be assigned a class C network address. In a class C address, the first three parts of the 32-bit IP address (the first 24 bits) are the network number and the last part (the last 8 bits) is the host address. A class C address also begins with a number between 192 and 223. The following example is a class C address:

```
200.32.47.1
```

The network number assigned is 200.32.47, and the host number is 1. You can assign other host numbers among the systems at your location as the following: 200.32.47.2, 200.32.47.3, 200.32.47.4, and so on. (You can't use 0 or 256 as host numbers because those numbers are reserved.)

For class A and class B addresses, the network numbers are shorter, and many more host numbers are available. Class A addresses begin with numbers between 0 and 127 and use only the first part (8 bits) as the network number. Class B addresses begin with numbers between 128 and 191 and use the first two parts (16 bits) as the network number.

By default, TCP/IP assumes that all hosts on your network can be reached on the same physical network. If this is not true, you have to configure your system to do *subnetworking*. Subnetworking tells your system to take part of the host number as the network number, thereby allowing more physical networks for your network number, but fewer hosts within each network.

If you have configured your set of systems to do subnetworking, you also must have one or more systems connecting your several physical networks. A system set up to connect many networks and pass messages between them is called a *router* (or sometimes a gateway).

For further information on setting up routers and subnetworking, see the TCP/IP Administration manual that comes with your version of UNIX.

Exercises

1. Assume that you have executed an nslookup command. Here is a response to the nslookup command:

```
Server: moniker.valdosta.peachnet.edu
Address:168.18.130.100
>
```

Respond by typing **set all** at the prompt (>). (Remember that the name of the server and the address of the server differ from one network to another. The response on your machine is different.)

   a. Explain what is meant in the preceding response by the word Server.

   b. Explain the four numbers listed next to the word Address in that response.

   c. Suppose that one of the machines on your network is called random and you are to check on it. What would you type to find the commands available to you. How would you find information on random?

   d. Assume that you answered the preceding question and you issued the command to get information on a machine called victor. Here is the response:

```
Name: victor.valdosta.peachnet.edu
Address: 168.18.130.241
```

Why do these two servers share the same first three numbers? What if the last number was the same? What impact would that have on the network?

2. Assume that, after following the material in this chapter, you now know how to mount remote partitions on your file server. Specify the file name that contains the mounted partitions on your system. How would you add the following partition from a file server called grits to your machine?

```
"/usr/local"
```

3. Discuss the importance of mounting partitions on your local machine from a remote machine. Assume that you typed the command mount on your system and got the following listing:

```
% mount
/usr/local on grits:/usr/local read/write/remote on Sat Jul 22
    10:31:49 1995
/var/spool/mail on grits:/var/spool/mail read/write/remote on Sat
    Jul 22 10:31:49 1995
```

a. Explain in detail the rows of the listing. You could start with the last line as an example:

```
/var/spool/mail on grits:/var/spool/mail read/write/remote
```

b. What does the first /usr/local of the first line specify? Is this partition on the grits file server or on the local machine? What are the permissions that are accessible on the local machine towards /usr/local?

c. Assume that you wanted to unmount /usr/local but mistyped the partition:

```
%umount /usr/local
Warning: /usr/local not in mnttab
Warning: /usr/local no such file or directory
```

Explain both warnings and why they are relevant to umount.

d. Give the command that would unmount the /usr/local directory from the local machine.

e. Assume that you unmounted the directory /usr/local/, which contained the ftptool tool, and tried to use ftp. What happens?

f. Give the command that will remount the directory that was just unmounted in the preceding exercise (#e).

11

UNIX System Administration

Topics Covered

- Site Preparation
- System Maintenance
- Handling Problems and Repairs
- Addressing Computer Needs
- Starting the Computer
- Shutting Down the Computer
- Accessing the System
- Configuring Terminals
- Creating User Accounts
- Preparing Media for Data Storage
- System Backups

- Configuring Printers

- Managing System Operations

- Monitoring System Performance

- Getting Advanced Help

The responsibilities of the system administrator vary from system to system. On larger systems, the tasks can be divided among several people. Some smaller systems do not require a full-time system administrator, and in such instances, a user is assigned the tasks of the administrator. In a network environment, a system may be administered over the network by a network administrator. In either case, the role of the system administrator is very important and comes with a formidable list of system-level responsibilities.

Managing and maintaining the UNIX installation requires a good deal of time and skill. The installation of additional hardware, the tracking of software updates, modifying the kernel to ensure the support of new devices, and anticipating user needs are some of the tedious tasks.

This chapter takes a closer look at the system administrator's responsibilities and some of the UNIX commands that are used to handle them.

The fundamental duties are the same on all systems. The primary tasks fall into the following categories, each of which is discussed in detail:

- Installation of the computer and new software as needed

- System maintenance, including system backups

- Diagnosis and arrangement for the repair of computer problems

- Anticipation of the needs of the computer and the users

Along with the job of performing the primary tasks, the system administrator is expected to be knowledgeable about the computer, the version of UNIX it is running, and the principal activities that take place on the computer. The administrator also acts as a resource for the system.

Site Preparation

Some system administrators have the opportunity to be involved in the early stages of installing a new computer. This often includes the preparation of the site before the computer is delivered. For the installation of a small computer, is a sturdy table in a room with normal air flow all that is needed? When large computers are involved, site preparation is a bit more complex. The following is a list of some factors to consider:

- *Machine dimensions.* You must know the dimensions of the new machine so that you can best plan where it physically fits at your site.

- *Access.* It is best to put your machine where you can easily gain access to it. There will be occasions when you need to add a cable or access a connector. You want to have the machine situated where you can access these areas without moving the computer. Leave as much room as possible around the system so you can work comfortably.

- *Electrical power.* You should give special consideration to an uninterruptable power supply (UPS), which provides power to a computer for a short period of time (usually up to an hour) if the electricity goes out. Surge protectors also provide an important safeguard.

- *Ventilation and cooling.* Place the computer in a well-ventilated room. Each manufacturer specifies temperature guidelines. Keep in mind that the larger the computer, the more heat it generates. So a room that may appear to be adequately ventilated will warm up considerably once the computer is activated.

- *Humidity.* Each manufacturer specifies an acceptable range. If the humidity level is unacceptable, you may have to install a humidifier or dehumidifier.

- *Supplies.* At the time you purchase the computer, you should also purchase the necessary supplies. Supplies include blank disks and tapes, printer paper, cleaners, printer ribbons or toner cartridges, spare cables, and essential tools such as a screwdriver.

- *Documentation.* You should always have the documentation that came with the computer, a copy of your service contract, and the telephone number for technical support.

- *Console.* Take extra consideration when planning where to locate the console. Place it in a convenient and comfortable site. As the system administrator, you may spend a great deal of time at the console.

- *Security.* Select an area that is secure from theft and unwanted access to the information contained on the system. Find ways to access the room, or mount the system to prevent its removal. Many computer rooms are equipped with a combination lock and require special keys or pass cards for entrance.

253

11

- *Safety.* Select an area where the computer will be located so that it is safe from fire and water damage. Consult your local building codes to determine what equipment (such as smoke detectors and alarms) are necessary for your area.

- *Ergonomics.* When planning your computer area, think about ergonomics, such as table height, seating, and ventilation. These can make the system easier to use for long periods of time.

Once these factors are considered, take time to plan for growth. As you plan where your system will be placed, consider how you would handle the addition of more disks, a CD-ROM drive, or a tape drive.

System Maintenance

After the computer is in place, the system administrator should plan for the tasks necessary to keep the system running. Following are some helpful tips:

- *Regularly clean the equipment filters and disk drive heads.* Dirt on heads makes reading and writing data unreliable. A small handheld vacuum cleaner is a useful tool for cleaning the computer air filters. A head-cleaning disk can keep the disk drives operating well. The amount of dust you can see on the outside of the equipment often does not indicate the amount on the inside; you should check and clean the equipment on a regular schedule.

- *The system administrator should regularly check the hardware connections, concentrating on the cables and their connections.* Most cables are fastened with screws that make them stay tightly in place.

- *The system administrator should keep a log book and record everything that is done on the system.* This book should list backups, service calls, the name of the technician who worked on the computer, installation of new hardware and software, and any problems or crashes. It should also contain a complete description of the peripheral devices that are connected to the system, including terminals and modems. This log is good for diagnosing problems and assisting a new system administrator when taking over.

- *Keep any and all magnets out of the computer room.* Although just having a magnet in the same room as computer disks won't cause damage, it is still dangerous. Someone could lay a magnet on a disk without thinking, thereby damaging or erasing the contents.

Handling Problems and Repairs

A system administrator cannot handle and resolve every problem that occurs. For this reason, arranging support contracts on hardware and software is very important.

Support contracts can include on-site support from a vendor or third-party support company. By working with contracted support personnel, the administrator can assist in diagnosing the problem and then rely on the expertise of the support personnel to solve it.

When a system administrator is called in to diagnose a problem, he or she will require some information about the problem. The following list includes the information the system administrator should have before calling for help.

- What program or programs were running on the system at the time of the problem

- What versions of the operating system and programs are on the system

- A description of the hardware configuration of the system, and logs of recent changes in the system (this information is often found in the system log book)

- A full description of the error or problem

- How frequently the problem occurs

- A method to reproduce the problem, if possible

Addressing Computer Needs

The system administrator must also manage and allocate system resources. As the number of users increases, or the amount of work the current users do on the system increases, the administrator should consider the expansion of file systems, the addition of printing devices, an increase in mass storage capacity, and the possible addition of communication lines. All these considerations depend on the needs of the users of the system.

For example, if a new group of users will start working on the computer system, the system administrator must make estimates on how much disk space these users will consume and how much they will load down the system. If the current disks do not have enough space for the expected usage or the system is already heavily loaded, the system administrator must plan for the purchase of additional disk space or a more powerful system. If extra space is not added, the system at best will slow down for everyone because there is not enough memory and disk space to run efficiently.

Starting the Computer

The term for starting the computer is the *boot* procedure. In most cases, turning on the computer causes it to go through the boot procedure. Although there is rarely a need for human intervention, the system administrator may be asked to enter the current time and date.

The following steps trace the boot process so that you can get an idea of what goes on behind the scenes:

1. The *bootstrap program*, a very short, simple program located on block 0 of the first hard disk, is read and executed by the computer.

2. The UNIX kernel loads the bootstrap program into the computer. The kernel is stored in a file in the root directory under the name /unix, /xenix, or some similar name.

3. The kernel configures itself by setting up its memory and testing for the presence of various types of hardware.

4. The *init process* is started by the kernel and controls the creation of login processes as long as UNIX is running. Once this is accomplished, the kernel has finished its role in starting the system. The rest of the procedure is controlled by init.

5. init also starts various *daemons* (background processes) along with a shell to execute the initialization script or scripts. Although the names of the scripts vary with the type of UNIX system, /etc/rc (described shortly) is common. Scripts /etc/rc0 through /etc/rc6 are also common.

6. Finally, init switches to multiuser mode and begins starting gettys, which in turn enables the users to log in.

A special shell script called /etc/rc is run by the init process. (rc stands for run commands; the exact name of the script or scripts varies on different versions of UNIX.) Here are some tasks that rc performs:

- Loading the system date and time. Depending on the system, rc may take the date and time from a battery-operated clock or ask the user to enter it.

- Using fsck to check the file systems for any problems.

- Mounting file systems on the appropriate directories.

- Starting daemons such as print spoolers and `cron` (which can run programs automatically at specific times).

- Initializing network services.

- Running the preserve program, which recovers any work in progress in `vi` if the system goes down.

- Deleting all files in the `/tmp` and `/usr/tmp` directories. Because these directories are intended for temporary files only, most UNIX systems clean them out each time the system starts.

System administrators can add their own command to `rc` to perform security checks or other tasks that are useful and should take place as the system boots.

Shutting Down the Computer

The practice of turning on a computer running UNIX in the morning and then turning it off at night is not common. Unlike most PCs, computers that have UNIX as their operating system are designed to be turned on and run continuously until a problem occurs. You should not turn off a UNIX computer by simply shutting off the power, because the UNIX system is always in the process of performing tasks whether there are users on it or not. To turn off the computer, you must let it finish any activity in progress and prepare itself to be turned off.

Most versions of UNIX use the `shutdown` command. The format of the command varies from one version of UNIX to another. The typical command, for System V, is

```
shutdown -i0 -g300
```

The `-i0` option requests a full shutdown, and the `-g300` option gives a five-minute grace period to have users finish their work and log off. Your UNIX system may have different options for the `shutdown` command. Check your system documentation for the proper shutdown options.

For many systems, `shutdown` is a shell script that performs the following tasks:

1. Disables logins to prevent new users from logging in.

2. Sends out a message to all users at regular intervals, urging them to finish what they are working on and log off.

3. When the grace period expires, the system daemons shut down.

4. Writes all the temporary information kept in memory to disk and closes all files. This ensures that all data is stored safely and the file systems are organized.

5. Signals the init program to terminate. At this point, UNIX has completed the shutdown process.

> **NOTE** *The time period from the end of the grace period to the actual halting of the CPU is about one minute or less.*

Accessing the System

The UNIX system provides built-in methods to keep the activities of users separate and distinct. One of the responsibilities of the system administrator is to assign a login name and set up an account for each user. The account is a record of who the user is and what he or she can access on the system. In most systems, each user is assigned a password in conjunction with the login name. The password serves as a verification of the user's login name.

Even the system administrator must have an account on the system. This account is set up in the system administrator's name. In addition to the regular account, the system administrator must also have access to the root or superuser account.

The root login is different from other user logins in two ways:

- root is not subject to any UNIX security. root has access to all files no matter what the permissions are set to. The only files that root cannot read are encrypted files. However, even encrypted files can be deleted by the root account.

- root is able to perform some operations that deny all other users access (for example, the installation of a new device or a system shutdown).

Obviously, the root account is very powerful. Along with this power comes responsibility. A single command that root executes can destroy a disk or crash a system. Most of the system administration tasks can be performed under your regular system administration login name. It is suggested that the root account be used sparingly and that extreme caution be taken when using the root login.

> **NOTE** *As with any login, the* root *login has the option of a password. With regular user accounts, a forgotten password can be handled by the system administrator. If the* root *account password is forgotten, there are serious consequences. In some instances, you can be locked out of the system and be forced to reinstall the operating system. This is a very inconvenient process because it also requires reconfiguring the system, reinstalling software, and so forth. Just copying the system from a backup tape won't work because you no longer have the* root *password. So take your passwords seriously. Don't forget them and don't let other people know what they are.*

Configuring Terminals

UNIX systems today generally support two main categories of terminals. The first is the system console, which is required for the system to operate, and the second is the user terminal, which is optional.

The system console is often a graphical terminal that can run a windowing system, such as X Window, and is used when the system is booted. On many small UNIX systems, the console is often the only terminal on the system, and it is located on the desk of the main user. Because the console is configured when the system is installed, system users do not usually need to know how to configure it.

For each additional person who wants to use the system directly, a terminal must be added to the system. The system must be given information about the terminal. On most UNIX systems, this requires that you enter information in several files in the /etc system directory.

Depending on the version of UNIX you are using, different files need to be modified to configure terminals. Modern versions of Berkeley UNIX use the file /etc/ttys, whereas UNIX System V uses the files /etc/inittab, /etc/gettytab, and /etc/gettydefs. The names and formats of these files vary depending on the exact version of UNIX you are running, so consult your system documentation before modifying any of these files.

Creating User Accounts

Before a user can be given an account, the system administrator needs to find out what group the user belongs to, what the user needs access to, what degree of access is needed, and where the user's home directory resides.

11

To successfully create an account, the system administrator needs to have special knowledge of the file systems, the password file, and the group file.

The *passwd* and *shadow* Files

The password file in most System V versions of UNIX is a combination of two files: /etc/passwd and /etc/shadow. The passwd file does not contain the password; instead, it points to the shadow file, which contains the encrypted login passwords (see Figures 11.1 and 11.2).

Figure 11.1

Contents of a passwd file.

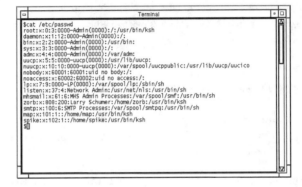

```
$cat /etc/passwd
root:x:0:3:0000-Admin(0000):/:/usr/bin/ksh
daemon:x:1:12:0000-Admin(0000):/:
bin:x:2:2:0000-Admin(0000):/usr/bin:
sys:x:3:3:0000-Admin(0000):/:
adm:x:4:4:0000-Admin(0000):/var/adm:
uucp:x:5:5:0000-uucp(0000):/usr/lib/uucp:
nuucp:x:10:10:0000-uucp(0000):/var/spool/uucppublic:/usr/lib/uucp/uucico
nobody:x:60001:60001:uid no body:/:
noaccess:x:60002:60002:uid no access:/:
lp:x:7:9:0000-LP(0000):/var/spool/lp:/sbin/sh
listen:x:37:4:Network Admin:/usr/net/nls:/usr/bin/sh
mhsmail:x:61:6:MHS Admin Processes:/var/spool/smf:/usr/bin/sh
zorb:x:808:200:Larry Schumer:/home/zorb:/usr/bin/ksh
smtp:x:100:6:SMTP Processes:/var/spool/smtpq:/usr/bin/sh
map:x:101:1::/home/map:/usr/bin/ksh
spike:x:102:1::/home/spike:/usr/bin/ksh
$
```

Figure 11.2

Encrypted passwords in the shadow file.

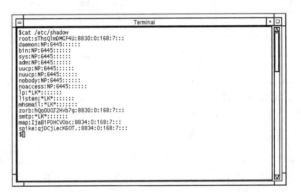

```
$cat /etc/shadow
root:sThsQlmDMGF4U:8830:0:168:7:::
daemon:NP:6445::::::
bin:NP:6445::::::
sys:NP:6445::::::
adm:NP:6445::::::
uucp:NP:6445::::::
nuucp:NP:6445::::::
nobody:NP:6445::::::
noaccess:NP:6445::::::
lp:*LK*:::::::
listen:*LK*:::::::
mhsmail:*LK*:::::::
zorb:hQoOUQT2Hvb7g:8830:0:168:7:::
smtp:*LK*:::::::
map:IjaB1PDHCVOoc:8834:0:168:7:::
spike:qjDCjLecK6OT.:8834:0:168:7:::
$
```

No matter what the length of the password represented, the encrypted password is always 13 characters long. UNIX has the means to encrypt a password in 4,096 different ways. Therefore, if two users have the identical password, their encrypted passwords look completely different.

Some systems do not require the use or assignment of a password. In such instances, the password field is empty and is displayed empty. The user is not required to supply a password to log in.

> **NOTE** *A system administrator is the only person allowed to modify the password and shadow files; however, because so many UNIX commands depend on the information contained in these files, all users must be able to read them. Because the passwords are encrypted, reading the files does not reveal the users' passwords.*

The *group* File

Groups of users, the group name, and the numerical group id are listed in the group file (/etc/group in most UNIX versions). Each line in the group file contains four fields, such as the following:

```
documentation:NONE:330:amanda,vinnie,nick,rick
```

The first field is the name of the group (documentation). The second field is the encrypted password; anyone who knows the password can become a member of the group. This example has the word NONE, indicating that there is no valid password for this group. This also limits the members of the group to the users listed. The group's numerical id is 330. The fourth field lists the members of the group.

Adding New Users

As system administrator, part of your job is to add new users to the system and set up their accounts. This process takes place after the terminal is connected. You must create a home directory for the user and modify several files. For example, suppose that Amanda M. User has just joined your group as a documentation editor. To complete the process of adding her to your system, follow these steps:

1. Select a location for the home directory. Because there may be several disks connected to the system, you decide where to place Amanda's home directory. Some factors to consider when making your decision are what file system has the most available space, where the other documentation accounts reside, and what area of documentation she is working in. In this case, suppose that you decided on /usr3 file system.

2. Modify the password file. The password file must contain a line for each user. This line contains information required by the system. For Amanda, the line looks like this:

```
amanda::3013:240:Amanda M. User:/usr3/amanda:/bin/ksh
```

11

The number in the third field, 3013, is the numeric user id. This number can be selected from any number that is not already in use. The second number (in the fourth field) is the numerical group id, which can be obtained from the /etc/group file and is associated with the group that Amanda is assigned to. The second field is the encrypted password. In this instance, the second field is blank because there is no password assigned for Amanda to log in. The next step explains how to assign a password.

3. Assign a password using the UNIX passwd command. This command is entered at the system prompt, and the system administrator enters the assigned password. The system administrator instructs the new user to commit this password to memory or to change it to something more familiar using the passwd command.

   When you use the passwd command, the system prompts you for your current password. In this case, the user has no password, so you are not asked. Then you are prompted for the new password. To make sure you typed it correctly, the program prompts you to reenter the new password.

   Once the password is entered, the line in the password file changes and now contains an encrypted password:

   ```
   amanda:1VPbSUWAA.8iA:3013:240: Amanda M.User:/usr3/amanda:/bin/ksh
   ```

4. Modify the /etc/group file. In this step, Amanda's name is added to the list of users for her group in the /etc/group file. A new line must be added for the group if Amanda is the first member of a new group.

5. Use the UNIX mkdir command to create a home directory for Amanda. Amanda should be the owner of the directory. To make her the owner, use the chown command. Next use the chgrp command to assign the directory to Amanda's group, and use the chmod command to set the permissions appropriately (probably using 755). Here are these steps:

   ```
   # mkdir /usr3/amanda
   # chown amanda /usr3/amanda
   # chmod 755 /usr3/amanda
   ```

6. Create a .profile file. The .profile contains all the information that is specific to an individual user. This file can be copied from another .profile and customized to the specific needs of the user. For the most part, this file should contain the necessities. Customization can be done by Amanda.

7. Configure /etc/inittab or /etc/ttys. Depending on the version of UNIX (UNIX System V uses inittab and Berkeley UNIX uses ttys), an entry must be made to one of these files to make the terminal prompt for a login.

This may not be necessary if the terminal was in use before Amanda took ownership.

Most systems have a tool that is available to perform these tasks. These tools vary. UNIX V System 4 (or SVR4), for example, lets you add a user just by using the adduser command. useradd has the following common options:

Option	Description
-c *comment*	Short description of the user's login; also the user's full name.
-d *dir*	The home directory of the new user. Its default is set to base_dir/login.
-e *expire*	Specifies the expiration date for a login.
-g *group*	Specifies the new user's primary group and is usually a name such as "doc," "admin," and so on.
-m	Creates the user home directory if it doesn't already exist.
-s *shell*	Full pathname of the program used as the user's shell on login. If it is empty, it defaults to /sbin/sh.
-u *uid*	The UID of the new user, usually the chronological number after the number assigned to the last-added user.
-D	Displays the default values: group other (GID of 1) base_dir /home skel_dir /etc/skel shell /sbin/sh inactive 0 expire Null (unset)
-b	base_dir: the default directory for the system if -d dir is not specified.

11

The general format of a useradd command is

```
% useradd [options] login
```

where *login* is the user login name. The command

```
% useradd -m -d /home -g 200 -c "George Meghabghab" gmeghab
```

adds a user with a home directory home and a group that belongs to number 200. The full name is commented out as George Meghabghab, and the login name is gmeghab. After the user gmeghab is added, the command passwd is issued to create a new password.

Deleting Users

It is sometimes necessary to delete users from the system. People may transfer, leave the company, or stop using the computer on the job. When a person leaves the system, they usually leave their work behind. The system administrator can choose to disable the login by placing a word, such as VOID, NOLOGIN, or GONE, in the password field of the line in the /etc/passwd file. This prevents anyone from logging in with that particular login.

There may be times when the system administrator has to completely remove a user from the system. In this case, take the following steps:

1. Keep backup files of the user's home directory. This is a precautionary measure so that the files can be retrieved later if needed. (For example, the user may have had the only copy of an important document in his or her home directory.)

2. Remove the home directory. After the backup is complete, remove the home directory and all existing files. This task can be accomplished with the use of the rm -r command.

3. Remove the entry from the password file. Enter the password file in the edit mode, find the entry for the user, and delete it.

4. Modify the /etc/group file. Enter the /etc/group file in edit mode. Search for all the entries that contain the user's name. Delete the user's name from these entries and, in cases where the user is the only member of the group, delete the group as well.

5. Modify the /etc/inittab file. If no one is going to use the terminal, delete it from the /etc/inittab file.

These steps can be accomplished in SunOS 5.4 through the userdel command. The general format of a userdel is

```
% userdel -r login
```

where login is the same login used in the adduser command. The -r in the command means that the user's home directory will be removed from the system. The next command deletes gmeghab from the system:

```
% userdel -r gmeghab
0
%
```

To verify that the command `userdel` exited properly, check the following exit value list:

Value	Meaning
0	Success
2	Invalid command syntax
6	The login to be removed doesn't exist
8	The login to be removed is in use
10	The login is removed but the `/etc/group` file is not updated
12	Cannot remove the home directory

A user name can be taken off temporarily for a variety of reasons:

- *Disciplinary reason*. The user did not follow some of the guidelines for using his or her account.

- *Miscellaneous*. The user is temporarily absent from school because of sickness.

The `usermod` command allows a temporary freeze of the user's access to a particular account. The general format of `usermod` is

```
% usermod [options] login
```

where *options* are the same options used in `useradd`. To freeze `gmeghab`'s account, for example, an expiration date can be stamped on the account:

```
% usermod -e "/08/31/95" gmeghab
```

This would deny `gmeghab` access to his account until August 31, 1995.

Preparing Media for Data Storage

Copying files from a hard disk to any form of media requires some preparation. For example, before a disk can be used with UNIX, it must be formatted so that it can store files. The formatting process divides a disk's tracks into sections called *sectors*. The UNIX kernel can translate a file's directory location to a sector or series of sectors. When a disk is new, it has no sector divisions. The formatting process can be compared to drawing horizontal lines on a blank sheet of

11

paper. The formatting process organizes a disk's blank surfaces into clearly divided areas where information can be written.

Having a number of formatted disks available, especially for creating backups, is a good idea.

System Backups

The practice of creating system backups is critical to the system's well-being. No matter how careful users are, there are times when a file is accidentally destroyed; without a backup copy, endless hours of work can be lost. A backup is simply a copy of the files that exists on the system. These file copies are stored on a tape or disk and can be restored (copied back to the system's hard disk in the event that a user finds a file missing or damaged).

Files may be lost as a result of the following:

- Hardware failures, especially disk drives

- Bad disks

- Program bugs

- Human error, when a person deletes the wrong file

- Computer viruses, worms, or theft

- Power surges, fire, or lightning

An unwritten rule is that on large systems, the system administrator is responsible for making backups. Usually on PCs, or small UNIX systems, users are required to make their own backups.

The system administrator decides how often backups are made and what medium is used. This decision comes after a careful evaluation of the daily workload and the most economical type of medium.

Selecting Backup Media

The primary storage devices for UNIX systems are fixed or hard disk drives. The system administrator must select an alternative, removable medium on which to store the backed-up files. The UNIX environment allows for the use of three types of media: floppy disks, tapes, and hard disks. The most economical is the floppy disk. Most computer systems come with a floppy disk drive, and the cost of the floppy disk is minimal. The disadvantage to using floppy disks is that the process is rather slow. Tapes are another alternative. While tapes are more expensive, they are more convenient. The most convenient of all media is the hard disk drive; however, this medium is the most expensive. Nonetheless, many systems have more than one hard drive and storing backup files on another hard drive is worthwhile. Some systems use a *mirroring* technique in which two hard drives are written to simultaneously. If one drive goes down, the other one is available with the same data.

> **NOTE** *When using hard disks as a backup medium, you can copy the data either to a second disk drive that is permanently attached to the system or to a removable drive. Most modern UNIX systems also allow you to use a writable optical drive (similar to a CD-ROM) as a backup medium.*

As system administrator, you must choose the best backup medium that your budget can accommodate.

Scheduling Backups

UNIX "stamps" newly created or recently modified files with the current time and date. The time and date is used by most system administrators to determine which files to include in a particular backup. Because user files can change daily, these should be backed up daily. System files do not change often and do not need to be backed up as often as data files.

The system administrator must determine the best time to perform the backup. Usually, an automatic process is established that uses a schedule to perform backups when the system is not in use. The best time is normally at night when the user load is minimal or nonexistent.

> **NOTE** *Although it is reassuring to know that regular backups are made of the data files, it is important to remember that there are no guarantees that a deleted or overwritten file can be restored from the backup. If a file exists on the backup, the backup file is an older version of the file and may not contain the most recent changes.*

11

Decisions on a backup schedule are best left to the system administrator who has weighed the pros and cons of more frequent backups versus less frequent backups. Backups cost time and money. Some factors that may aid the system administrator in his or her decision are the following:

- *Risk factors*. How reliable is the hardware on your system? Are your programs usually bug-free? What is the knowledge level of your users? Is your electrical power consistent? Any of these questions that produce a "yes" signifies that you are not in need of frequent backups. Each "no" answer increases your need for frequent backups.

- *Cost factors.* What would be the cost of data loss? If the data lost were sales invoices, entries would be time-consuming to duplicate, but the data could be reentered. However, if the data lost were hotel reservations, the cost to the owners of the hotel would be high.

Backing Up and Restoring Files

UNIX has several commands that enable you to perform backups. Many manufacturers of tape or optical backup hardware also supply special programs that work well with their drives.

Three types of operations are involved:

- *Making or creating the backup is the most common operation.* This operation is performed regularly and consists of copying files from your file system to a backup medium.

- *Listing the contents of a backup helps the system administrator determine which files are stored on the backup and the date the backup was made.* This operation can be performed on an as-needed basis.

- *Restoring backup files from the medium back to the file system.* This operation is performed only after files are lost or erased.

The *tar* Command

The original UNIX backup command was tar. This command was a tape archive utility that was meant to maintain tape archives and do the copying. The cpio command is the next-generation backup command.

The tar command now works with floppy disks as well as with tape. The tar command has some benefits and some peculiarities. For instance, tar handles each file put to floppy disk with a 1K boundary. This means that if the file you are backing up has one byte in it, tar allocates a 1K minimum, thus wasting 999 bytes of space. This can result in a massive waste of space if you are backing up many small files.

However, tar can be told what blocking factor to use. And you can tell tar the size of the files you are backing up, so large backup streams can be chopped up into lots of small pieces.

> **NOTE** *The* `tar` *command backs up in one continuous process. Before beginning a backup with* `tar`*, make certain you have enough formatted floppy disks. If you do not have enough floppy disks formatted, you have no choice but to break the process and start over. Also, backing up your data may take a while, so make sure you have enough time available to do this task.*

The syntax of the `tar` command is

```
tar options directories
```

Note an example:

```
tar cvf /dev/fd0 /usr2 /usr3
```

The options specified in the example call for a creation of a new backup (c for create). `tar` lists everything as it goes along (v for verbose), with the file name of the device (`/dev/fd0`) followed by the list of directories to be backed up (`/usr2 /usr3`).

> **NOTE** *The* `tar` *command options are not preceded by a dash (-) as is the case with other UNIX commands because the "options" are not really options. Some of them must be present with every* `tar` *command.*

If files are going to be retrieved from a backup disk, the x (extract) option is used in place of the c option:

```
tar xvf /dev/fd0
```

You can also use the `tar` command to retrieve certain files from the backup medium by listing the names of the files on the command line:

```
tar xvf /dev/fd0 /usr/amanda/memo/barney.1
```

You can list the files stored on a backup with this variation of the `tar` command:

```
tar tvf /dev/fd0
```

The following are common options for `tar`:

Option	Description
c	Creates a new `tar` file
r	Writes a new archive at the end of the device

(continues)

Option	Description
t	Lists the contents of the archive
x	Extracts the archive
f	Uses the next argument as the place where the archive is to be placed
v	Verbose output

The *cpio* Command

Although the tar command is easy to use and sophisticated enough for most backup purposes, it has some limitations in choosing files for backup. For example, you cannot tell tar to back up all files whose names begin with a, nor can you request a backup of all files that have been modified in the last week. These tar command's limitations resulted in the creation of the cpio command.

The overall action of the cpio command is similar to the tar command with some major differences. Because cpio does not have definite boundaries, files can be split between two floppy disks. However, this can present a problem. Suppose that the third floppy disk in a set of five becomes corrupted; all files on floppy disks after three are useless. The entire backup image is lost.

To produce a backup, enter the cpio command as follows:

```
cpio -ocv >device
```

The -ocv options are used so often that it may be difficult for a system administrator to define their meanings. The -o option tells cpio to create a backup, the c option instructs cpio to write header information in character format, and the v option tells cpio to list files as it backs them up.

> **NOTE** *For each file that cpio backs up, it writes a header on the floppy disk. The header contains the file name and information about the file. The header can be written in binary or character format. The binary format is the default.*

The cpio command does not list the files or directories that are to be backed up. The cpio command relies on the find command to produce the list of files for backup. If you are going to backup the /usr directory, you must issue the find command in the following format:

```
find /usr -print ¦ cpio -ocv>/dev/fd0
```

This command line orders the find command to produce a list of files and directories in the /usr directory. The command then pipes this list to cpio for backing up the listed files to the /dev/fd0 floppy drive.

You can also use the find command to select other criteria for backup files. For example, you can ask for files that were modified in the past week to be backed up:

```
find /usr -mtime -7 -print ¦ cpio -ocv >/dev/fd0
```

> **NOTE** *In all examples, the* cpio *command remains the same, but the variation of the* find *command denotes which files are selected for backup.*

Periodically, you can back up a list of files. You can have this list in a file. The cpio command reads the list from the file and performs the backup on these files:

```
cpio -ocv <backup.list >/dev/mt0
```

If a file contains the list of files you want to back up and you reference that file, there is no need to use the find command.

Retrieving all files from a cpio backup is possible with the following syntax line:

```
cpio -icvdmu </dev/fd0
```

Once again, these options should be second nature to the system administrator. Table 11.1 lists their meanings and, in parentheses, what the option stands for:

Table 11.1 *cpio* **Restore Options**

Option	Description
i (input)	Restores a backup
c (character)	Uses character headers
v (verbose)	Lists the files as they are restored
d (directories)	Creates directories as needed
m (modify time)	Date-stamps the restored files with the dates they had when they were backed up rather than with the current date
u (unconditional)	Restores files even if they already exist on disk

Consolidating File Blocks with *copy* and *dcopy*

The dcopy command is used for backups from one hard disk to another. This command is available on UNIX System V. Because the data blocks that make up a file on a hard disk become scattered over time, UNIX requires more time to access the file. When dcopy copies the files, it stores together all the data blocks for a file, which results in the copy being more efficiently arranged than the original. For this reason, many system administrators perform a dcopy regularly.

The copy command, available on the Berkeley UNIX systems, performs the same operation as dcopy.

Duplicating Disks with *volcopy*

The volcopy command rapidly copies every block from one disk to another disk. The resulting copy is the exact image of the original. Therefore, the receiving disk must be the same size and type as the original. One disadvantage of the volcopy command is that it copies every block on the disk, even unused space. The result is that copying disks that are mostly empty takes a longer period of time.

Tips for Successful Backups

Because there are a number of techniques that are available to minimize the hassle of performing backups, care must be taken to weigh the trade-offs involved in selecting one technique over another. Pay particular attention to the integrity of the backup. Here are some helpful tips to consider when making, maintaining, and using backups:

- *Back up data only*. Backing up only user files can result in a huge time savings. Because most UNIX systems contain a large number of files and programs that never change or that can easily be replaced, there is no need to back up these files frequently. You should always have a complete backup of the entire system available, however.

- *Mix full backups with incremental backups*. Incremental backups make copies of only those files that have changed since the last backup. The find command has the capability of selecting only files that have changed within a specified period. You might set aside a day each week to perform full backups and continue with incremental backups for the rest of the week. This strategy cuts down on backup time.

- *Rotate backups*. Alternating the medium you use for backup is a good idea. Some system administrators use one set of media one day, another set the next, and continue on with alternating these two sets. This method can prevent the wearing out of one particular medium, and when the time comes to restore data, the medium is not damaged nor has errors. You should have several sets of tapes and floppy disks available and back up one time on a tape and the next time on floppy disks in a repeating cycle.

- *Store some backup sets off-site*. This prevents destruction of backup sets in the case of fire, theft, or any other damage to the site.

- *Perform backup verification*. You should check your backups periodically. It is not safe to assume that because you went through the steps, the backups are usable. Perform a simple test by listing the contents of the backup or restoring a small file.

- *Label everything*. Make certain that each set of backup media is labeled. Indicate when the backup was created, who made it, what it contains, and how it should be restored.

> **NOTE** *The use of more than one file system is commonplace on a UNIX system. This practice is possible by mounting additional file systems to a branch of the root file system. It separates user files from system files by giving the user files their own file system. Accessing the mountable file is accomplished by using the UNIX* mount *command. The separate user file system is often named* /u *or* /usr2. *The system administrator uses a backup command to copy entire file systems. The practice of having separate file systems for user files makes the file-system backup command ideal for backing up only user files.*

Configuring Printers

11

After terminals, printers are the most common output device connected to UNIX systems. When printers are connected to a UNIX system, they are configured by the system administrator so that users can print to them.

One printer is identified by its device name as the primary or default printer in the UNIX system. This printer handles all printer output generated by a program. In fact, any job that is sent to the printer is handled by the default printer unless the system administrator configures alternative or additional printers.

To configure additional printers, the system administrator must identify each printer by name and tell the system how it is connected to the system. The printer names are used as part of a print command by the user. The printer service then routes output to the named printer.

With a multitasking/multiuser system it is possible to send more than one job to the printer at a time. Because output can be accepted from only one program at a time, UNIX uses a print-queuing mechanism, sometimes called print spooling. The *print spooling* process collects print jobs as they come in from users' requests. It holds the job until the previous job has finished, and then sends the next job to that printer. Naturally, someone has to tend to the management and maintenance of the print queue; this is a task for the system administrator.

When many print jobs are waiting in the print queue, the system administrator may be called on to adjust the priority of pending print jobs. The system administrator can look at the jobs in the queue (using the lpstat command), decide to reposition jobs in the queue, and cancel a print job that is too large or will take too much time during the course of the regular workday. If a printer must be taken out of service, rerouting the print jobs to another printer is necessary. All these options enable the system administrator to maintain printers while printing activity is going on without disturbing the print function.

In UNIX, you use the lp command to send jobs to a printer:

```
% lp file1
request id is SPARCprinterII-513 ( 1file)
```

This command prints file1 on the default printer because no printer was specified. In this case, the default printer is called SPARCprinterII.

If you decide that you want to cancel the printed file, use the following command:

```
% cancel SPARCprinterII-513
request SPARCprinterII-513 cancelled.
```

To verify that the printer is printing file1, use the lpstat command to display the current status of the print queue. A queue (first-in-first-out) is needed because UNIX printers are shared by many people and UNIX needs a "printing method" to organize jobs in order of arrival. Using the lpstat command with no options displays all users' print requests. In this case, an lpstat yields the following:

```
%lpstat
File Number          owner(user)   Nb of Bytes Date Printer Device
SPARCprinterII-513     gmeghab  9387           Oct 19    SPARCprinterII
%lpstat -a
SPARCprinterII accepting requests since Tue August 29 14:03:35 EDT 1995
```

This information tells you what printers are configured or attached to your machine (in this case, there is only one, the SPARCprinterII) and that the latter started accepting requests for printout since August 29, 1995.

If you decide to print on a printer other than the default printer, use the lpstat -a command. This shows the names of all the printers configured for your system.

Formatting Your Text Files

The pr command is another useful command that enables you to format a text file before printing. You can add pagination, change the default number of characters per width page, change the default number of lines per page, indent all lines by *n* characters, add a header on every page, and double-space your document. Here are some of the possibilities with the pr command:

```
% pr -l 40 -w 60 -o 5 -h "nice try george" -m file1 file2 -d ¦lp
```

This command sets the page length to 40 lines, the width to 60 characters, the left margin to 5 characters per line, and the header nice try George on every page. It also merges two files—file1 and file2—into columns and pipes the command to the lp command to be printed.

Of course, you can cat a file, pipe it into pr, and then use lp to print it, as in

```
% cat listing ¦   pr  ¦   lp
```

The file listing will be opened, prepared for printing, and then sent to the printer.

Adding Printers to Your System

The command lpadmin is available for use by a system administrator to configure printers that are added to your system. Assume that you are to add a printer called SPARCprinterII to your list of printers. You become a superuser and execute the command to add a new printer or to reconfigure an existing printer. The general format for adding a new printer is the following:

```
#  lpadmin -p printername options
```

The most common *options* are -v, -U, and -s for a new printer. In the command

```
#  lpadmin -p SPARCprinterII -v /dev/bpp0
```

the option -v means that a device is associated with a printer. The device is a pathname of a file to which the lp command can write. The device name can be associated with more than one printer. If the option -v is not given, the option -U corresponds to a dial-up number over which the lp command transmits the file to the printer. The preceding command created a new printer SPARCprinterII on a device that is attached to your machine named /dev/bpp0.

Suppose that you want to print on a remote printer shared by other machines. Assume that the printer is to be called SPARCprinterI and is served by a machine called doc. Here is the lpadmin command you will use:

```
#  lpadmin -p SPARCprinterI -s doc!SPARCprinterI
```

The lpadmin command will generate a configuration file that looks like this:

```
Content types:  any
Printer type:   SPARCprinterI
Remote:         doc
```

Of course, you can change the name of the printer on your machine (victor) and call it SPARCprinterII instead of SPARCprinterI. The lpadmin command will then be

```
#  lpadmin -p SPARCprinterII -s doc!SPARCprinterI
```

This command creates a configuration file for a printer named SPARCprinterII on the machine victor, which will print on a printer named SPARCprinterI on a machine called doc.

The next step is to enable the SPARCprinterII printer's queue. You use the command lpc to start or stop a printer, enable or disable a printer's spooling queue, and display the status of the printer's queue. Note the following example (make sure you become a superuser before executing lpc):

```
# /usr/ucb/lpc
lpc > ?
Commands may be abbreviated. Commands are:
abort enable    disable    help restart    status    topq    ?
clean exit down quit start stop  up
lpc> status
SPARCprinterII:
queuing is disabled
printing is disabled
lpc> up SPARCprinterII
SPARCprinterII:
queuing is enabled
SPARCprinterII:
printing is enabled
lpc> status
SPARCprinterII:
queuing is enabled
printing is enabled
lpc> exit
# exit
%
```

The preceding is an example of a session that enables queuing and printing on the printer SPARCprinterII.

Managing System Operations

In UNIX terminology, a *job* is a program that is scheduled to be executed at a specified time—thus, the use of the phrase *scheduled event*. The system administrator can initiate jobs to run unattended at a convenient time. The difference between a job and a program is that a program runs when a user enters the program's name on the command line; a job's execution can be delayed until a later time.

A job may be slated to run at midnight by the system administrator. If the job will be time-consuming, there is no need for the system administrator to be present at the terminal to start the program. A job can be something as simple as a command, or it may consist of several tasks that are linked in a shell procedure file. Often, these jobs are set up in the crontab file and are run automatically by the system cron program.

There are a variety of occasions that might warrant the use of a job. The use of the sync command is one of those occasions. This command tells UNIX every few seconds to write the contents of buffer-based files to the disk. Using the sync command ensures that only the last few seconds of disk file activity will be lost in case of a system power failure.

Monitoring System Performance

The system administrator has the task of checking the efficiency of the system. Monitoring the amount of disk space available can be accomplished with the use of the df command. The df command tells how much space is available on each file system. Depending on the output of the df command, the system administrator decides what files need to be deleted to free the disk space. If the problem becomes chronic, adding disk drives may be necessary.

Most versions of UNIX provide tools to monitor the performance of the computer. You can become acquainted with these tools by reading the manuals that come with your UNIX system.

Getting Advanced Help

Every day new forums concerning different aspects of computing are created. These include user groups, system administrator groups, and publications that are both online and offline. Such groups prove to be very helpful because their members' knowledge is acquired by hands-on experience. Some of the groups are UniForum, USENIX, and other local groups.

You may decide to subscribe to publications that focus on the UNIX community. Excellent magazines are available, and classes in system administration are available also. Of course, the technical support group that is available for each version of UNIX is normally listed in the contract you receive when you purchase the software.

Exercises

1. What command would you use to list all printers available on the network? Give the command that lists the status of all the listed printers. How would you add a printer named SPARCprinter to the list of printers that is accessible from your computer?

2. As a system administrator, you are asked to have a machine called victor serviced by a printer called SPARCprinterII. victor does not have a printer connected to it. Give the steps, in order, that enable victor to print on the printer SPARCprinterII.

3. If gmeghab belongs to a primary group, called cs, how would you add gmeghab to the group neural_networks? How would the group membership of gmeghab appear? Would the /etc/group file reflect the fact that gmeghab now belongs to two groups? Show how this representation looks.

4. What is the purpose of the following command:

   ```
   %shutdown -y -I5 -g0
   ```

   a. How is this command different from % shutdown -I0 -g300?

   b. How is this command different from % shutdown -y -iS -g0?

5. As a system administrator, how would you start a system as a single-user system?

6. As a system administrator, how would you start your system as a multiuser system?

7. Explain the meaning of the following list of file names in the /dev directory:

   ```
   ls -lL
   total 15
   crw-rw-rw-  1 root      11,  44 Mar  2 09:52 arp
   crw------  1 gmeghab  84,   1 Mar  2 15:18 audio
   crw------  1 gmeghab  84,   3 Mar  2 15:18 audioctl
   drwxr-xr-x  2 root          512 Mar  2 15:18 cua
   brw-rw-rw-  1 root      36,   2 Mar  2 09:52 diskette
   brw-rw-rw-  1 root      36,   2 Mar  2 09:52 diskette0
   ```

```
crw-rw-rw-  1 root      50,  99 Mar  2 09:52 win99
crw-rw-rw-  1 root      81,   0 Mar  2 09:52 winlock
crw------   1 root      15,   0 Oct 25  1994 wscons
crw-rw-rw-  1 root      13,  12 Oct 25  1994 zero
crw------   1 root      11,  71 Mar  2 09:52 zsh
crw-rw-rw-  1 root      71,   0 Mar  2 09:52 zsh0
crw-rw-rw-  1 root      71,   1 Mar  2 09:52 zsh1
```

   a. What does the letter L in ls -lL stand for?

   b. Issue the command ls -als arp. Tell what happened. Why are the permissions different? Explain.

   c. What does the first character c stand for in the permissions, as in arp in the list?

   d. What does the first character b stand for in the permissions, as in diskette in the list?

   e. What happened to the number of bytes that usually appear in the fourth column of an ls command? Check the arp row.

   f. What do the two numbers that are separated by a comma in the fourth column represent?

8. As a system administrator, you are always worried about the growth of your system getting out of control.

   a. What steps would you take to keep files under control?

   b. Give the names of directories that usually keep trashed files destined to be eliminated.

   c. Give the find command that will find the names of files that exist in /var and /var/tmp and that were not accessed for the last 72 hours; the files should also have core in their names.

12

Working with UNIX and the Internet

Topics Covered

- Understanding the Internet
- Newsgroups, Mailing Lists, and Interest Groups
- Using Telnet
- Using FTP
- Using Gopher
- Other Services
- Getting Connected

The Internet, a network of more than 10,000 networks, connects more than a million computer systems and users on every continent throughout the world. It is the foundation of the "Information Superhighway" (the national information infrastructure in the United States). Since 1992, the Internet has experienced an exponential growth rate—at least 10 percent each month.

Networks and systems connected to the Internet can exchange many types of information, including e-mail, files, programs, images, and audio files. Any system on the Internet can offer services to others. Users can access libraries, databases, government information resources, financial data, and programs that make accessing other systems easier.

With so many users, services, and resources available on the Internet, being a part of the Internet is increasingly important. Almost all UNIX systems either include the software and hardware necessary to connect to the Internet or enable you to obtain these components easily. After you are connected to the Internet, you can access a number of resources and services, including those described here:

- *Electronic mail.* Send e-mail to sites on the Internet and other networks.

- *Interest groups.* Communicate by e-mail with a group on a common topic.

- *Newsgroups.* Similar to interest groups, but more like a bulletin board system; communicate between systems rather than users.

- *Telnet.* Log in to other systems and run programs to access information at those sites.

- *FTP.* Transfer files between computers.

- *Gopher.* Locate and retrieve information by using a menu system.

A number of other services and tools, such as Archie, Wide Area Information Services (WAIS), World Wide Web (WWW), and Mosaic, enable users to easily move around the Internet and locate sources.

Understanding the Internet

Information flows through the Internet in the form of *packets*. An e-mail message from one system to another, for example, is broken up into a specific number of packets, depending on its size, and sent out on the Internet. Each packet is numbered, has the address of its destination, and is routed through different networks. The target system receives the packets and, after they all arrive, assembles the packets into the e-mail message. This means that the two systems don't have to be tied together with a direct connection to exchange information. One system sends information to the Internet, and another system receives the information from the Internet. Each is connected to the network, and they exchange information through the Internet.

The Internet is a diverse collection of networks that don't all use the same hardware or software for local communications. To communicate and exchange information with other networks on the Internet, all use the *Internet Protocol (IP)*. The protocol sets the conventions so that packets can be exchanged among systems.

A number of other protocols are associated with IP. One important one is *Transmission Control Protocol (TCP)*. Two systems use this protocol to communicate with each other when a user on one system wants to run a program or log in to another system. In other words, TCP allows a user on one computer connected to the Internet to start a terminal session on another computer on the Internet. The necessary information for this terminal session is exchanged as packets, just as in the case of electronic mail. Both of these protocols are important, and people often refer to TCP/IP when they talk about the Internet.

Most of the services on the Internet (such as FTP, Gopher, and Archie) run as *client-server applications*. One computer system runs a program that acts as a server. Another computer system runs a matching program that acts as a client. For example, when you invoke the command archie, you start a *client* program, named archie, on your computer. This contacts a *server* program, also called archie, on another computer. You type commands to your client, which sends the information to the server. The server interprets those commands and responds to your client. That way, one server can work with several clients.

The Internet was developed so that users and systems at universities, research institutes, governments, and military organizations could communicate with each other electronically. Individual sites paid fees for Internet connections and were required to pay for maintenance on the systems that supplied information and user support. The U.S. Government funded much of the Internet's infrastructure. Now, however, many commercial organizations and individuals use the Internet as well. Many services and much information are free in that you don't need to pay to retrieve the information or use the services. Most users of the Internet share a spirit of cooperation and sharing.

Among the heaviest uses of the Internet is electronic mail. Using e-mail for communication has many advantages:

- Reports, data, or documents reach their destinations quickly, usually in a matter of seconds or minutes.

- You don't need to worry about interrupting someone if you send a message, and you aren't necessarily interrupted as you receive messages. The computer system receives them.

- You don't need to play "phone tag" or make an appointment to communicate with someone.

- You can deal with the messages you receive at a convenient time.

- You can send electronic mail at times that are convenient for you.

See Chapter 7, "Electronic Mail," for more details on sending and receiving e-mail.

Host Names and Domain Names

Each network connected to the Internet has a unique name, called a *domain name*. Individual computers on a network have *host names* that include the domain name. An example is given in the next paragraph. The host name is usually given in a recognizable form but corresponds to a numeric address called the *IP address*. This address routes information. If you use a domain or host name to access a site on the Internet, that name is translated to the numeric address. The translation is done by a program called a *name server*, or your system consults a table of names and addresses kept in the file /etc/hosts on your system.

An example of a host name is ike.engr.washington.edu. Each portion in the name is separated from another by a period (.) and represents a different level of the name. The name on the far right (edu) is the most general and says that this host is in the domain edu. In this case, edu identifies the site as educational or academic. Most universities and colleges are identified in this way. The next portion to the left, washington, gives more specific information about the host or domain name. This one happens to be at the University of Washington. These two are the most general portions of the host or domain name. The names are assigned by an agency that registers each network on the Internet. That agency also assigns the numeric address (IP address) to the network. Each host has to have a unique IP address, and there is one central agency to contact to register domain names. The other portions, engr and ike, are assigned locally—in this case, at the University of Washington. The next portion (engr) may identify a department, and the last portion (ike) often identifies a specific computer system. (Chapter 7 provides more details on domain names and addressing.)

Some domain or host names have only three fields—for example, marvel.loc.gov (the host name for one system at the Library of Congress). The top-level domains in the United States are divided into several categories, as shown in the following table:

Domain	Category	Example	Site
edu	Educational sites	mwc.edu	Mary Washington College
com	Commercial sites	novell.com	Novell
gov	U.S. Government sites	whitehouse.gov	The President's residence
mil	U.S. military sites	ddn.mil	Defense Data Network
org	Other types of organizations	eff.org	Electronic Frontier Foundation
net	Network resources	internic.net	Internet Network Information Center

Domains outside the United States usually have a two-letter code that identifies the country—for example, jp for Japan, uk for the United Kingdom, and ch for Switzerland.

The address of a site or computer system on the Internet appears as follows:

    host_name

The address of an individual appears as follows:

    local_address@host_name

In the address mybuddy@coco.holdon.com, the local address is mybuddy, and the host name is coco.holdon.com. (The local address portion is often the login id of a user.) See Chapter 7, "Electronic Mail," for specific details on addressing e-mail.

12

Finding E-mail Addresses

No universal address book exists for the Internet. Because mail is routed automatically based on the host name, however, keeping a record of where to find an individual isn't necessary. If the Internet continues to grow at its present rate, any universal address service would be expensive to maintain and update. It's not hopeless, though. The following list describes several ways to find someone's e-mail address:

- Reply to the message through e-mail. Most e-mail systems enable you to reply to a message you receive. If the message came from another site on the Internet, the e-mail system creates the correct address for the reply. Just check the "Reply To" header in the e-mail message.

- Call and ask for the address.

- Look for the address on a business card, resume, or letterhead.

- Consult membership lists or documents on the Internet.

- Write to the postmaster at the remote site. UNIX e-mail systems accept mail addressed to postmaster. If you know the host name portion of someone's address but aren't sure of the local name portion, send e-mail to postmaster@host_name.

> **NOTE** *Note that the person who ends up reading these messages can usually answer a request for an address, but may have a number of other tasks of higher priority to perform first. Be polite, and don't be pushy about finding an address this way.*

- Use an automated address service or address book on the Internet. You can access several by using Gopher and HyTelnet. No single service or book is best for every request. Experiment to find which suits you best. To find such services by using Gopher, enter the following command:

      gopher gopher.tc.umn.edu

  Choose the menu item Phonebooks.

  To find such services using HyTelnet, enter the following command:

      hytelnet

  Choose the menu item <SITES2>, and choose the menu item <DIR000> (Whois/White Pages/Directory Services). More than 60 different directory services or sites for you to access are listed under DIR000.

Sending E-mail to Other Networks

The Internet is not the only network that provides e-mail services. A number of proprietary commercial systems provide e-mail and other information services. Some of these are not completely compatible with the Internet, but you can usually exchange e-mail between the Internet and these systems. This exchange is possible by means of a *gateway*—a computer system or software that transfers mail from one network to another. Because many of these systems have their own syntax or formats for addresses, you need to know ways of translating a person's account name or address to a format that you can reach through the Internet. To send a proposal for a brochure to a customer whose account on CompuServe is 1234,988, for example, you would send the proposal to `1234.988@compuserve.com`.

Table 12.1 shows how to reach users on some other networks.

Table 12.1	E-mail Addresses for Sending E-mail from the Internet	
Network	**Example User/Account**	**Address to Use**
America Online	`My Friend`	`myfriend@aol.com`
Applelink	`friend`	`friend@applelink.apple.com`
AT&T Mail	`friend`	`friend@attmail.com`
BITNET	`friend@site`	`friend@site.bitnet` or `friend%site.Bitnet@cunyvm.cuny.edu`
BIX	`friend`	`friend@bix.com`
Calvacom	`MF34 (My Friend)`	`ms34@calvacom.fr`
CompuServe	`1234,899`	`1234.899@compuserve.com`

(continues)

12

Table 12.1	Continued	
Network	**Example User/Account**	**Address to Use**
Connect Professional Information Network	`FRIEND`	`FRIEND@connectinc.com`
Easylink	`1234899`	`1234899@eln.attmail.com`
EcoNet	`friend`	`friend@igc.apc.org`
FidoNet	`my friend at 9:8/7.6`	`my.friend @p6.f7.n8.z9 .fidonet.org`
GEnie	`friend`	`friend@genie.geis.com`
GeoNet	`friend at host`	`friend@host.geonet.de`
MCIMail	`My Friend (123-7654)`	`1237654@mcimail.com` or `My_Friend/1237654 @mcimail.com`
Prodigy	`friend`	`friend@prodigy.com`
SprintMail	`My Friend at some_organization`	`/G=My/S=Friend/O= some_organization /ADMD=TELEMAIL/C=US /@sprint.com`

Some of the entries may need further explanation; these are described in the following list:

- *BITNET.* You want to send e-mail to someone whose BITNET address is `friend@CHOCOLATEVM1`. Depending on how your local mail system is set up, use one of the following addresses:

  `friend@CHOCOLATEVM1.bitnet`

  `friend%CHOCOLATEVM1.bitnet@cunyvm.cuny.edu`

- *MCIMail.* You want to send e-mail to someone whose MCIMail address is `My Friend (123-7654)`. You can use one of the following addresses:

  `1237654@mcimail.com`

```
My_Friend@mcimail.com

My_Friend/1237654@mcimail.com
```

- *SprintMail.* You want to send e-mail to someone whose SprintMail address is My Friend at Chocolate, Inc. use the following address:

```
/G=My/S=Friend/O=ChocolateInc/ADMD=TELEMAIL/C=US/@sprint.com
```

Newsgroups, Mailing Lists, and Interest Groups

With so many people connected to the Internet, you may naturally expect that certain individuals have common interests or want to share information about common topics. Several thousand groups have formed to share information, hold discussions, and ask questions. These groups are called *mailing lists, interest groups*, or *newsgroups*. The software technology to support these groups was initially developed on networks that either predated the Internet, such as UUCP networks, or are of different types, such as BITNET.

These groups deal with a variety of topics. Some are specialized, such as the interest group E-EUROPE, which deals with communications with businesses in Eastern Europe, or the newsgroup comp.arch.bus.vmebus, which deals with hardware and software for VMEbus systems. Others have a more general audience, such as the group TRAVEL-L, which deals with tourism and traveling, or the newsgroup named rec.humor.funny. Some are *moderated*, which usually means that a volunteer moderates or examines messages before they are sent out for everyone to read. This process weeds out irrelevant messages.

Participating in mailing lists, interest groups, or newsgroups can be beneficial. You may perform any of the following tasks:

- Monitor discussions or news about a specific topic.

- Learn about professional, business, or personal opportunities.

- Make contacts for further e-mail discussions or other matters.

- Communicate with experts in a specific field.

- Ask questions of several—perhaps thousands—of other users about a topic you're researching or difficulties you're having with hardware, software, or other types of technology.

- Share your expertise with others who use the Internet.

One means for exchanging information this way is called *Usenet news*. It was initially developed to work on UUCP networks. Usenet can be thought of as a software system to receive and transmit collections of messages called *news* or *articles*. The articles are identified as belonging to a particular category called a *newsgroup*. The articles are passed from one system to another. They are delivered to a computer system, not to an individual. Users on a participating system can selectively read, post, or respond to articles in a newsgroup. There are several thousand newsgroups with millions of participants throughout the world.

Another system is called a *LISTSERV*. It was initially developed on BITNET. A LISTSERV system is similar to an e-mail mailing list. Users can add or remove their e-mail addresses from a list. After a user subscribes, he receives mail on the topics to which he subscribes. The communication with this sort of list is on a per-user basis. Communications come and go in the form of electronic mail addressed to individuals. Several thousand lists cover a wide range of topics.

In some cases, interest groups have been set up on Internet systems using software similar to the LISTSERV software on a BITNET system. The Usenet news system is more efficient in the sense that only one copy of a message is received at each site. With an interest group, all the subscribers at a site receive the same message. Many interest groups are available as Usenet news. When several users at a site get information from the interest group this way, they cut down on the amount of e-mail traffic and the space dedicated to saving messages at their site.

Newsgroups

Usenet was started as a means to share news and other information among users on UNIX computer systems. The news is a collection of messages in which each message is designated as belonging to one or more newsgroups. Each site that participates in Usenet has a list of newsgroups that it receives and a list of groups that it sends to another site. In this way, newsgroups are passed around the Usenet community of computer systems. Users at each site select which newsgroups they want to read; at many sites, users also can reply to, follow up, or post articles in a newsgroup. Usenet is very much like an Internet-wide bulletin board.

Administrators at a site can select which groups they receive, but don't have control over which articles are received or sent out. Usenet doesn't have a central control; all control is local. This local control is one of the reasons Usenet is so popular and diverse. Local control also adds to its strength as a source of information, help, and news. After an article is passed along, it most likely gets worldwide distribution.

> **NOTE** *Posting, sending a follow-up, or replying to an article on Usenet is a public act. Your e-mail address is attached to your reply or posting. It is then distributed to everyone who subscribes to that newsgroup throughout the world.*

Several thousand newsgroups are available through Usenet news. The collection of articles that a system receives is called a *newsfeed*. A good deal of traffic often occurs at a site in a single day, and this traffic can require several megabytes of space. Selectively choosing newsgroups cuts down on the system resources allocated to news.

The newsgroups are arranged in categories. Here are descriptions of some of the major categories:

- `alt`. Anything goes.

- `bit`. Groups available through LISTSERV on BITNET.

- `comp`. Groups relating to computers, computing, and computer science.

- `news`. Topics dealing with the news network itself.

- `misc`. Topics that don't fit into other categories.

- `rec`. Topics or groups that are recreational in nature.

- `sci`. Issues in the sciences.

- `soc`. Social issues and assorted cultures.

Table 12.2 gives a small sampling of newsgroups.

Table 12.2   A Sampling of Newsgroups

Newsgroup	Description
`alt.artcom`	Artistic Community, arts and communication
`alt.business.multi-level`	Multilevel (network) marketing businesses
`alt.humor.best-of-usenet`	What the moderator thinks is funniest (moderated)
`bit.listserv.travel-l`	Tourism

(continues)

Table 12.2 Continued	
Newsgroup	**Description**
comp.dcom.telecom	Telecommunications digest (moderated)
comp.security.unix	Security issues on UNIX systems
comp.sources.unix	Complete UNIX sources (moderated)
comp.unix.admin	Administering a UNIX system
comp.unix.dos-under-unix	MS-DOS running under UNIX by whatever means
comp.unix.questions	A good place to ask questions
comp.unix.sys5.r4	UNIX System V Release 4
comp.virus	Computer viruses and security (moderated)
misc.entrepreneurs	Discussion on operating a business
news.announce.newusers	Great place for new users to get information (moderated)
rec.food.cooking	Cooking, food, and recipes
sci.research	Research methods, funding, and ethics
soc.culture.misc	Discussions about social cultures

Articles are read by using software called a *newsreader*. Several different popular newsreaders are available. Some of them are rn, trn, and tin. The last two arrange articles in *threads*. A thread is a series of articles on the same subject. To elaborate on the use of any of them would require too much space here. Ask your system administrator whether Usenet or Internet News is available on your system. If either system is available, ask what newsreader program is available, what groups your site receives, and how you can get some local assistance.

A good group to start with is news.newusers.questions. If Usenet news is available to you, enter the command

```
tin news.newusers.questions
```

and you are ready to read some FAQs (frequently asked questions) as a new user and start subscribing to the thousands of newgroups that are available. You also can use e-mail to subscribe to such groups, as discussed in the next section.

The way you deal with the articles you receive through Usenet is probably similar to how you work with e-mail.

Usenet can be a valuable source of information, help, or just plain fun. It enables you and other users to access a worldwide collection of experts and information.

Interest Groups and Mailing Lists

Interest groups or mailing lists, like newsgroups, are valuable sources of information, news, or help. You communicate with the list by e-mail. More than two thousand interest groups are available on the Internet. Many of these groups were formed and are managed from BITNET networks, but gateways between the two network systems enable you to subscribe to these lists. The lists cover a wide variety of topics such as art, business, computers, food, humor, literature, and travel. Most of the lists are managed by software; some are digests of e-mail that the group receives, and some are moderated by volunteers.

Interest groups are particularly useful if you want to discuss issues with experts or others outside your organization. You can think of an interest group as a public forum for discussing or posting information or questions. Messages that are sent to the group may be read by any member of the group, although some groups are moderated to screen out irrelevant material. Many of the groups keep archives of past messages and provide other services, such as the names and e-mail addresses of other subscribers or members.

You need to be aware of several points as you work with interest groups or mailing lists. Naturally, you need to know the names of lists. Many lists also offer services to the members, and it's useful to know what is available. Because lists are managed by software, often the address you use to join or leave a list is different from the address you use to contribute to the list. This is particularly true when several lists are managed by the same software. You need to be aware of the following items:

- How to identify or choose a group or list

- The address you use to subscribe to a group or list

- The address you use to contribute to a group or list

- Services available from a group or list

- How to unsubscribe from a group or list

Finding Interest Groups or Mailing Lists

Several sites on the Internet keep lists of interest groups and mailing lists. These lists are quite large—usually more than one megabyte—so you may want to check with your system administrator to see whether one is available locally. Your colleagues or professional contacts also can be good sources for some lists. The following is a list of interest groups:

- CDROM-L. Issues related to using, producing, and installing CD-ROM systems.

- E-EUROPE. Eastern Europe Business Network.

- GIGGLES. Humor.

- TRAVEL-L. Issues of tourism.

- UNIXAPPL. UNIX Applications Mail List.

- UNIX-SRC. UNIX software in a source, not executable, form.

After you locate such a list, you usually first see a short description of the list and information about how to subscribe. The following entry is a sample of what you may see after accessing one of these lists:

```
Group Name:    CDROM-L
DESCRIPTION:  Mailing list for the discussion of software
and hardware issues related to CD-ROM.
To subscribe to CDROM-L send the message
        SUBSCRIBE CDROM-L your full name
to LISTSERV@UCCVMA.UCOP.EDU.
```

Subscribing to a List

To subscribe to a list, you need to know the address of the person or software that handles subscriptions. Software known as LISTSERV handles most interest groups or mailing lists. When you send a subscription to a LISTSERV, you aren't communicating with a human. Your message has to follow strict rules because a computer program interprets it.

In the following example, Carol Carlyle subscribes to the list CDROM-L:

```
$ mailx listserv@uccvma.ucop.edu
subscribe cdrom-l Carol Carlyle
.
$
```

Substitute your name for Carol Carlyle. Make sure to press Enter after each line. No Subject: portion or other information is necessary. The software at uucvma.ucop.edu interprets your message and makes you a member of the list. Remember that your e-mail address is passed along with any electronic mail; the system knows where to find you.

Getting a Response from the List

In a short time, you get a response from the list you joined. Be sure to save the response for future reference. It tells you the services available, the address, and how to leave the list.

The following response is similar to one you might receive after subscribing to CDROM-L:

```
Dear networker,
Your subscription to list CDROM-L (CD-ROM) has been accepted.
You may leave the list at any time by sending a "SIGNOFF CDROM-L"
command to LISTSERV@UCCVMA.BITNET (or LISTSERV@UCCVMA.UCOP.EDU).
Please note that this command must NOT be sent to the list address
(CDROM-L@UCCVMA) but to the LISTSERV address (LISTSERV@UCCVMA).
The amount of acknowledgment you wish to receive from this list upon
completion of a mailing operation can be changed by means of a "SET
CDROM-L option" command, where "option" may be either "ACK" (mail
acknowledgment), "MSGACK" (interactive messages only) or "NOACK".
Contributions sent to this list are automatically archived. You can
obtain a list of the available archive files by sending an "INDEX CDROM-
L" command to LISTSERV@UCCVMA.BITNET (or LISTSERV@UCCVMA.UCOP.EDU).
These files can then be retrieved by means of a "GET CDROM-L filetype"
command, or using the database search facilities of LISTSERV. Send an
"INFO DATABASE" command for more information on the latter.
Please note that it is presently possible for anybody to determine that
you are signed up to the list through the use of the "REVIEW" command,
which returns the network address and name of all the subscribers. If
you do not wish your name to be available to others in this fashion,
just issue a "SET CDROM-L CONCEAL" command.
More information on LISTSERV commands can be found in the LISTSERV
reference card, which you can retrieve by sending an "INFO REFCARD"
command to LISTSERV@UCCVMA.BITNET (or LISTSERV@UCCVMA.UCOP.EDU).
Virtually,
The LISTSERV management
```

Notice the following elements in the preceding response:

- To use the commands mentioned, send them to the LISTSERV.

- To leave the list, send the message SIGNOFF CDROM-L to the LISTSERV at the address LISTSERV@UCCVMA.BITNET or LISTSERV@UCCVMA.UCOP.EDU.

- To contribute to the list CDROM-L, use the address CDROM-L@UCCVMA.BITNET.

- To see an archive of messages to the group, send the message INDEX CDROM-L to LISTSERV@UCCVMA.BITNET.

- To see a list of members of the group or list, send the message REVIEW CDROM-L to the LISTSERV.

12

- To keep your name from appearing on the membership list, send the message SET CDROM-L CONCEAL to the LISTSERV.

- To get more information about LISTSERV commands, send the message INFO REFCARD to LISTSERV@UCCVMA.BITNET.

Signing Off a List

You may find that you're getting too much mail from the interest group or mailing list. You may find also that the group doesn't meet your needs at some point. To remove your name from the list, you need to send a sign-off message to the LISTSERV. Remember, the message doesn't go to the group!

Retrieve the message you received from the LISTSERV when you subscribed and follow the instructions. This usually means that you must send e-mail to the LISTSERV with a message that contains only signoff and the list's name.

To sign off (unsubscribe) from the list CDROM-L, type the following commands and press Enter after each one:

```
$ mailx listserv@uccvma.bitnet
signoff CDROM-L
.
$
```

You need to send the message from a system that has the same address as the one you used to join the LISTSERV. If you have difficulty, send a message to the group to ask for help.

Using Group Services

The message you receive from the LISTSERV when you join the group contains information on how to use some of the services available to the group. You can obtain archived files of messages or other information, get a membership list, and get an extensive list of all available services. To send a command to the LISTSERV, send e-mail messages. Table 12.3 lists some messages and the corresponding LISTSERV results.

Table 12.3 LISTSERV Commands	
Message	**Action**
signoff *your_name*	Signs off or unsubscribes from the group.
index *list_name*	Receives a list of archived files for the list.

Message	Action
review *list_name*	Receives a membership list for the group.
set *list_name* conceal	Removes your name from the public membership list.
info refcard	Gets a list of commands you can use with a LISTSERV.

Using Telnet

One of the original services on the Internet is Telnet. By using the command telnet, you can log on to another computer on the Internet. Of course, you need to have a login name and password on another system, or another type of permission to use the other system. A number of sites have established login names and passwords for others to use to access information or software at the site.

A large number of sites allow access through Telnet. Sites include libraries throughout the world, network service centers, campus-wide or company-wide information systems, weather stations, professional and business organizations, government agencies, and some commercial services. These sites benefit everyone. So many sites exist that you need a guide to help you find resources. Two helpful resources are the Updated Internet Services List maintained by Scott Yanoff, and the program HyTelnet by Peter Scott. Get a copy of Yanoff's list by sending the e-mail message yan-inet to yanoff@csd4.csd.uwm.edu.

To try HyTelnet, type this command:

```
telnet access.usask.ca
```

Use the login name hytelnet.

Accessing Telnet

Type the command **telnet**, type an Internet address, then and press Enter:

```
telnet localhost
```

You see a list similar to the following:

```
Trying..
Connected to localhost.yoursite.yourdomain
Escape Character is '^]'
login:
```

Now you can log on to your own system!

One very important thing to note is the message `Escape Character is '^]'`. This message means that the Escape Character is Ctrl-]. (The caret stands for the Ctrl or Control key.) Hold down the Ctrl key, press the key labeled], and release both keys. Use this escape sequence to issue local commands to Telnet—the most important of which may be `quit` to terminate a Telnet session. If you press Ctrl-], you see something like this:

```
telnet>
```

Type **quit** and press Enter to return to your normal shell prompt.

When you use Telnet, you start a client/server process. Your local machine, the client, requests another system to act as a server. The TCP creates a *virtual connection* between the systems. After you log in, it's as if you are at a terminal directly connected to the remote system. You aren't directly connected, but it seems that way.

Sometimes the connection operates slowly, and you may want to terminate the connection. You may be using an unfamiliar system, and you feel lost with no way to log out. That's when it's a good idea to use Ctrl-] or whatever is the escape character. This action turns you back over to your system to issue a `quit` command.

On most systems, you need to give a login name to use a Telnet connection. Some systems, however, use port numbers to allow users to log on. The port number corresponds to a specific program that you start when you include the port number in the `telnet` command. To log on, issue the command `telnet`, followed by the Internet address of the remote system and the port number, and press Enter. For example, to receive a weather report or other weather information for various parts of the United States, enter the following command (here the port number is 3000):

```
telnet wind.atmos.uah.edu 3000
```

As another example, to get the NBA (National Basketball Association) schedule, enter the following command (port number 859):

```
telnet culine.colorado.edu 859
```

You can type **q** to quit, or use ^].

Using HyTelnet

HyTelnet is a hypertext browser for finding resources available through Telnet. Peter Scott wrote and maintains HyTelnet (e-mail `aa375@freenet.carleton.ca`). The UNIX software that you need to run it on your system was written by Earl

Fogel (e-mail `fogel@herald.usask.ca`). The software is available "free" on the Internet. To try it, enter the following command:

    telnet access.usask.ca

Use `hytelnet` as a login name.

A large collection of Telnet-accessible sites is listed and arranged in categories. HyTelnet uses a hypertext interface to enable you to go from one item to another, either in a top-down fashion as you do in a menu system, or from one topic to another by using the arrow keys. Use the right-arrow key to go to a topic and the left-arrow key to return to a previous topic. In addition to listing topics and sites, HyTelnet also lists the login and logout steps necessary to go to and return from a site. It also allows you to automatically issue a `telnet` command without having to type `telnet` followed by an address. After you are finished working at a site, you're returned to the HyTelnet program. HyTelnet allows you to navigate the Internet efficiently and effectively, using a hypertext interface added to Telnet.

Starting HyTelnet

If you don't have the HyTelnet software on your system, you need to Telnet to a site that allows you to run the program. If you have the software on your system, type **hytelnet** and press Enter. You see a screen similar to the following:

```
Welcome to HYTELNET version 6.6
October 10, 1993
        What is HYTELNET?          <WHATIS>
        Library catalogs           <SITES1>
        Other resources            <SITES2>
        Help files for catalogs    <OP000>
        Catalog interfaces         <SYS000>
        Internet Glossary          <GLOSSARY>
        Telnet tips                <TELNET>
        Telnet/TN3270 escape keys  <ESCAPE.KEY>
        Key-stroke commands        <HELP>
.................................................
Up/Down arrows MOVE    Left/Right arrows SELECT    ? for HELP anytime
m  returns here    i  searches the index    q  quits
.................................................
HYTELNET 6.6 was written by Peter Scott
E-mail address: aa375@freenet.carleton.ca
```

Selecting Topics

The topics you can select are surrounded by angle brackets (< >). Use the up- and down-arrow keys to move from one topic to another. The current topic appears in reverse video. For example, the topic <SITES1> holds information about library systems available on the Internet. To move to the next topic, press the down-arrow key. You see <SITES2> in reverse video. You can press ? for help at any time.

To check other sources, press the down-arrow key to highlight <SITES2> and press the right-arrow key. Pressing the right-arrow key takes you to another section of the HyTelnet system. To return from that section, press the left-arrow key. You see the following list:

```
Other Telnet-accessible resources
<ARC000>  Archie: Archive Server Listing Service
<CWI000>  Campus-wide Information systems
<FUL000>  Databases and bibliographies
<DIS000>  Distributed File Servers (Gopher/WAIS/WWW)
<BOOKS>   Electronic books
<FEE000>  Fee-Based Services
<FRE000>  FREE-NETs & Community Computing Systems
<BBS000>  General Bulletin Boards
<HYT000>  HYTELNET On-line versions
<NAS000>  NASA databases
<NET000>  Network Information Services
<DIR000>  Whois/White Pages/Directory Services
<OTH000>  Miscellaneous resources
```

Connecting to a Resource

Look at Miscellaneous resources for an example of what is available. Use the down-arrow key so that <OTH000> is highlighted, and press the right-arrow key. The following is an abbreviated version of what you see:

```
Miscellaneous Telnet-accessible systems
<OTH001> American Mathematical Society's e-MATH
<OTH002> American Philosophical Association
<OTH080> American Type Culture Collection
<OTH003> ASSET: Asset Source for Software Engineering Technology
<OTH053> Business Start-Up Information Database
<OTH069> Canadian Department of Communications Information System
<OTH085> CENET, the Cornell Extension NETwork
<OTH101> EDIN: Economic Development Information Network, Pennsylvania
-- press space for more --
```

The line -- press space for more -- indicates that there are other pages of sites to contact.

If you select <OTH053> Business Start-Up Information Database in the middle of the screen, you see the following:

```
                Business Start-Up Information Database
TELNET HERMES.MERIT.EDU or 35.1.48.159
Which Host? mdoc-vax
Username: NEWBIZ
                W E L C O M E   T O   T H E
    M I C H I G A N   D E P A R T M E N T   O F   C O M M E R C E
            I N F O R M A T I O N   N E T W O R K
Welcome to the Business Start-Up Information Database
New Business Info
```

```
                    Information for New Businesses
        1    Licensing Information for Specific Types of Business
        2    Checklist for Starting a Business
        3    Information for Employers
        4    List of Business Development Centers
        5    Business Financing Information
        6    Help - How to Use NEWBIZ
        EX   Exit
```

You also see TELNET HERMES.MERIT.EDU in reverse video. If you press Enter or the right-arrow key now, you are asked if it's okay to Telnet to that site. Press Enter again; HyTelnet attempts to make the connection. Before you do, be sure to write down the information that appears just below telnet HERMES.MERIT.EDU. It tells you that to log in, you have to specify mdoc-vax as the host and use NEWBIZ as the user name. If the connection gets hung up or you're lost, remember to use Ctrl-] to get the telnet> prompt and type **quit** to return to HyTelnet.

Quit HyTelnet at any time by pressing q on any HyTelnet screen.

Using FTP

One of the original services on the Internet was designed to allow transferring files from one system to another. It goes by the name FTP, which stands for *file transfer protocol*. Files of any type can be transferred, although you may have to specify whether the file is an ASCII or binary file. They can be transferred to any system on the Internet provided that permissions are set accordingly. FTP offers these advantages:

- It's very useful to transfer files from one network in an organization to another.

- It's an effective way to get a geographically dispersed group to cooperate on a project.

- It's a potent and popular way to share information over the Internet.

FTP isn't just the name of the protocol; it's also the name of a program or command. You issue the command by typing **ftp**, followed by the address of another site, and pressing Enter. You're then prompted for a user name and password. If you have a login name on more than one system on the Internet, you can use FTP to transfer files from one system to the other. You transfer files by issuing commands from one system to the other; these commands allow you to list directories and copy files in either direction.

Working with UNIX and the Internet

FTP is an effective and popular way to share software and documents on the Internet. Site administrators usually enable *anonymous FTP* when they set up FTP. Users at other sites use FTP to contact this anonymous FTP site, using the username anonymous. They can then copy files that are explicitly located in certain directories back to their systems. Some anonymous FTP sites also have a directory named incoming so that these anonymous users can deposit files as well.

FTP Basics

FTP works as a client/server process. You give the command ftp using a remote address, such as the following:

```
ftp newday.horizon.com
```

The FTP running on your system is a client to an FTP process that acts as a server on newday.horizon.com. You issue commands to the FTP process at newday, and it responds appropriately.

To see a list of all FTP commands, type **?** and press Enter during an FTP session. You probably need only a few of these commands now, and you may find that you need only a few for most of your FTP work. Table 12.4 lists some FTP commands.

Table 12.4 FTP Commands

Command	Action
cd *directory_name*	Changes to *directory_name* on the remote system. For example, to change to a directory named pub, type **cd pub**. To change to the parent or previous directory, type **cd**.

dir	Lists the current directory. You see a sequence of letters and dashes before each entry. If the first letter is a d, that's a subdirectory of the current directory. For example, a listing for a file named coco and a directory named bobo looks like this:
	
	`dr-xr-xr-x    1024    bobo`
	`-r--r--r--    9867    coco`

get *file_name*	Retrieves the file named *file_name* from the remote system to your current directory on your local system.
put *file_name*	Puts the file named *file_name* from your local system into the current directory on the remote system.

Command	Action
lcd *directory_name*	Changes to *directory_name* on your local system.
ascii	Switches to ASCII mode for transferring text files; abbreviated as asc.
binary	Switches to binary mode for transferring nontext files such as programs, word processing files, or compressed files; abbreviated as bin.
quit	Terminates the ftp session.

> **NOTE** *You can safely transfer any file between UNIX systems in binary mode, and some files must be transferred in binary mode. Usually, you need to issue the command* binary *after you connect with an FTP server. But there are exceptions! If you are using FTP with a system that isn't a UNIX system, you have to transfer text files in ASCII mode.*

Suppose that you have the login name of the user on newday.horizon.com and you want to use FTP for some file transfers. To make most transfers, use the following steps:

1. Enter this command to contact newday.horizon.com:

   ftp newday.horizon.com

2. After you see the prompt User:, give your user name on the remote system (newday.horizon.com):

   User: tuser

3. After you see the prompt Password, give the password for the user on the remote system (for security reasons, the system does not display the password as you type it):

   Password: can't tell

   If the user name and password are correct, you are connected to newday.horizon.com with an FTP server process waiting for your commands. You may see a message from newday similar to the following list:

   Connected to newday.horizon.com
   220 newday.horizon.com ftp server ready

```
Remote system type is UNIX
Using binary mode to transfer files
ftp>
```

To terminate the current FTP session and return to the prompt, type **quit** or **bye** and press Enter.

Getting a File from Another System

Suppose that the remote system has a file named `data.raw` in a directory named `collects`. To retrieve this file, use the following steps. As you issue the commands, you receive some responses from the server, indicating that it's carrying out your orders. The responses are not shown here.

1. Use the command `cd` to change to the directory named `collects`:

   ```
   ftp> cd collects
   ftp>
   ```

2. Use the command `dir` to list the current directory to see whether the file is there:

   ```
   ftp> dir
   drwx--x--x   2 tuser other    1024 Jan  7 11:30 Mordata
   -rw------   1 tuser other    3346 Aug  9 11:51 bigs
   -rw------   1 tuser users  14444 Jan  9 16:32 data.chk
   -rw------   1 tuser other   33673 Dec 12 11:11 data.raw
   -r--r--r--   1 tuser other    1234 Dec  7 15:23 zorroe
   ftp>
   ```

3. Use the command `get` to retrieve a file:

   ```
   ftp> get data.raw
   ```

   The remote system transfers the file to your current directory. Information about how many bytes transferred and the rate of transfer appear.

Transferring a File to Another System

Transferring a file from your system to a remote system is done with the FTP command `put`. To transfer a file named `final.rpt` from the directory `reports`, a subdirectory of your current directory, use `ftp` to start an FTP server on the remote system and follow these steps:

1. Use the command `lcd` to change the directory on your system:

   ```
   ftp> lcd reports
   ```

2. Use the command `put` to transfer the file `final.rpt` from your system to the remote system:

   ```
   ftp> put final.rpt
   ```

The file transfers, and you receive feedback about how many bytes were sent and the rate of transfer.

Anonymous FTP

Using anonymous FTP, you can access many files on the Internet. Internet users share terabytes (trillions of bytes) of documents; software (both source and executable) for DOS, Macintosh, UNIX, VM/CMS, and Amiga systems; images; and so on. Using anonymous FTP to access these files is just like using any FTP session, except for the following requirements:

- You need to know the address of a site that allows anonymous FTP.

- You must use anonymous as the user name.

- You give your e-mail address as your password.

To connect to a site, you need to know these things:

- The name of the file you want to retrieve

- The directory of the file

- The address or host name of the anonymous FTP site

Follow these steps to get your own copy of the file how.to.ftp.guide from the directory pub/nic/network.services.guides from ftp.sura.net:

1. Start an FTP session with the remote site:

   ```
   $ ftp ftp.sura.net
   ```

2. Specify anonymous as the user name.

3. Give your e-mail address as the password.

4. Use the cd command to change to another directory:

   ```
   cd pub/nic/network.services.guides
   ```

> **TIP** *Many anonymous FTP sites contain a file named README, which contains information about available files. To read that file (or any text file) without retrieving it, type* get README ¦pg *and press Enter.*

5. To check that the file you want is in the current directory, use the dir command to list the contents of the current directory:

   ```
   dir
   ```

6. If you're using FTP on a UNIX system, issue the `binary` command so you can successfully retrieve a text file or a file in some other format (if it isn't a UNIX system, you need to know whether the file is in text format):

```
ftp>binary
```

7. Use the `get` command to retrieve the file:

```
ftp>get how.to.ftp.guide
```

If you see any other files you want to retrieve, you can get them now.

Working with Compressed Files

Files are compressed to save space at anonymous FTP archives and to decrease transfer times. These files must be retrieved in binary mode and uncompressed at your site. There are several programs for compressing/uncompressing files. You can decide which to use by looking at the name of the file. Table 12.5 lists the three common compression programs, how to identify which was used, and what to use to uncompress it.

Table 12.5	Compression Programs	
Program	**File Name**	**Use**
compress	gotit.Z	uncompress gotit
zip	gotit.zip	unzip gotit
gzip	gotit.gz	gunzip gotit

The compress and uncompress programs are part of the usual UNIX software. Others are available by anonymous FTP on the Internet.

> **NOTE** *Sometimes a collection of files is put together using a UNIX utility named* `tar` *(tape file archiver). This really doesn't save any space, so the archive, as it's called, is usually compressed. For example, you might see a file named* `greatstuff.tar.Z`*. To uncompress it after you retrieve it, type* `uncompress greatstuff.tar` *and press Enter. To extract the archive, type* `tar -xf greatstuff.tar` *and press Enter. The* `tar` *file* `greatstuff.tar` *is still there; compress it again or delete it.*

UNIX software for HyTelnet, as well as a version of unzip, is available by anonymous FTP at `ftp.usask.ca` in the directory `pub/hytelnet/unix` in the file `hytelnet.tar.Z`. To retrieve this software and prepare to install it, follow these steps:

1. Access FTP:

   ```
   ftp ftp.usask.ca.
   ```

2. Give anonymous as the user name, and your e-mail address as the password.

3. Change directories:

   ```
   cd pub/hytelnet/unix.
   ```

4. Switch to binary mode:

   ```
   binary.
   ```

5. Get the file:

   ```
   get hytelnet.tar.Z.
   ```

6. Quit FTP by typing **quit**.

7. Uncompress the file:

   ```
   uncompress hytelnet.tar.
   ```

8. Extract the archive:

   ```
   tar xvf hytelnet.tar.
   ```

Searching for FTP Files with Archie

You can use anonymous FTP to access millions of files. Finding the files you want is difficult without some tool to help. One useful tool is the software Archie. Use it by sending a file name or a part of a file name to an Archie server. The server returns the location of those files at anonymous FTP sites.

Archie was developed at McGill University, Canada, by Alan Emtage, Peter Deutsch, and Bill Heelan. It is an effective and popular tool that has several server sites on the Internet. A site list is available through HyTelnet or in the Updated Internet Services List. You can access sites by e-mail, Telnet, and Gopher and by running an Archie client on your system. You can get a copy of the source program, in C, of an Archie client by anonymous FTP at `ftp.sura.net`. Look in the directory `pub/archie/clients`.

When you use Archie, you contact a server and send it a request. To search for a file, send the file name or a portion of the file name. You can request an exact match or use what you sent as a pattern to be matched somewhere in the name of a file. The commands you use are different depending on whether you access the server by e-mail or use your client.

Accessing Archie by E-mail

To access Archie by e-mail, send a message addressed in the following way:

```
archie@internet_name_of_archie_server
```

The names of three Archie servers are the following:

`ds.internic.net` (run by AT&T)

`archie.unl.edu` (University of Nebraska)

`archie.insec.pt` (Portugal)

You can send e-mail to `archie@ds.internic.net`, `archie@archie.unl.edu`, or `archie@archie.insec.pt`.

When you send e-mail to an Archie server, the subject is treated as part of the message. The message includes the commands you use. To get a complete list of commands to use with an e-mail request to Archie, send e-mail to a server, with the message consisting only of the word `help`:

```
$ mail archie@ds.internic.net
help
.
$
```

You don't need to know all the commands to start searching. The following example demonstrates how to find a file whose name is `how.to.ftp.guide`:

```
$ mail archie@ds.internic.edu
set search sub
find how.to.ftp
.
$
```

Use the command `find` followed by a string, `how.to.ftp` in this example, to locate anonymous FTP sites. You can use `set` in one of the following ways:

- Use the string to make an exact match: `set search exact`.

- Use the string as a substring: `set search sub`.

You eventually receive mail from an Archie server that is similar to the following:

```
Host seq1.loc.gov   (140.147.3.12)
Last updated 07:38 24 Jan 1994
    Location: /pub/IUG
        FILE   -rw-r--r--   6325 bytes  23:00 24 Apr 1992
```

```
     how.to.ftp.guide
     Host sunsite.unc.edu    (152.2.22.81)
     Last updated 08:05 22 Dec 1993
         Location: /pub/academic/agriculture/sustainable_agriculture
             incoming
             FILE    -rwxr-xr-x    7814 bytes  23:00  6 Oct 1992
             how.to.ftp.guide
     Host ftp.sura.net    (128.167.254.179)
     Last updated 07:32 18 Aug 1993
         Location: /pub/nic/network.service.guides
             FILE    -rw-rw-r--    6327 bytes  14:28 24 Mar 1993
             how.to.ftp.guide
```

Now you have three sources for the file how.to.ftp.guide. They arc at seq1.loc.gov in the directory /pub/IUG, sunsite.unc.edu in the directory /pub/academic/agriculture/sustainable_agriculture/incoming, and ftp.sura.net in the directory /pub/nic/network.service.guides.

> **TIP** *Archie searches can take a long time and return many matches. You can run the command as a background process, redirect the results to a file, and look at it later.*

Using an Archie Client

The sites that run Archie servers prefer that you use an Archie client to query their database. An Archie client is a program that is run on your system configured to contact a specific Archie site. Use it by typing a command such as

```
archie [-options] string_to_match
```

where *string_to_match* can be matched exactly or be used as a substring.

Table 12.6 gives some of the Archie options.

Table 12.6	Archie Options
Option	**Effect**
-c	Searches substrings, paying attention to upper- and lowercase. For example, archie -c Ethics returns information about a file or directory with Ethics in its name, but no information for one with ethics in its name.
-e	Searches for an exact match (this is the default). For example, to find files or directories that exactly match the string ethics, use archie ethics.

(continues)

Table 12.6 Continued	
Option	**Effect**
-s	Searches substrings, ignoring upper- and lowercase. For example, `archie -s ethics` returns information about a file or directory with `ethics`, `Ethics`, or `eThIcS` in its name.
-t	Sorts the results from the most recent to the oldest.

To conduct an Archie search for files or directories whose names contain the string business, enter this command:

```
archie -s business
```

The following list is similar to what you see:

```
Host ftp.germany.eu.net
    Location: /pub/comp/msdos/mirror.garbo
    DIRECTORY drwxr-xr-x        512  Dec 19 09:00  business
Host nic.near.net
        Location: /docs
    FILE -rw-rw-r--    30647  Aug 10 19:04  internet-business-
        journal.txt
```

The first item gives a directory named business in the directory /pub/comp/msdos/mirror.garbo at ftp.germany.eu.net. You might want to start an anonymous FTP session to ftp.germany.eu.net, change to the business directory (cd /pub/comp/msdos/mirror.garbo), and see what files are there (dir). The second item lists a file named internet-business-journal.txt in the directory /docs at nic.near.net.

> **TIP** *When you use the option* -s, *you are likely to have lots of listings returned. To read one screen at a time, use* `archie -s string ¦pg.`

Using Gopher

With all the information available on the Internet, it's sometimes difficult to find what you want. HyTelnet can help you locate information available by Telnet, and Archie can help you find files available by anonymous FTP. A more recent tool for navigating the Internet is Gopher.

Gopher lets you search for and retrieve information by using a menu system. After you select a file, it appears on-screen. After you've seen it, you can save it on your local system, print it on your local system, or e-mail a copy to an Internet address. You can also download the file; this method is particularly useful if you access the Internet by dialing into another system directly connected to the Internet.

Understanding Gopher

Gopher runs in a client/server mode. You start a Gopher client on your local system and then send commands to a Gopher server. The server displays menus and interprets your commands.

One characteristic of Gopher is that all the resources in a menu entry don't have to be on the server. It's relatively easy to create menus that are nothing more than Gopher connections to other servers. This procedure enables you to access one server, go to a large variety of sources on the Internet, and return to that server.

The software for Gopher is available by anonymous FTP. There is a copyright associated with it, like most information on the Internet. Check the information at the source to see whether there are any charges for using it in your organization.

You can easily have either a Gopher client or a server on your system. It's also relatively easy to add menu entries and teach others how to add entries. Gopher is useful if you want to set up an organization-wide information system.

Entries on a Gopher menu are files, directories, or Internet services. You can initiate Telnet sessions, Archie searches, and other searches from a Gopher menu entry.

You can access Gopher by either running your own client or by using Telnet to go to a site that has a Gopher client. To use Telnet, enter this command:

```
telnet consultant.micro.umn.edu
```

Use Gopher as the login name. You can also use HyTelnet to access a variety of Gopher sites. The next section explains how to use a Gopher client. The commands you use there are the same as those you use if you access Gopher by Telnet.

Using a Gopher Client

To use a Gopher client, type **gopher** and press Enter. The gopher command connects you with a Gopher server, which was set when your client was configured.

To "point" your client to a specific site, type **gopher**, followed by the location of a Gopher server, and press Enter. For example, if you type the command

```
gopher gopher.internic.net
```

you're likely to see this:

```
Root gopher server: gopher.internic.net
--> 1. Information about the InterNIC/
    2. InterNIC Information Services (General Atomics)/
    3. InterNIC Registration Services (NSI)/
    4. InterNIC Directory and Database Services (AT&T)/
Press ? for Help, q to Quit, u to go up a menu     Page: 1/1
```

Entries that end with a slash (/) are directories. To move to a directory that has an arrow (-->) in front of it, press Enter. You see another menu. A good place to start here is with item 2. To select an item, type the item number and press Enter.

If you select a file, the file appears one screen at a time. When you have seen it all, use m to mail a copy by e-mail, D to download the file, s to save the file on your local system, or p to print the file. If you press Enter, you return to the menu.

The line at the bottom of the screen lists some actions you can perform when you see a menu. Here are some useful actions:

- To get help, type **?**. You see a list of all commands you can use to move through the menu system.

- To quit, type **q**. This command returns you to your shell prompt.

- To go up one menu, type **u**. This command is useful when you use many levels of menus.

Gopher is easy to use, and it's a valuable tool to help you access resources and services on the Internet.

Other Services

This chapter deals with a number of tools and services available on the Internet. Several of them are text-based applications, but some are available with a Windows interface. Several of these are dedicated to only one site, such as Telnet or FTP, whereas others, such as Gopher, access several sites.

A number of other services are available on the Internet to help you find resources and services. They have been developed to help with the problem of navigating the Internet, or to bring together information from different sources for search and retrieval. The World Wide Web is the answer for all these services and is probably the future of all possible business and information transactions on the Internet. These services are summarized here:

- *WAIS*. Wide Area Information Service.

- *WWW*. World Wide Web.

- *Mosaic and Netscape*. Graphical interfaces that are hypertext information browsers and WWW clients.

Use WAIS when you want to search several databases for articles that deal with a topic you specify. When you use WAIS, you're presented with a menu of two hundred or more databases. Select what you want to search, and enter a search string. WAIS then searches databases on different Internet sites. It returns a list of articles or items that contain your search string. Save the articles on your system, or send them to yourself or someone else by e-mail. You have to enter the Internet address. WAIS is very useful when you need to do research.

The World Wide Web provides all the services of Gopher, FTP, Telnet, and anonymous FTP in a wonderful process known as *hypertext*. The way hypertext works on the Web is even better than the way hypertext works with HyTelnet. Hypertext enables you to move through the network—from one Internet domain to another, and from one computer network to another—searching for things, people, information, services, and businesses, and even shopping without knowing where any of them are. The Web's hyptertext is set up in a special form called HTML (or html) for Hypertext Markup Language.

You search the Web using either a line-oriented browser or a graphical browser such as Netscape. Line-oriented browsers are accessible through HyTelnet. When you use the WWW, you have the advantage of using a hypertext interface to move from topic to topic. This interface provides a means of linking various sources of information on the Internet. You feel as if you are using one system, but you can easily travel throughout the Internet by choosing a highlighted topic. These browsers are seldomly used now because they are text-oriented.

The graphical browsers make it fun to search for information on the WWW. Mosaic and Netscape are two of the most popular browsers. Mosaic was the first to provide a graphical interface. It runs in X Window, in Windows on a PC, or in a Macintosh environment. With graphical browsers, you use a mouse to go from screen to screen, or choose topics on-screen. The topics can be text, images, or sound files. Whether you work in a UNIX environment, a graphical Web browser such as xmosaic, or a Windows environment on your PC, you will be able to move from your *home page* (your access point to the Web) to other new places and look up new things.

You must have a direct link to the Internet to use a browser such as Mosaic or Netscape. A *direct link* means that you access the Internet either through a network board in your computer or through a SLIP or PPP account if you access the Internet via a modem. Mosaic must run on your own system. You can get the xmosaic software by anonymous FTP from `ftp.ncsa.uiuc.edu`.

Although Mosaic was popular in the beginning, it lacked many of the features that Netscape provides. Netscape is now the Web browser of choice.

Web sites can be located using a *search engine*. A search engine is a site that searches the WWW for sites containing information you specify. Some of the more popular search engines are Infoseek, Lycos, Open text Index, Magellan, Excite, Alta Vista, Yahoo, and Web Crawler. These search engines act like spiders that collect information from different home pages, Gopher sites, and FTP sites. Depending on the search engine you are using, the precision of the search and the quality of the results will vary considerably. Some of the engines can search through 20 million URLs in a few seconds, and then filter and retrieve the information you want, which may be obtained from a few thousand URLs of the 20 million searched.

Getting Connected

Getting connected to the Internet can be time-consuming or as simple as calling someone with a connected site and getting an account on his or her system. If your organization is connected to the Internet, see your system administrator or your network administrator to arrange for your station to be connected.

If your organization isn't connected to the Internet, you have to go through the process of evaluating the costs and benefits of different types of access. Will you need to be connected by a dedicated line and provide your own hardware, software, and administration? This approach often has the benefits of faster transfers and access to the Internet, but the cost is usually more than $20,000 per year. Will a dial-up connection to some other site be sufficient? This method is less expensive but often not as fast as a dedicated line.

Individuals can access Internet through a number of commercial systems. This usually means dial-up access; you're charged the same way as for any commercial service. You need a modem and communications software, and you pay for the time and storage space you use. Two types of dial-up access are available. The least expensive is called a *shell account*. With a shell account, you use your modem to call a UNIX system and get login privileges. Your system is not directly connected to the Internet, but you can access many Internet services and resources. The other type of access is called *SLIP* (Serial Line Internet Protocol) or *PPP* (Point-to-Point Protocol). With SLIP and PPP, your system is connected directly to the Internet, and a host name is assigned to your system. SLIP or PPP is preferable to a shell account if you want to take advantage of some of the graphical user interfaces (GUIs), such as Mosaic or Netscape.

Regardless of how you connect to the Internet, you need software that implements TCP/IP. This software comes with most UNIX systems. If you don't have it, you can purchase it through a number of sources. If you don't use a modem or serial connection, you also need to purchase networking cards and cables.

Access to the Internet is becoming more common. It may soon be available in the same way as cable TV services. One contact is the InterNIC (1-800-444-4325). This agency is responsible for Internet connections in the United States. Other sources include books on the Internet, such as Que's *Using the Internet* and *The Internet Resource Quick Reference.*

Exercises

1. Using some of the search engines available through Netscape, search the Internet and find the following information:

    a. A Congressman from southern Georgia is Saxby Chambliss. When did he graduate from the University of Georgia? What is his daughter's name?

    b. A local high school needs a giant robotic arm to help clean the roof of its gymnasium. The principal needs to contact the chief of the ER4 Robotics Systems Technology Branch at NASA. Who should she call?

    c. Who flew with Neil Armstrong to the moon? When did the trip occur?

    d. Xerox PARC (the Palo Alto Research Center) invented modern networking. When was PARC founded?

    e. Linux is a version of UNIX that runs on personal computers. Who maintains the Linux Documentation Project?

    f. OCEANIC is an Oceanography resource provided by whom?

    g. *Dilbert* is Mark's favorite cartoon. What is Dogbert's ambition?

    h. Why did the Second Continental Congress declare their reasons for separating from England?

2. What is the difference between HyTelnet and Telnet?

3. What is a client/server model? Give four examples of Internet tools that fit into this category.

4. Is the World Wide Web a client/server model?

5. What are the differences or similarities between `rlogin` and `telnet`?

6. What are the differences and similarities between the commands `telnet` and `ftp`?

7. What are the differences and similarities between `rcp` and `ftp`?

8. Define gateways and routers. Can a gateway be a router? Can a router be a gateway?

9. Is one router enough to claim that you have designed an Internet site?

10. You have mailed three users belonging to the same mailing group the same file name message. Assume that these users are located in the U.S. in three different locations. What determines which user receives the message first? Last?

11. Valdosta State University is considered to be an Internet site on the Information Superhighway. What would this imply from the Internet point of view?

12. While reading the file name `hosts` in the `/etc` directory of a machine named `grits` on your network, you discovered the following listing:

```
127.0.0.1 localhost loghost
131.144.8.206 grits grits.valdosta.peachnet.edu mailhost
131.144.8.253 netware
168.18.130.12 admit
131.144.4.10 peachnet
131.144.8.20 s1500.vsc.peachnet.edu leonard
128.192.1.7 uscn cyber
128.192.1.5 uga ibm
```

   a. The first line is

   ```
   127.0.0.1 localhost loghost
   ```

   What does this imply for anybody connected to the network? What kind of relationship is there between `grits` and the `localhost` and `loghost`?

   b. Analyze the second line:

   ```
   131.144.8.206 grits grits.valdosta.peachnet.edu mailhost
   ```

   What would this imply to any machine connected to the network?

c. Some of these IP addresses contain just one name after the sequence of four numbers. Does this mean anything?

d. From the number 127 of the list of four numbers on the first line, determine whether localhost is a global network:

```
127.0.0.1 localhost loghost
```

What does the first 0 mean? What does the second 0 mean? What does the last number 1 mean?

e. Some machines share the same first number. What are they? What does this mean for the whole network?

13. Your local workstation is called victor. victor's /etc/hosts file reads as the following:

```
127.0.0.1 localhost
168.18.130.241 victor loghost
131.144.8.206 grits
```

a. What is the relationship between victor and localhost?

b. What is the relationship between victor and grits?

c. victor shares a few numbers with one of the machines in question 12. What are the numbers? What do they mean?

14. Suppose that you issue the command

```
%netstat -i
```

on your machine, and you get this result:

```
Name  Mtu  Net/Dest     Address    Ipkts      Ierrs Opkts      Oerrs
Collis    Queue
lo0   8232 loopback     localhost 89683878   0     89683878   0       0
0
le0   1500 131.144.8.0  grits      416716295 39960 296857110 61458
12733819 0
```

a. What does the first line mean?

b. What does the second line mean?

c. Now suppose that you issue the following command:

```
% ifconfig le0 down
```

What would this command do? How would you correct the situation? Give the command that will correct the ifconfig command to rectify the le0 situation.

Index

Symbols

\# (pound sign) prompt, 38
\$ (dollar sign) prompt, 37-38
% (percent sign) prompt, 38
& (ampersand), 224
* (asterisk), 224
; (semicolon), 209
< > (angle brackets), 299
@ (at sign), 153, 189
{} (braces), 207
| (pipe), 9, 16, 58
~ (tilde), 51

A

absolute method,
  permissions, 88-90
absolute references, 50-52
accessing
  Archie by e-mail, 308
  file permissions, 69
  FTP (file transfer protocol)
    sessions, 302
  Internet sites, 284-285,
    314-315
  system, 258
  Telnet, 297-298
  UNIX, 32
accounts, users, 258-261
adding
  functions to C programming
    language, 224-226

printers to system, 275-276
text, 122-125
users, 261-264
addresses
  automated services, 286
  e-mail, 148-149
    finding, 286-287
    Internet, 150
    UUCP, 149
  networks, 248-249, 287-288
  on the Internet, 284
adduser command, 263
advertising, *see* exporting
alias command, 158
aliases
  creating, 158
  editing, 158
  in C shells, 175-177
  in e-mail, 151-152
allocating memory, 95
alphanumeric values, 210
America Online, 287
American National Standards
  Institute (ANSI), 206
ampersand (&), 224
angle brackets (< >), 299
anonymous FTP (file transfer
  protocol), 305-306
ANSI (American National
  Standards Institute), 206
Applelink, 287
application programs, *see*
  software

Archie, 308-309
archie command, 283
arrays, 188, 211-212
arrow keys for cursor
  control, 119
ascii command, 302
ASCII text files, 55
assembly language, 18
assigning
  passwords, 262
  variables, 187-189, 213
asterisk (*), 224
at sign (@), 153, 189
AT&T Mail, 287
attributes
  directories, 79-82
  files, 57, 79-82
automatic logins, 37

B

background execution, 6,
  15, 42, 65, 186
  see also multitasking
backups
  commands
    copy, 272
    cpio, 270-271
    dcopy, 272
    tar, 268-271
    volcopy, 272

printers, 273-276
  adding, 275-276
  commands, 274
  naming, 276
  queues, 274-276
  remote, 276
  text files, formatting, 275
printf() function, 208
printing
  e-mail, 157
  values of variables, 172
process states, 181-183
processes, 13
  background, 42, 186
  checking, 177
  communicating, 55
  executing, 181
  foreground, 186
  idle time, 101
  job numbers, 183-186
  killing, 181
  linking, 58
  monitoring, 101
  parent, 180
  permissions, 86
  piping, 58
  priority numbers, 183
  semaphores, 55
  status, 182
  stopping, 177
  system information, 177-181
  tracking, 181
  users, 180
  variables, 190
processing, see executing
processors
  clustering, 8
  CPUs (central processing
    units), 12
  peripherals, 12-13
  ports, 13
  RAM (random-access
    memory), 12
  terminals, 7
Prodigy, 288
Programmer's Workbench, 19
programming languages, C, 206
programs, 13
  background, 15, 65
  cat, 66
  communicating, 13
  ending, 64
  executable, 54, 277
  foreground, 16, 65

launching from any
    directory, 176
  mail, 164
  MH (Mail Handler), 164
  MIME, 164
  MUSH (Mail User's
    Shell), 164
  NMail, 164
  parallel, 16
  ZMail, 164
prompts, 37-38
protocols, 21
  TCP/IP, 233-234
ps command, 178-181
put file_name command, 302
pwd command, 39, 66

Q-R

queues, printers, 181
  disabling, 276
  enabling, 276
  status, 274
quit command, 302
quitting, see exiting

RAM (random-access
    memory), 12
random-access memory
    (RAM), 12
rcp command, 235-250
read modes in mailx
    program, 152
read permissions, 84, 87-88
read-ahead/write-behind file
    access, 47
reading e-mail, 154-157
"real estate," see screens;
    windows
real numbers, 210
rebooting computers, 101
receiving
  binary files in mailx
    program, 160-161
  data on the Internet, 283
  files, 238-239
  responses from mailing
    lists, 295-296
  text files in mailx
    program, 159-160
recovering
  directories, 77
  files, 77

redirecting input, 72-73
references, 50-52
regular expressions, 71
regular files, 15, 54, 68
relative references, 50-52
Remote File System (RFS), 22
remote printers, 276
remote systems
  applications, 241-243
  connecting, 233
  connections, 242-243
  files, 237-240, 304-305
  FTP (file transfer
    protocol), 304
  logins, 232, 241
  mounting, 243-247
removing, see deleting
renaming, see naming
repairing files, 48
repeat loops, 199, 202
repeating
  commands, 131
  emacs text editor
    commands, 137-139
replacing, 126-128, 138-139
replying to e-mail, 154-156
resources, 277
restoring backups, 271
retrieving files, 269, 304
returning values, 226
review list_name LISTSERV
    command, 297
RFS (Remote File System), 22
rlogin command, 241
rm command, 75
rmdir command, 75
root directory, 39, 50
root login, 258-259
rotating backups, 272
rsh command, 242-243

S

S (process state), 179
saving
  aliases in C shells, 177
  e-mail, 156-157
  emacs text editor, 136-138
  operating systems, 11
  vi text editor, 115-119
scalability, see multiprocessing
scanf() function, 209

329